Away at War

A Civil War Story
of the Family Left Behind

By Nick K. Adams

To Pamela —
I hope you enjoy my telling of
this true family story of separation,
hardship, and loss...

Nick K. Adams

Strategic Book Publishing and Rights Co.

Strategic Book Publishing and Rights Co., LLC
USA | Singapore
www.sbpra.com

For information about special discounts for bulk purchases, please contact Strategic Book Publishing and Rights Co., LLC. Special Sales, at bookorder@sbpra.net.

ISBN: 978-1-68181-992-1

DEDICATION

To all my former students at Discovery Elementary in Gig Harbor, WA, who listened so attentively to the Civil War letters of Corporal David Brainard Griffin. Your interest was my inspiration for the creative process that translated those letters into this story.
Thank you!

Corporal David Brainard Griffin (taken in Nashville, TN, September 29, 1862)

INTRODUCTION

From September of 1861 through September of 1863, my great-great-grandfather Griffin wrote at least 100 letters from the fields of battle back to the family he left behind on the southeastern Minnesota prairie while he fought in the American Civil War. That collection is available in my earlier publication: *My Dear Wife and Children: Civil War Letters from a 2nd Minnesota Volunteer.*

Beyond describing what he was thinking, experiencing, and feeling, many of Griffin's letters contain responses to what his family had written him about what they were encountering and accomplishing without him on their farm and in their meager "shanty," which for them was home. It is that information which I have lifted to make the guiding outline for this novel. An 1882 work, entitled *History of Fillmore County, Minnesota,* also provided me numerous bits of local color for the period.

Most of the events I describe, as well as the people and the places they inhabit – and even the content of many of the conversations which occur – are true in substance, as reported in the Griffin correspondence. I have only given them whatever shape was required so that the young family's story could flow.

I invite you, dear reader, into the lives of this family who represent the high personal cost that waging war – for whatever cause, good or evil – inevitably produces.

Chapter One

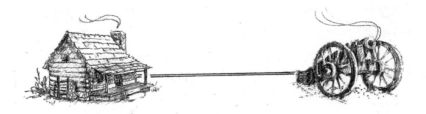

September Morn, 1861

Two young girls, five and seven, hovered beside their mother on the porch of their rough-cut Minnesota prairie home. Submerged in the utter quiet and dark that surrounded them, miles from any neighbors, all three stared up into the vast star-lit sky. They shivered, perhaps more from their uncertain future than from the advancing night's chill air.

A third child, a six-month-old boy, was fast asleep inside the log dwelling, oblivious to the turmoil then churning the emotions of the female members of his family. Far beyond his infant comprehension lay the fact that the only other male member in the family, his father, was gone, gone to war, a war, yes, to preserve the Union, but a war that now severed the fatherly protection, comfort, and strength his presence had always provided.

So, mother and daughters pondered. *How would all the daily chores get done? What about the spring and summer field work if he wasn't back as he promised? And him, where was he this night? Or where might he be all the nights until his return? And worst of all, what would happen to them if he didn't return? Could they even survive without him?*

Tears escaped down the three faces as each struggled at her own level, with no clear answers to their questions. All Ma could offer was a soft assurance: "We'll be all right. He'll come back, then everythin'll be good again. We're just not gonna think about bad things for now."

With that, they circled into a comforting embrace, reentered the single room they called their "shanty," and faced individually that first of many nights of fitful sleep and troubled dreams.

***

That day had begun much earlier, not long after the sun had broken through the mist laying heavy across their prairie wilderness. The younger of the two daughters, Ida May, was hiding in the hayloft of the barn, unwilling to face this day of separation. As she softly sobbed, she called up the memory of that spring evening five months before. Her father had ridden back from town with news of a war about to begin. She could still see him as he jumped off Ol' Jim, waving a newspaper over his head. He had called his wife and two young daughters together in the yard to tell them what had happened down in South Carolina.

Not quite five at the time, this was Ida May's earliest clear memory of life on the southeastern Minnesota prairie. It was no doubt imprinted by the intensity of the emotional exchanges that began that night between her parents.

She was far too young to understand the issues that caused South Carolinian troops to fire on the small island Federal fort in Charleston Harbor that April of 1861. Neither could she understand the consequences of the events which followed. For instance, her father had brought home additional newspaper stories about "Secession," "War," and "Bull Run." But what *was* clear to her was how passionate her parents became over those events—her father more angry, her mother more fearful.

Then six weeks ago her father, Brainard Griffin, brought home some news the consequences of which she *did* understand. President Lincoln had asked for a hundred thousand more volunteers to go fight in this war. After only a brief deliberation, her father had decided he must say yes to the president's call.

That's when the *real* trouble between her mother and father began, for Philinda Minerva did not want her husband to go. The issue wasn't discussed; it was argued, loudly and constantly. It was even argued in front of their three children: Ida May, her two-years older sister, Alice, and their six-month-old baby brother, Edgar Lincoln. The two sides were basically: "What will happen to our Union if I *don't* go?" and "What will happen to your family if you *do* go?"

Now she was up in the barn remembering it all, for the day of her father's departure to join up had come—Wednesday, September 23, 1861—and she didn't want to face it. Deep down she knew that her hiding wouldn't keep him from going, but at five what else *could* she do?

"Ida May! Ida May!" Alice's voice grew louder and more insistent with each call as she approached the small red barn. Their milking Jersey, Rosie, and her twin male calves, named Dime and Duke, had been led out to pasture following the morning milking. They joined the eight head of yearling beef cattle being raised for cash on the prairie grassland not yet plowed for growing grains. Both sows and their litters of nearly grown pigs had disappeared even earlier to forage in the nearby stand of red oak, sugar maple, and hickory nut trees. And all thirty-something chickens, of various sizes and colors, had scattered from their coop attached to the barn at the first light of day. Their clucking and scratching for bugs and seeds in the tall prairie grass surrounding the house would continue until nightfall. So the barn where Ida May hid, with its broad twin doors shut, was for now empty, quiet, and nearly dark inside.

Opening one of the doors just a bit, Alice stuck her head in. "Ida May, I *know* you're in here! Come on out—now!" Her voice then softened to a gentle pleading: "Pa's got to leave soon, and he *so* wants to give you a good-bye hug."

Ida May stirred, then edged out to show herself from behind the mound of hay eight feet above her sister. Her dark eyes and even darker twin braids were an identical match to Alice's. That was true also of her white cotton pinafore over a green-brown patterned wool dress. But the strings of dusty tear tracks that smudged her face, and the bits of hay that clung to her hair and clothes, made her overall appearance now quite different from her older sister's.

"But I don't *want* Pa to leave," she almost wailed as she crawled over to the wooden ladder, where its top rung rested just above the loft's square opening. Her wordless snuffling displayed her inner turmoil as she swung her legs over the side and began her careful descent.

Alice entered the barn and moved to the ladder's end to help Ida May step down the last few rungs to the barn floor. "I know," she said, "but Pa feels he's *got* to go. You know that. An' you also know he's promised to be back in just a few months."

Gently reaching out to take Ida May's small hand, Alice turned back toward the twin doors and the fall day's early morning light and led her troubled younger sister along the short pathway to the house—their "shanty," as they all called it—to rejoin the other members of their family.

Edgar Lincoln, still in his warm nightwear, was on the floor near the center of the shanty's single, multipurpose room. He was being watched by his cousin, Eliza Churchill, who was sitting close by on a short three-legged stool. Laughing with glee, he was rolling his rag ball around the wood-planked floor. Each time he did it he scooted on his bottom after it, only to push it away again, and laugh again. Though he was oblivious to the raw emotions which surrounded him, Eliza was sensitive to the conflicting family responses to this significant morning.

Her uncle and aunt, the children's parents, occupied the pine settle—a high-backed bench—beside the open fireplace, which still served as both the sole source of heat and the family's cookstove. The adults were lost in their own thoughts, gazing into the small fire, already required even in the daytime that late September on the northern prairie. Both were afraid to speak for fear of reopening the wounds caused by their impending separation.

Their nearly trancelike gaze was interrupted as their daughters came into the room from the large porch that fronted their house. Alice came in first, followed immediately by Ida May. Both girls paused to tickle their little brother, increasing his glee even more. They also glanced at their slightly older, orphaned cousin as she silently disappeared up the ladder to the sleeping loft the three girls shared to give the family a last few minutes of privacy. Alice and Ida May then crossed the room to the fireplace to face their parents.

"Found her," Alice stated matter-of-factly. "She was hidin' in the barn all right, just like you thought."

Ida May just stared at the floor, unable to look at her father as she fought back the tears which were building to flood again.

Brainard rose to his feet as his daughters approached, but he remained silent. His given name was David Brainard, though he chose to go by his middle name, just as his wife, Philinda Minerva, did. Noting the tearstained cheeks of the younger daughter he loved so deeply, all he was able to choke out was her name. "Ida, my Ida." At that, he stooped to gather her tightly to him.

Her anguished sobs burst forth again, and she buried her face in his shoulder, her body trembling with unspoken fears. With great tenderness, he continued, "It breaks *my* heart, too, to leave your ma, my babies, my home. I'm crying inside, just like you are, my sweet Ida May."

At this second speaking of her name, she lifted her eyes to look directly into his. They were as dark as hers, and equally intense. She blinked, sniffed twice more, and wiped her nose on the back of her wrist. Then she reached back to him with her little arms to fully return the comforting hug she had so desperately needed.

"Well," he said, relieved by the temporary reunion, "Can't a man get some breakfast in him a'fore he sets off for war?"

Chapter Two

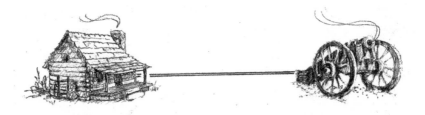

Pa's Farewell

The room soon filled with the crackling sound and smoky goodness of bacon frying. The home-cured slices, cut from the previous year's butchering, sizzled in a skillet set on an iron tripod over the hot coals in the fireplace. Nearby, the tops of baking-powder biscuits browned in the lidless Dutch oven, adding the wholesome smell of fresh bread.

Alice began setting the small table for five, while her mother brought up from the cellar the bowl of eggs she had hard-boiled the day before. By the time Alice had finished her task by pouring three small cups of fresh milk, Minerva had set out the homemade butter and the first jug of this year's honey for their biscuits. The fresh honey had been gathered in the comb the week before from the bee tree Brainaird had been lucky enough to locate in the woods above their home.

"Reckon I can't start the tea to boil for your pa and me till the bacon's done cookin'," she told Alice, setting the kettle aside. "But we've already drunk one pot before morning chores. Guess tea for us isn't so important now as food for the family anyways."

Brainard took this opportunity to "play horse" one last time with Ida and Edgar before he left. His snorts and their peals of laughter drew looks of shared pleasure on the faces of the two preparing breakfast. It was a special moment of family love among them all.

"Everything's nearly ready," Minerva whispered to Alice, giving a nod that released her daughter to join the others on the floor. She had seen the longing desire in Alice's eyes.

With Alice now included, the floor play switched from rides on their father's back to the three children trying hard to all pile on top of him as he wriggled and rolled. The happy sounds of this horseplay soon drew Eliza back down from the loft, and she joined in the playful scuffle.

Their roughhousing was halted, however, when Nerva called them to come eat. Though all responded quickly to her call, they were still giggling and squirming as they gathered behind their chairs at the table. "Enough now," their mother warned, "'tis time to eat."

Alice boosted Edgar Lincoln up to stand between his parents on his mother's chair. There perched, he gave one hand to each parent to steady himself. When the rest of the hands around the table completed the circle, as was their custom, the family bowed their heads in prayer. Brainard's grace was longer than usual, and included pleas for the watchful protection of his family during his absence as well as for his safe return.

The somberness of the moment was plain as they sat down, close but not crowded, reminded by the prayer that none of them knew when they would all eat together again. Edgar perched comfortably in the crook of his mother's arm to nurse, still too young for bacon and biscuits, or for worries about the looming separation.

Between bites Brainard explained, "I'll get to Mr. Colby's in Spring Valley tonight, an' head out early for Chatfield a'fore I aim for the river. Some of the boys there said they'd join me, so I won't be alone."

Chatfield was a little more than twenty miles as a crow would fly across Fillmore County. It would be a considerably longer trip for

Brainard, however, because he was planning to walk the winding country roads up to Spring Valley before heading northeast the following day as the road continued on to Chatfield. By "the river," he meant the Upper Mississippi, which ran down from the state capital. On it, he and his friends would be able to get transportation north to the enlistment fort just outside St. Paul.

"I thought you had to walk all the way to Fort Snelling," responded Nerva. "Just to the river? That won't be so bad."

"Will you get on a *boat*?" asked Alice, with a bit of awe in her voice on the final word, as she loved all things having to do with water.

"Yep. A paddle-wheel steamer most likely. It'll run us all the way up to St. Paul, an' Fort Snelling is just a short walk from there."

"An' then you'll come back?" Ida May's deepest hope hung in the question she asked.

"No, sweet Ida. Then I'll have to stay and be a part of the great army that will save our Union from bein' torn apart. I'll have a uniform an' a musket, and an important job to do. You'll be very proud of me, just you wait and see."

That said, Brainard rose from his chair. "Anybody wanna check out the farm one last time with me?" His daughters jumped to their feet and checked with their mother, who nodded agreement as she continued to nurse Edgar Lincoln. They then rushed to his side, each taking a hand. Eliza graciously stayed behind to help her aunt, allowing her cousins a few more precious moments with their soon-departing father.

Around the farm they went, four hands across, with a lightness of spirit that belied the fact he was leaving them later that morning. They began by inspecting the short fence lines and the animals they contained. One by one, doors were then opened into the few small outbuildings to check their contents and soundness.

Finding all to be well, their father asked, "What do you say, girls, we mosey on down to check on the orchard now?" The three turned from the small cluster of buildings and crossed over to the rutted lane that lead away from the farm.

Along one side of this lane the first owners of the farm had planted six apple trees. For only the second year, they were now heavy with a season's worth of red-striped fruit. "I can almost smell the pies your ma's gonna make from these apples."

"Won't you be sorry not to get any," Alice teased.

"Oh, I'll be back a'fore they're all gone. I'll get my share of pie. Maybe some of your share, too," he said, returning the tease.

Their eyes swept across the Griffin land on both sides of the lane. To the west of the apple trees lay both the fenced-in hay meadow and the recently harvested and plowed acres of land annually planted to oats and wheat. To the east sat the two acres of still-standing, but starting-to-droop cornstalks, where the cattle now wandered for forage. And beyond the cattle and corn waited the tall, dark-headed stalks of sorghum, yet to be cut and processed into molasses.

"That's a big chore I've got to leave for you to do without me." Brainard sighed, waving his hand across the field of sorghum. His lingering gaze into his daughters' eyes that followed, however, spoke the confidence he had that they and Nerva could get it done.

Hands on their shoulders, he then turned the girls so all were facing back up the lane. Now they could see the creek that ran down from the woodlots on the hillside above them and crossed the lane about halfway to their shanty.

"I suppose our pigs up in those woods are in hog heaven by now, stuffed an' snortin' in their sleep. You girls'll have to have full charge of them, so your ma won't have to worry about 'em none."

"We can do that fine, can't we, Ida May? But it'll be butcherin' time soon, won't it, Pa?"

"You're right on that, Alice. You won't have to watch 'em long."

Their eyes scanned the horizon to the north. Through breaks in the trees they caught glimpses of the rolling hills beyond, acres and acres of native prairie grass that they cut for hay. None of that land had yet been plowed into cultivation. All these pieces made the setting for their life together so tranquil—hard, always hard, but tranquil. At least until that day.

The three walked up the lane and stopped by the family's large vegetable garden. Nearly half of it was given over to the potatoes that grew so well there and were thus an important food staple.

Alice turned to her father and asked, "What will you miss most, Pa?"

Sweeping both girls into his arms, he answered with a laugh, "My wife and babies, of course," and he swung them around several times.

"No," Alice came back when she was again on solid ground, "I meant about the farm. What *here*," she said as she traced her open palm around them in an arc, "will you miss most?"

"Well, you've stumped me," he answered as he plopped down at the edge of the garden and dragged them down beside him. "My animals? My barn and sheds? My fields? My orchard? My woods? My shanty? Guess I'll have to say my shanty, 'cause that's where my family will be."

Pulling them up again as he returned to his feet, he raced them, all three laughing with glee, back to the house.

They found that while they were out Nerva had cleaned up the breakfast things and Eliza had settled Edgar Lincoln into his morning nap by gently rocking him in his mother's padded rocking chair. They also noticed that Nerva had laid out on the table the items Brainard had yet to pack before he left: a clean shirt, an extra pair of wool socks, his shaving mirror, straight razor and lathering soap, a writing box of paper, pencils and a penknife, and his Bible. All of this he would roll up in a single woolen blanket, tied at both ends, so he could carry it draped across either shoulder.

"Looks like I'm just about set," Brainard announced after placing his few essentials in the center fold of the blanket and rolling and tying each end with twine, ready to leave. "It's time, Nerva. It's time."

The girls had watched their father's final preparations, each leaning into one of their mother's hips, with her arms casually laid along their shoulders. Edgar Lincoln was by now sound asleep in Eliza's lap, his baby blond hair tousled across the crook of her arm. When Brainard bent down to kiss his son and softly stroke his cheek one last time, his eyes also caught Eliza's. His warm smile and silent nod thanked her for the loving care she gave his son. As he turned away from the rocker, Alice and Ida May began to cry and rushed to hug their father. Their mother then joined them, and the family embrace lasted until Nerva backed away to allow what happened next.

Squatting on his haunches, Brainard drew each girl in turn to himself, starting with Alice. To both he whispered the same message: "I love you. Take care of each other an' your ma, an' 'specially little Edgar. I'll be back just as soon as I can. I promise."

This quieted them, and each indicated she had heard by giving him an extra squeeze around his neck, followed by a kiss upon his clean-shaven cheek.

Then Brainard rose and moved to where his wife stood alone. They embraced, but not so tightly they couldn't still see one another's face. Their eyes held each other at least as strongly as their arms did, until she broke the spell with her words, "You just make sure you get yourself back to us, you hear? That's all I've got to say!"

Nodding his promise, he placed a final farewell upon her trembling lips, turned, hoisted his lightly packed bedroll onto his left shoulder and slipped it over his head and under his right arm, and started for the door. Ida May rushed to beat him there, at first pretending she wouldn't let him pass, but then opening the door and standing aside. The three followed him onto the front porch, off which he lightly stepped and turned to wave good-bye.

Their calls of "good-bye," "take care," and "I love you" filled the chill air as he began briskly walking the wagonway that led the twelve miles up to Spring Valley, then on to Chatfield and beyond, to whatever adventures none of them yet knew.

Often he turned back to wave again at his family still standing and calling to him on the shanty's front porch, but he finally disappeared into the undulations of the southeastern Minnesota prairie. The last "good-byes" sent both directions became soft, almost whispered, more like prayers than farewells.

When she couldn't see him anymore, Ida May struggled out of her mother's grip and raced across the closest hayfield toward the nearby oak and hickory woodlot occupied by the pigs. She knew from that higher ground she would be able to look down on the wagonway as it wended its course westward before turning north.

Arriving as quickly as her short legs and stout heart could propel her, she was rewarded with one more glimpse of her father. He was by then moving rapidly away from all so dear to him. When he heard her call of "Pa!" he realized she had chased after him to the wooded overlook above, and his heart began to beat as wildly as his returning wave. Deeply touched by her utter devotion for him, he finally understood what had driven her to hide as their morning began.

As he then continued on his way, David Brainard Griffin renewed with even greater conviction his vow to himself: "*I will come back!*"

Chapter Three

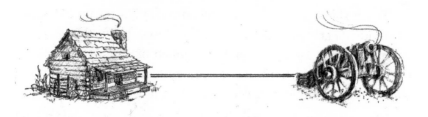

Harvest Time

Minerva knew it would be easier for idle hands and minds to brood over Brainard's departure than for busy ones, so she had plans for the girls that would take several days to accomplish.

Ida May had barely returned, breathless, from the high-ground woodlot when her mother set in. "Alice, Ida, we've got heaps to do yet in the garden 'afore winter comes. An' even more'n usual with your pa gone. Now, you girls go fetch the diggin' tools an' the stack of baskets from the shed whilst I check on little Edgar. I'll bring Eliza an' meet you by the root vegetables right away." Having said that, she turned to enter the house, while her daughters headed toward the low storage shed along the far side of the barn.

Ida May's mind was still stuck with the vision of her father receding along the wagonway. Grabbing Alice's hand to stop her big sister, she blurted, "Pa'll be all right, won't he, Alice? He'll be safe an' come back home, won't he?"

"Of course he will. Don't you be a'worryin' your little head none 'bout that." Alice reached out and smoothed the top of Ida May's black hair as she spoke with a reassuring smile, though she had been troubling herself with the same question. Taking her younger sister's hand, they continued to the shed, gathered the requested harvest items, and arrived back at the largest section of the garden patch just as their mother did.

"Eliza's got Edgar Lincoln a'sleepin' away in his crib. Poor little tyke's wore out from all your pa's horseplay. She'll be out right smartly. Oh, here she comes now." The sisters called out to their cousin before putting down the baskets and tools and ran to the porch to accompany her to the garden.

"Well, let's start with pullin' the carrots an' turnips," instructed Nerva. "My, won't they make good soup. We'll pull together as we work down the rows. Then they can dry out in the sun a bit before we top 'em."

"Will we be doin' the potatoes too, Aunt Minerva?"

"Their tops look like they still need a few more days to die back, Eliza, so we'd best leave 'em till next week. As for the pumpkins an' squashes," Nerva added as she pointed with her hoe to the far edge of the garden, "they can wait till a good frost hardens 'em. All that's left then are the parsnips. Them'll need to be covered with extra dirt 'cause we'll leave 'em to sweeten over the winter and dig 'em in the spring."

They set to work, and the indicated root vegetables pulled easily from the rich, loose soil. Both rows of each were soon harvested, with all those hands pulling. They laid the roots out, green tops still attached, close to the holes in which they had grown, and the strings of alternating colors on the dark earth would have looked like a child's painting from the edge of the garden.

Handing the older Alice and Eliza sharp knives, Nerva instructed them, "You two cut off the tops and put the roots in the baskets. Be sure you leave an inch or so on each, an' keep the carrots an' turnips separate. An' you be real careful of them knives, as I don't want to deal with any cut off fingers today." Taking it as the serious joke it was meant to be, the girls assured her they understood. "Any wormy ones, just put 'em with the tops for the pigs," completed her instructions to them.

Turning to her younger daughter, she continued, "Ida May, you gather up all the cut tops an' carry 'em to the trough by the barn for the pigs' supper. Won't they love that. I'll start diggin' the onions."

Alice and Eliza started carefully cutting and piling while Ida May began carrying the nutritious tops as directed. The two older girls took turns singing some rhyming songs they had learned at school as they worked. Ida May could only think about her pa. As she walked between the garden and the barn, she tried to imagine how far he had gotten, what he had seen, or who he might have met along the way. She didn't remember ever being beyond Alba or her grandparents' farm, except one trip up to her Aunt Mary's house in Spring Valley, so her extended thoughts were quite hazy.

When all the carrots and turnips were cut, six wicker baskets were piled high with long, straight, bright orange roots. Five more were overflowing with purple-white globes as big as fists. Alice gave a big sigh of amazement. "Can you believe all this, Eliza?"

"Granma's garden's done just as good as yours this year. Wonder if they're a'harvestin' at home like we are here?" As Eliza spoke, she tried to raise one of the baskets by its handles. "Whew. These're much too heavy for us to cart to your cellar, even if both of us are a'liftin'. We'll have to wait for your ma's help."

Meanwhile, since the onion tops had been broken back the week before to start the drying process, Nerva had to use her small wooden spade to dig rather than pull the onions. They, too, were laid out in the sun, but they would have to stay there for several days for the outside skin to cure before they could be gathered up for safe winter storage. She had only completed digging two of the long rows of these savory roots by the time the girls finished loading up all the baskets with their harvest.

Looking at the sun, which was already as high overhead as it would get on the northern prairie in late September, Nerva said,

"Let's stop for a bite of lunch. Edgar's most likely awake by now. We can do the carryin' an' the rest of the diggin' this afternoon."

The girls, tired but happily distracted, agreed at once and all four workers trooped over to the well to wash in a bucket of water drawn up, cold and clear, for that purpose.

As they approached the porch they could hear the light whimpering of the baby, so the girls hurried in to fuss over him while Nerva paused to survey the morning's work. She nodded with satisfaction and felt assured her husband would have been quite pleased with the harvest. She then followed the girls inside.

"Be good to the little'un, will you?" she called to them, "whilst I fix us up a bite to eat."

"Could we eat outside, Aunt Minerva? Please? It's such a nice day," inquired Eliza.

"I reckon that'd be all right. Sure, why not? We'll have us a little picnic down by the apple trees." After a pause, she added, "Won't that make Brainard wish he were here."

Soon the whole lot of them were traipsing down the short lane toward the small orchard that had been planted a year or so before the Griffins had arrived in Minnesota. The girls took turns carrying Edgar Lincoln, who appeared to be delighted to be outdoors again. Behind them, Nerva carried a sitting blanket over one arm and a packed picnic basket in the other hand.

The butter, soft cheese, and dill pickle slices for the sandwiches were all homemade, along with the bread itself, and those would very soon become chores for her daughters to undertake. That would free up time for Nerva to do more of the things Brainard had done. Water, drawn and carried by Eliza, and apples, picked by Alice, completed the meal. Edgar Lincoln was content to nurse, then lay on the blanket looking up into the apple trees and the puffy clouded sky beyond. He soon drifted off, like one of the clouds, to sleep again.

"Ma, where do you s'pose Pa is by now?" inquired Ida May, also lying on her back, idly enjoying this brief respite from the day's chores.

Concern for the family's immediate future was evident behind Nerva's eyes, but she quickly disguised it and answered her young daughter's question with a laugh. "Oh my, he must be halfway to Spring Valley by now. That's where he'll spend the night, at Mr. Colby's. He's prob'ly stopped along the way by some creek, eatin' his sandwiches too."

"What do we still need to do this afternoon?" Alice asked. For Ida May's sake, she was deliberately shifting the subject away from her missing father.

Her mother was already repacking the basket, but stopped to reply. "Besides finishin' diggin' the onions, we just need to carry the full baskets down to the root cellar. Then there's still the regular evening chores, of course."

***

With three of them digging, and five-year-old Ida May carefully laying out the large, fragrant roots, it didn't take long to complete harvesting the last of the onions. "There, that's done," proclaimed Nerva, as she looked with growing satisfaction at the four long rows laid neatly out to dry. "They'll be so tasty in our soups this winter."

"They sure will," answered Alice, remembering how bland the cooking had become by the end of winter when last year's onions ran out.

"Shall we carry down the carrots and turnips now?" Eliza asked.

"Ida May, you go ahead of us an' open the trapdoor. Make sure the way's clear. Eliza, dear, you get us a light down below, that's a good girl. Don't worry none if little Edgar awakens. It's a bit past his feedin' time anyway. Just leave him be till I get there. You both go on now. We'll be right behind you!"

Ida ran up to the shanty's porch and pushed aside the washstand from near the entryway so she could raise the door in the floor that led down a ladder into the cellar. She then peered down into the cellar's darkness below.

It was more cave-like than a real cellar because Brainard had not yet put in the usual wood siding and floor when he had dug it out. Along three of the dirt walls he had, however, nailed together shelving for the various jugs, baskets, and other containers that stored the family's winter food. The fourth wall was fronted by barrels of fruit and salted meats. Since it was below ground as well as beneath the insulation of their house, it was consistently cool and dry, summer and winter.

Eliza lit two candle stubs in the fireplace's low fire, and carefully holding the flamed candles together in one hand, descended the ladder and stuck the stubs into sconces on the wall at the bottom. With their light now flickering away the darkness in all but the corners of the small room, she looked up for the arrival of the harvest.

Edgar Lincoln began to whimper loud enough for Ida May to cross the room to his crib when Nerva and Alice arrived carrying the first basket between them. All Ida May could offer her baby brother at that moment was the comfort of her presence.

The step that followed, requiring two to carry the basket of carrots, would have been easy for Brainard, even by himself. But he was gone, likely already to Spring Valley for the night. There wasn't room for mother and daughter to go down through the trapdoor together. And because neither one of them was strong enough to handle a heavy vegetable basket by herself, they ended up tying a rope between the side handles and lowered each basket, one by one, into the cold storage area below, where Eliza waited to receive them.

When all the baskets were lowered, Alice joined Eliza below and they duly arranged them on the simple shelving. "Well, that's done," Alice said to Eliza while they climbed back up the ladder. As her head bobbed through the trapdoor, she asked, "What's next, Ma?"

"Them pigs," was her simple answer. "And soon's I've finished nursing Edgar Lincoln here, I'll take my milking stool and pail out to

Rosie in the pasture an' nurse her too." She laughed at her own joke and the two older girls joined in.

So all three girls, with Edgar again alternately carried by them, headed out across the pasture toward the woodlot where their pigs had been rooting around all day. Their job was to herd them all home to the supper of green tops Ida had carried to their trough. The herding sticks the girls wielded were hardly necessary as the pigs always seemed to know that supper awaited their return.

Edgar Lincoln chattered along in his usual lively way, still mostly unintelligible. But other than gentle encouragements to the pigs, the girls were mainly silent as they neared the end of the first day with Brainard gone.

Nerva had set a large pot of water to warm near the fireplace before she went out to do the milking. By the time everyone returned with their chores completed, this provided a refreshing cleansing of the day's dirt from hands and faces in preparation for the brief evening that remained.

Their light supper consisted of cornmeal cakes drizzled with a bit of honey, thin slices of fried ham, and fresh milk. A last burst of energy was spent playing with Edgar Lincoln on the floor while their mother cleaned up the supper dishes. By then, all three girls were ready for evening prayers and the climb up the eight-rung ladder to their sleeping loft above the fireplace. They changed into their long flannel nightgowns and tumbled into the low bed they shared. Its cornhusk mattress rustled familiarly as they snuggled in beneath two homemade quilts that would keep them warm through the lengthening chilly night. Holding hands, Ida May in the middle, they were soon asleep.

Nerva banked the fire in the fireplace with three of the largest chunks of wood Brainard had brought in before he left. She wouldn't have to get up to restack it until morning. Then, with Edgar Lincoln in her arms, she, too, slipped into bed. As she drifted into sleep, her thoughts wandered to her already faraway husband.

At the edge of those thoughts hovered the question both her heart and mind asked: *How will we ever get along till he returns?*

***

Although the care and feeding of all the farm animals required most of the family's time and attention, the harvest of their kitchen garden continued for the rest of that week and all of the next. Bushel baskets of harvested onions and potatoes followed the earlier carrots and turnips down through the trapdoor in the shanty's floor. After them came string-tied bunches of garden herbs, dried hanging upside-down beside the fireplace. The best of the ripe apples were carefully packed in straw in the barrels already below. Finally, strings of sliced apples, dried first in front of the fire overnight, were hung beside the herbs. In the middle of winter, they would be brought up, soaked in watered maple syrup, and baked into delicious apple pies.

During those long fall days, Edgar Lincoln was often left to entertain himself between naps, mostly by playing in the newly turned garden soil, where he could watch and be watched. But each evening he also thrived on the special attention of Ida May as she bathed away the day's accumulated dirt, while Alice and Eliza helped his mother with the barn and supper chores.

Occasionally he seemed curious about his father's absence, and would glance around the room with a toddler's quizzical look. *He's missing Pa*, Ida May often guessed when she saw this. So she would hug and rock him, whispering soft words in his ear, until his not-clear question was temporarily forgotten again.

Chapter Four

A Letter from Pa

The nearest settlement to the Griffins was called Alba. It lay a little over a mile away, by the same narrow, winding wagon track upon which Brainard had walked away to war. Hardly more than a crossing of roads, it consisted of only three homes, a single-room schoolhouse, and a blacksmith shop. Alice and her two Churchill cousins had begun attending that school the year before. The smithy was operated by the large-framed but always jovial Hiram Winslow.

A mile on the other side of Alba was a tiny general store attached to the home of Andrew Peters. It lived up to its name by being filled with small amounts of a large number of things needed in a prairie home: hardware for house and farmstead; sewing materials by the yard; barrels of foodstuffs, dried as well as locally produced; tins, jars, and sacks of edible ingredients; various iron and crockery housewares; leather goods, like boots and harnesses; and hunting and butchering supplies.

This store, to which everyone for miles around came, also served as the local post office, with Mr. Peters its postmaster. Twice a week a postal wagon from the twenty-five-mile distant county seat of Preston delivered and picked up the mail.

Nearly two weeks had passed since Brainard had left his family and farm for Chatfield, St. Paul, and the War of Secession beyond, when a man rode up to the Griffin homeplace. It was Allen Chipman, their neighbor to the east. He had often traded labors with Brainard, and had agreed to help Nerva however he could.

He slid off his horse and sauntered up to the front porch, glancing at their newly harvested kitchen garden as he passed. The still day of early October caused the morning's fall chill to linger, so he had on his long woolen overcoat and a scarf wrapped twice around his neck and tucked into his coat's front. "Howdy, Nerva. You doin' all right?" he asked when she answered his knock on the door.

She nodded with an uncomfortable smile, a bit unsure of herself and his errand, as she hadn't asked him to come for anything.

"See you've got yo'r garden stuff most about brought in," he continued. "Well, just stopped by to tell ya' yo've got a letter at the post office from yo'r man."

At that news, Philinda Minerva's wan smile brightened to a full grin. "Oh, thankee, Mr. Chipman, ever so much for that good news," a prayer-like clasp of her hands beneath her chin further expressing her gratitude. Turning into the room, she asked, "Did you hear that? Pa sent us a letter. Alice, I want you to go right now and fetch it home for us."

Alice was already halfway across the room to get her winter coat and hat hanging on the peg where she had placed them after completing her morning chores when she answered. But the softened tone of her "Yes, Ma" had nothing to do with the exciting news of a letter from her Pa. It was just that she worried as she calculated how long and alone the round-trip to the post office would be.

Sensing the hesitation in her elder daughter's voice, Nerva continued, "Why don't you take yesterday's butter to sell, an' bring home a small sack o' dried cherries er plums, whatever he's got, and I'll bake us a little party cake to celebrate when you get back?"

The evident pleasure of the combined tasks broke through her reservations, and Alice's face fairly beamed as she slipped into her coat and hat. "I'll get the butter and go," she said with increased enthusiasm.

Mr. Chipman had already returned to his waiting horse and started again toward his own home by the time Alice came running out the door, a small, cloth-wrapped bundle retrieved from their cellar hitched under her arm. Calling "good-bye" to him, she hurried in the opposite direction, with an occasional skip or hop in her step as her excitement grew.

From the many times she had walked to school—which was only halfway to the general store—she knew the round-trip would take her well more than an hour. But she didn't care. *Pa's all right! He's written us a letter!*

The mud-rutted lane to Alba crossed several shallow creeks and traversed intensely colored woodlots of maple, hickory, and oak as it wound across the undulating prairie toward the settlement. The few nonmigrating birds—mostly chickadees, waxwings, and several kinds of winter finches—were flitting from tree to tree looking for this day's nourishment. Rabbits, as well as other creatures, larger and smaller, quietly crept into hiding as the young girl approached. But seven-year-old Alice was mostly unaware of her surroundings as she passed by. She was totally focused on carrying out these all-important tasks for her family.

Nearly breathless from her self-imposed pace as well as her excitement, she eventually entered the village store and approached the broad counter. Only recently had she grown tall enough to see over it.

Mr. Peters, ruddy cheeked and green-aproned as always, smiled down at her with the friendly warmth of a low hearth-fire. He lived

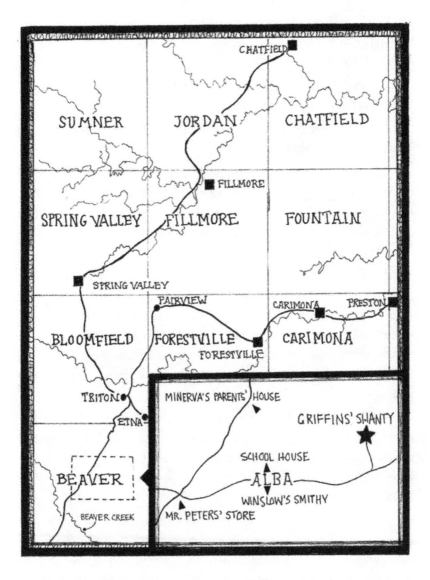

Map of western Fillmore County, MN with Beaver Township insert

alone since the passing of his wife several years before, but was never lonely because he enjoyed the company of all the folks who came in regularly to talk and trade goods and pick up their mail.

"Well, if it ain't little missy Griffin," Mr. Peters said, leaning his very large forearms forward on the countertop. "I do believe I've got a letter for your ma from your pa."

"I know, Mister Peters. That's why I've come. To fetch it home." Her breathing was finally returning to normal.

"And what's that 'ere bundle you're a'totin'?" he asked, pointing a wagging index finger at her.

"Butter," said Alice. "Fresh yesterday. Ma said to sell it for some dried cherries or plums so's she can make us a party cake to celebrate the letter from Pa." There was a pause, then "If you please," she added, as she raised the cloth-wrapped bundle and set it on the counter.

Reaching below the countertop into the wooden box containing the mail awaiting pickup, the clerk retrieved the desired letter and held it as he turned to the shelving behind him where the cooking ingredients were stored in glass and crockery jars, most of them tightly stoppered. His right hand hovered between two of them while he asked over his shoulder, "Cherries or plums, you say? I've got some of each. Which one do ya' want?"

Alice thought for just a moment, remembering with both her mind and her mouth her mother's cakes that celebrated special family occasions. She blurted out, "Cherries, please." Although she loved all her mother's party cakes, she knew her pa most especially loved the ones made with cherries.

After filling a small paper sack with the dried fruit, Mr. Peters held out his hands to Alice, the sack in one, the letter in the other. Alice, with only the slightest hesitation, reached both hands for only the letter and held its edges carefully as she read her mother's name, written large in the middle, then her father's name, written smaller up in the top corner.

To: Mrs. Philinda Minerva Griffin

Alba Post Office

Fillmore County, Minnesota

From: Pvt. David Brainard Griffin

Company F, 2nd Regiment MV

Fort Snelling, Minn.

"Pa," she whispered as she slipped it into her large apron pocket. Before turning to leave, she glanced up at the smiling storekeeper/postmaster still patiently holding the sack of dried fruit. Alice blushed, reached for the cherries and added them to the pocketed letter.

Then, with thanks called back to Mr. Peters as she ran out of the store, she began the return journey home. But the letter didn't stay in her pocket. Many, many times during that trip she drew it out to reread the names on the envelope, and whisper over and over again, "Pa."

***

Their cousin, Eliza, had walked the three miles back to her grandparent's home the day before, after her two-week stay, so just her own daughters were seated at Nerva's feet after the evening chores and supper. Both of them had snuggled up as close as they could get. The double-sized sheet of writing paper, filled front and back, was smoothed out on their mother's lap, and each girl had a small plate beside her, a few odd crumbs of the last of the cherry party cake yet to pick up. Edgar Lincoln slept peacefully beside his mother on the settle, tired from his day's play with Ida May and full from his evening feeding. The fire would keep the room warm for another hour or so, and then they would all need to be under their covers.

"Read it again, Ma, please?" begged Ida May. "I'm going to remember everything he writes us."

And Alice added, "I do hope Pa's all dressed up in his uniform when he gets his likeness taken. Won't he look different?"

So Nerva moved their single kerosene lantern closer and began to reread to them all that their father had told them on paper about what he had seen and done on his trip from home up to Fort Snelling: first on foot to Chatfield, where he was joined by several friends, then all of them by wagon across to Winona, and then by paddle-wheeled steamboat up the Mississippi River.

She read a second time his description of his new "outfit," which he said consisted of *"one overcoat, one dress coat, knapsack, canteen, haversack, and two pairs of shirts, drawers and socks, and one pair of shoes, one hat and one cap."* She heard them repeat their groans as he announced: *"We expect to start from here sometime next week for Washington, so I cannot come home before I go."* And she watched them turn and grin at each other again when he promised: *"I have not got my likeness taken yet. I will try to get it done before I write again. I will write before we go from here."*

She hoped his closing words, which were a great comfort to her, would cheer her daughters as well. And they did:

"While we are separated, we cannot help but think of one another, but we must be contented as it is. I shall write to you as often as I can, and all the news that I can think of. You must write to me as often as you can, and write how you all get along. Kiss the babies for me as often as you can. Tell them their Pa thinks of them pretty often and wishes he could see them all. Good-bye. Be a good girl and think of me, your friend and husband,

D. B. Griffin."

Nerva's voice choked a bit as she finished the letter and refolded it into its envelope. All three pairs of eyes glistened as a result of the reading, tears that were a mixture of joy and longing, of close family and painful separation.

"Well," concluded Nerva, "he got there safely, and he's gonna do all right. So are we. We'll be fine till he comes back. Now you young'uns get into bed a'fore the room gets cold."

When all the children were settled in for the night, Nerva was finally able to let flow the welling tears she had bravely kept back from her little ones. They were mixed tears. Some were simply relief at the news of his safe arrival. Others came from the uncertainty of his future in this war that had taken him from them. But also, and perhaps the largest share, originated in all the unknowns she now faced without him. For nearly half an hour she allowed this cleansing. Then she too, emotionally comforted and exhausted, lay down to rest, alone.

Chapter Five

Pa Writes Again

Two weeks later, Nerva bundled up her children against the late October chill for an important bartering trip into Alba. The three were loaded into the straw-covered bed of the family's small farm wagon, along with six one-gallon crocks of their freshly made apple butter, two squealing but tightly tied hogs, and a picnic basket for a lunch break during their half-day excursion. Ol' Jim, the prairie family's only horse for either pulling or riding, was all hitched up, ready to go.

The muslin covered crocks of apple butter were part of the batch she and the girls had cooked down the week before. They had used those apples from their crop that were not nice enough to keep whole or slice and dry on strings before the hearth. The washed, peeled, and chunked apples had been piled into Nerva's spiky legged iron kettle just off the front porch.

The kettle's "spider legs" allowed for a small fire to burn beneath it. Throughout most of the next two days it had been Ida May's responsibility to tend that fire with small bits of wood. Not only did she need to make sure the fire was constantly burning, she also had to keep it low enough so as not to scorch the kettle's contents.

All that while, Alice and their mother had taken turns stirring the apple pieces with a large wooden paddle. Once, when Nerva handed the paddle back to her daughter, her eyes had misted over, and, with a slight choke in her voice, had reminisced, "I can still see yo'r pa—years ago now, when we was first married—sittin' on our old porch back in Vermont a'whittlin' this out for me." The awe on Alice's face as she took the paddle was reward enough for this revealed memory.

The softly blurping sauce had slowly thickened as it cooked down into the sweet brown preserves the family loved on their winter's morning biscuits. Over that time span, even little Edgar Lincoln had discovered the sheer delight of licking warm apple butter from his tiny fingers.

Altogether, ten crocks had been filled, with a small bowlful left over for immediate consumption. Four of those had been covered with muslin and taken down to the root cellar to add to their winter stores, while the remaining six were now on the wagon, to be traded in town for supplies.

As for the hogs, Mr. Chipman had stopped by earlier that morning to help Nerva catch, truss up, and load the two squealers. Like everything else on the Griffin farm, they were part of the produce upon which the family lived.

Their two mama sows had raised fourteen piglets between them. Brainard had already sold a neighbor four of the little ones at weaning time. Of the ten that remained, two had simply not come back from their daily foraging trip to the close-by acorn and hickory nut woods, four were to be butchered and salted down in a month or so for the family to eat, and the two that were trussed up in the wagon were ready to be sold. The last two, the runts, wouldn't be ready for market until the end of the year.

The familiar three-mile trip to Mr. Peters' store was uneventful. They met no one on the country lanes they took, and the world seemed to be already quieting itself down for its annual long winter's nap.

Edgar Lincoln fell asleep between his sisters almost as soon as the wagon had begun moving, but Alice and Ida May chattered along the way about the January start of the school term. Ida May desperately wished this term would mark the beginning of her formal education. She lamented that she had yet another whole year to wait.

Nerva's plan for part of their bartering trip would be to trade for new shoes for the children as well as for fabrics she would make into school clothes for Alice and work dresses for both girls. She knew she had plenty of things already laid by for Edgar Lincoln to grow into, so she wouldn't have to focus on him just yet. They also needed additional cash to pay the monthly schooling fee for Alice.

Alba, itself, was as quiet as the trip from the farm. They didn't even meet anybody as they continued on to their final destination at Mr. Peters' store. Nerva urged Jim up to the hitching post in front. When they finally arrived, her words changed to "Whoa there, easy now," then she jumped down to tie his lead harness to the rail.

Alice and Ida May had nudged Edgar Lincoln awake as soon as they had seen Mr. Peters' place in the distance so that all three were ready to be helped down. They immediately headed into the store, Edgar Lincoln happily riding piggyback on Alice's shoulders. "Keep watch on your brother, now," Nerva reminded her girls as the three disappeared inside.

"Hello there, young Griffins!" was Mr. Peters' greeting to the children as they entered. "Law me, this *is* your lucky day!"

"How's that?" asked Alice as the siblings moved up to the counter. Three expectant faces smiled up at the always jolly store clerk for his answer.

"Why, 'cause you've gotta 'nother letter from your pa, that's why. Just come in today. But I'm guessing you didn't even know it!"

"No, sir, Mister Peters," said Ida May. "We just brung in some of our fresh-made apple butter an' a couple o' tied-up hogs to trade with you."

"Is that a fact? Then this here's *my* lucky day too, for I've got customers askin' 'bout *both* them items! Your ma still out with the wagon?" he asked. Responding to the girls' unison nods of affirmation, the clerk headed toward the store's front door, adding, "There's some hard candies in the dish there for ya' to suck on whilst I help your ma unload."

***

When the dress fabrics were chosen, cut, and folded, the new shoes fitted and wrapped, the necessary school supplies bundled up, and the remaining value in exchange for the apple butter and hogs paid in cash, Mr. Peters handed Nerva the newly arrived letter. After a quick heart-tugging glance at the familiar script, Nerva let the girls briefly hold and examine the envelope containing more news from their father. One by one they turned it over and back, marveling at the neatly handwritten words that had directed the letter from him to them. Ida May finally held it out for Edgar Lincoln to see as she whispered: "It's from Pa."

"Ma, can we open it?" asked Alice, with a trace of awe in her voice.

"Please, oh please?" pleaded Ida May.

"Hush now," their mother replied. "Let's go find us a picnic spot like we planned and read it together there." She indicated which bundles Alice and Ida May were to carry, picked up Edgar Lincoln in her free hand, and led her young family to the door. From the doorway, all said their polite "thank you for the candies" and "good-byes" to Mr. Peters, then exited the store.

The girls eagerly climbed into the wagon themselves, scrambling up the wagon wheels and over the sideboard, then reached down to grasp their brother as he was handed up to them. Untying the horse, Nerva climbed up onto the driver's seat, and with a "Hud up, Jim," they circled back around toward home.

"I'm thinkin' of that sheltered place, right by the first stream crossing," she called over her shoulder to her children. "Spring Creek, I believe it's called. It's a bit chilly, but the day's nice enough. We'll be warm an' dry there whilst we eat our lunch an' read our letter."

The girls were elated by the prospect. Edgar Lincoln was only interested in continuing to lick the sticky sweetness off his fingers and lips.

During the twenty minutes it took to get there, the sisters speculated on the news their father had sent. "Bet he misses us," "Hope he's not sick or nothin' bad," and "What if he's comin' home!" were some of the things they had to say. Ten-month-old Edgar Lincoln occasionally looked up, smiled his boyish smile, and said the single word and memory "Pa" over and over to himself.

As soon as their mother pulled off the wagon road, Alice and Ida May were ready to jump down on their own. "Don't forget your brother," reminded Nerva, "nor our picnic basket."

"No, Ma," responded Alice as she picked up Edgar Lincoln to hand him down to her, while Ida May turned back to retrieve their lunch. Alice had already followed her brother over the sideboard and taken him from her mother when her younger sister swung the heavy basket down into Nerva's outstretched hands, then clambered over the edge herself.

A circle of smooth boulders in the small roadside clearing made perfect seats for the family, though Edgar Lincoln wasn't content to stay long, even for something to eat. Instead, he began crawling around the circle as fast as his little hands and knees would carry him. It was with a similar impatience that the girls waited, although more for the reading of the letter than the food. But Nerva insisted on carefully readying all before agreeing to open the precious letter.

When she finally did, the girls were munching silently on their biscuits and hard-boiled eggs, one on either side of her, looking on as the words on the page began to come to life.

"My dear Beloved wife and children,

I take my pen in hand once more and address a few lines to you and let you know how I am getting along. I am well . . . and have enjoyed myself as well as could be expected."

After looking with satisfaction into each other's eyes, both girls turned their gaze up to their mother's face as she continued reading his recorded details about the units of men at Fort Snelling and the variety of activities in the camp that filled their father's daily schedule. Then they gasped in unison, each with a hand raised to her open mouth, when Nerva read the words:

"The 2nd regiment starts from here Monday morning at 6 o'clock for Washington, so I expect this will be the last letter you will get from me until I get there . . ."

"He's not coming home? Not at all?" wailed Ida May.

Nerva quieted her with a calming hand gesture and continued reading, though her voice trailed off as she scanned the next few lines. She picked up again, with a decided choke in her throat at:

"I should like to hear from home and the little ones (kiss them for me), and may God bless and protect you all."

Nerva stopped and looked at the girls.

"Is that all, Ma?" Ida May looked quickly back at her sister for support.

"No, love. He wrote a bit more, uh, later in the day . . . He says he got his likeness taken, and had it sent to us. He adds:

"I should like to stand in some corner when you get it and see how you act, but I can guess." He mentions the friends he's with . . . and he wants to know how I'm a'gettin' along on the farm, now that I'm the boss." Then with a laugh she said, "And he reminds me I need to get the barrels made for salting down the pork before we butcher the hogs. An' he bids us all good-bye."

"Well, bless his heart," Nerva continued. "On the back he's got a note, *'To Alice and Ida Griffin.'* That's you, isn't it?" she teased.

41

"To us?" squealed Ida May, clapping her hands twice. Alice simply looked up imploringly into her mother's face, eyes squinched in anticipation. Nerva read it aloud, alternating her voice's direction between her daughters:

Now I will write to you a little. Pa would give a good deal if he could see you here today I would show you the soldiers when they come out on dress parade. They look pretty, I tell you. I see lots of little girls here every day and little babies. Kiss Edgar for me, won't you? There now, Pa is crying. Be good girls and help Ma take care of him, and when he grows up to be a man he will be good to you. Pa thinks of you a good many times every day. Pa has not undressed himself since he came away from home. He eats his dinners outdoors and sleeps on some hay in tents. Ma will tell you what they are. Now ain't that funny? Now you must write to Pa when Ma does, because Pa does not know when he will see you again. Kiss one another for me, and then kiss Ma for me. Now there, Pa will have to stop and go to work. I have to mend my trousers for they have not got any new ones for me. You would laugh at me wouldn't you, to see me sewing my breeches, but I make it go first rate, I tell you, but good-bye to Alice J, and Ida M. Griffin from their father,

David Brainard Griffin."

The girls did as he had asked, held and kissed each other with tears of sorrow and joy streaming down their faces. Then they both grabbed their mother as she corralled the still-circling Edgar Lincoln. The four shared more kisses between them all before piling back into the wagon and heading, emotionally exhausted, for home.

"Sleeping in tents" was the topic of conversation along the way.

Chapter Six

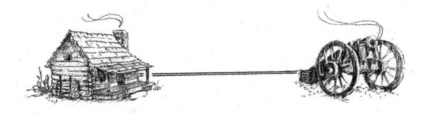

Fall Chores

Fall began to turn decidedly toward winter over the next two weeks. Minerva still did not have to waken more than once in the night to restack the fireplace, but each morning the frost covering the world outside their shanty got heavier and took a little longer to thaw. The colorful maple, oak, and hickory leaves had nearly all fallen, and with them the last of the summer's acorns and maple seeds, as well as the new crop of flavor-filled hickory nuts.

Alice and Ida May herded the family's four hogs, saved for winter meat, up the small wooded hill each afternoon, taking Edgar Lincoln in tow to give their mother a break. There the hogs fattened quickly on the rich harvest of seeds and nuts, which they rooted out each afternoon with considerable porcine shoving and snorting.

The girls had to compete with the hogs, trying to gather as many of the delicious hickory nuts as possible to keep for their mother's winter baking. Their young brother was never any help, for he preferred to sit in a gathered pile of crunchy fallen leaves. He would toss handfuls of them into the air and laugh as they sifted back down over him. But together Alice and Ida May managed to

43

bring back a nearly full basket every day when they shooed the hogs home. These baskets were then lifted up the ladder to the girls' sleeping loft, where the nuts could dry and cure from the rising fireplace heat before cracking.

It was also time for their storage cellar to receive the large blue-green winter squashes and sweet orange pumpkins. They were still attached to the vines that were by then withered a dry brown, but were easily cut free. Their "meat" would make many nourishing soups and savory pies during the long winter months ahead.

One Saturday morning in early November, Ida May asked at breakfast, "Ma, when are we gonna hear from Pa again?"

"I don't know, my love. I reckon it may be some time yet, for they're all on their way to Washington City. But here's somethin' I *do* know: It's cold enough now to butcher them hogs you've been takin' to the woods each day. An' we've *got* to make sure we get our barrels made first!"

Alice brought the wash basin with a kettle of fire-warmed water to the table to do up the breakfast dishes while Ida May played with Edgar Lincoln on the floor. Their mother, her morning milking already done, was about to head out to finish her barn chores when Alice asked, "Who will make the barrels for us?"

"I was a'thinkin' I'd ask Mr. Chipman. Mr. Wallace always done it a'fore, but they moved on last week. I was hopin' Chipman would then help us with the butcherin' too. I wonder what he'll want for all that? Half a hog, I 'spect. Hope not more'n that." She placed an index finger to her pursed lips in a pondering gesture and continued, "I s'pose I should go see him today to make 'rangements. But what'll I do 'bout you children?"

"Why not take Edgar Lincoln with you? He'd like the ride, an' he's not much help anyway," interjected Alice with a laugh at her own joke. "We'll be all right."

Ida May confirmed her sister's statement with a slow nod of her head, repeating, "We'll be all right, Ma." Then after a slight pause she added, "You won't be gone long, just to Mr. Chipman's."

"Well, I've been thinkin' I'd head over to Grampa's place too, an' ask if any of them would feel up to helpin' us a bit."

Her parents, Almon and Polly Griffin, had settled in the section a couple of miles beyond Alba soon after Brainard and Minerva had begun their homestead. They had moved, with their son, Allen, from the village in Vermont where both their daughter and her husband had been raised. Already slowed by their age, they now had their hands full, raising the two orphaned children of their oldest daughter. That's why at least one of the young girls, usually eleven-year-old Eliza, often spent weeks at a time at the shanty with Alice and Ida May. Her older sister, Hellen, at fourteen, was already a big help to her grandparents, both in the house and in assisting her Uncle Allen around the farm.

The grandparents' place was the opposite direction from Mr. Chipman's and would more than triple the length of her trip. But her daughters encouraged her to go anyway, for grandparents and cousins would be a welcome assist in the butchering process. "Besides," Nerva thought out loud, "then we could maybe help them get in the last of their firewood."

So it was decided. And after ample warnings to the girls about being careful and constantly on the lookout for the wandering wolves that were reported to be hunting ever closer to their homestead, Nerva climbed into the buggy with Edgar Lincoln, both bundled in their winter quilts. As Ol' Jim trotted smartly away, Alice and Ida May waved gay good-bye and began herding the hogs toward the woods for their afternoon feeding.

"Ma trusts us good, doesn't she?" Ida May inquired of her older sister as their sticks prodded the grunting pigs up the hill.

"She *has* to," Alice quickly responded. "Without Pa, we're all she's got! But you're right, it feels good inside that Ma knows we can be responsible."

As the pigs approached the woods, already snuffling for nuts and seeds, the sisters gave each other a quick, satisfying hug confirming their shared pride over the task they had been trusted with. And Ida

May agreed as Alice reminded her, "Be sure you keep on the lookout for wolves, like Ma warned."

Meanwhile, the arrangements Nerva needed to make went well at both stops. In fact, Mr. Chipman, anticipating Minerva's need for barrels, already had two of them made and waiting for her. To allow him time to make the other two, they agreed on the following Friday for the butchering date—weather permitting—with an early morning start. Her family also agreed to come, and her mother even promised to bring a basket of huckleberry muffins for a morning break and two loaves of fresh slicing bread for noon sandwiches. "We'll see you then next Friday," Polly promised her daughter, and after a round of hugs, Nerva and her son headed for home.

Because both errands had been accomplished so quickly, and the day was still clear and calm, Minerva decided to circle around the long way and stop at Mr. Peters' store to purchase the large sacks of salt and sugar they would need to cure the meat. That would save her a later trip back for them. Her *real* reason, however, was to check on the possibility of a hoped-for letter from Brainard.

Perhaps it was thinking about her absent husband instead of the road before her that caused Minerva to miss the turnoff for Alba. She absentmindedly continued on her southerly journey another half a dozen miles, almost to the Iowa border. She was shocked as she looked around the open prairie and for a brief moment had no idea where she was.

"Goodness me," she exclaimed to nobody in particular. "How did we get here? We must be purty near Iowa!" Edgar Lincoln had long since nodded off, his head resting on her lap, but when he heard her voice and felt the buggy suddenly stop, he awoke and began to softly whimper, desiring to be fed.

After taking care of her hungry son, Minerva turned the buggy around and retraced the miles back to the village where she should have taken the road to the right. When she finally arrived at Mr. Peters' place, somewhat shaken by the experience, she tied Jim to the hitching post and lifted Edgar Lincoln down and carried him into the general store.

"Afternoon to you, Miz Griffin," were the words that greeted Minerva when she walked in, but what quickly caught her attention were the two letters Mr. Peters held up, one in each plump hand. "Saw ya' ride in, an' thought ya' just might want these."

Minerva rushed to the counter and put Edgar Lincoln down at her feet so she could take the letters into her own hands. She looked back and forth at the treasured communications. Both were from Brainard. "Oh yes, Mister Peters, I surely do. Imagine that, *two* letters!" Placing them with a loving pat into the pocket of the apron she'd worn beneath her winter coat, she looked back up at the store clerk, remembering her other purpose for stopping. "I'll be needin' four sacks of salt and two sacks of raw sugar, as we'll be butcherin' our hogs next Friday."

"Got 'em round at the loadin' dock at the back, if you care to bring yo'r buggy around," he said. "Shall I just mark it down, or will this be cash on the barrelhead?"

"Mark it down, please, Mister Peters. We'll settle up later."

Edgar Lincoln, having been set down to wander on his own, crawled up to the familiar counter, pulled himself up on its glass front, and began eying the row of penny candy jars.

As Mr. Peters was writing the order in his ledger, he noticed the look on the young boy's face. Allowing his hand to pause briefly over each jar, he watched until Edgar Lincoln's face lit up to a full grin, so he dipped into that jar and handed the little one a piece of red striped peppermint candy. The sheer joy in the boy's eyes as he stuck one end into his mouth was thanks enough.

Watching what had happened, Minerva smiled and remarked, "I'll bring my buggy round to the back," and carried her son out the door.

***

Once home, Minerva guided the buggy into the barn, where the salt, sugar, and two new barrels would be stored briefly with the butchering equipment. She climbed out, then lifted down the sleeping form of her young son and carried him into the shanty, carefully laying him in his cradle to continue his nap. Returning to the porch, she began clanging the dinner bell to signal one of the girls to come in, and headed back to the barn to unhitch and feed Jim. She had hardly finished when Ida May came running all breathless into the yard, yelling ahead, "What's wrong, Ma?"

"Nothin's wrong, child. This time it's what's right." As she held the letters up, she said, "And what's right is I've got *two* letters from your pa. Now go get your sister, an' bring them hogs back, even if it's early yet, so's we can read 'em together. Go on now, scoot!"

"Letters?" responded Ida May. "From Pa?" She spun around and sped back toward the woods at a gallop, whooping all the way, "Alice! *Letters*, Alice! From Pa!"

Soon the girls had urged both sows and their now fully grown offspring home to their pen by the barn. Into the shanty they raced, to find their mother calmly waiting for them at the table, her hands quietly resting on the still unopened letters, as if already drawing strength from them. While Edgar Lincoln slept, Nerva opened the first envelope, and as she unfolded her husband's written page, a second page, smaller and folded, slid onto the table. "Why, this here one's addressed to you girls," she said as she glanced at its greeting.

Both sisters responded with murmured excitement, but immediately began encouraging their mother to read her own letter first.

"Lebanon Junction, Kentucky - October 24, 1861

I seat myself down on the ground, in a tent with a board in front of me to write upon, in order to write a few lines to you and let you know where we are and how I am getting along. You will see by the heading of this letter where I am. I am well as usual, and have not been sick as yet. I suppose you would like to know how I came here . . ."

Brainard then described the regiment's boat trip from St. Paul to La Crosse, followed by trains to Chicago and then Pittsburgh. He wrote of how heartened he was that all along the way they were cheered by flag and handkerchief waving crowds of excited citizens. But in Pittsburgh, he reported, their destination was changed, and they were ordered onto three Ohio River boats heading, with four other regiments, for the war front near Louisville instead, a trip of more than 600 miles. After arriving, he wrote, they had set up camp and began to wait for further orders.

The girls exchanged occasional glances of delight, but most of the time their eyes were glued to their mother's lips as she made their father's words come to life from the pages he had written.

Brainard concluded:

"We cannot tell when we shall go from here, nor where we shall go when we do. There is a good many rumors in camp . . . I hope that I shall hear from you before long, for I am anxious to hear from you all."

His brief note to his daughters, written the next day, had an appropriately different tone:

"My dear affectionate children, Alice and Ida Griffin,

As I have written a good lot to Ma, I will write a few lines to you. Pa is well this morning and he hopes that his little girls are well too and his little boy babe Edgar Lincoln. I live right by the side of the railroad and there is a train of cars a going by now. Last night one came by with a great lot of soldiers and twelve great big cannons to shoot the rebels with. Pa don't know but that he will have to go and help shoot them too. I have to go out every day and learn how to use a gun. We have a lot of music here every day. Two brass bands and two martial bands. Pa sees lots of little black babies here. They are just as black as the ground, and they are most of them slaves. Poor little things. Pa feels sorry for them. You must have Ma write to me for you. Now be good girls and mind Ma. I wish that I could see you this morning, and talk to you, and kiss you all, but I cannot, so good-bye, good-bye.

This from your father, Brainard Griffin."

"What are slaves, Mama?" asked Ida May, puzzled by her father's expressed sorrow over them. "And why are they black?" she continued, innocent because of her family's northern prairie isolation. "Did they get burned in a fire?"

"No, silly," answered her sister quickly. "They were brought here from Africa. They're different, that's all. Their skin is just dark, not light like ours. That's what I've learned at school. There's even pictures of 'em in books," she concluded, with obvious pride at being ahead of her little sister.

"And slaves, my dear . . ." Thus began the next quarter hour's series of questions and answers about how some people controlled and used others for their own profit, and how that resulted in the present conflict between the states, which required their father's absence.

When Ida May finally seemed content, Nerva picked up the second envelope and exclaimed, "Gracious me, we've still got another whole letter to read!" And so their time connected to their husband/father through pen and paper continued:

"October 29, 1861: I seat myself down once more to write a few lines to you. I am well as usual with the exception of a toothache. I had it all day yesterday and last night, but it has stopped now. There was a battle fought a week ago about 30 miles from here at a place called Wildcat, in which the Rebels were driven back with a loss of near a thousand men. Ours was less than fifty killed and wounded. If the Rebels had won the day, they would have marched on for Louisville, and if they had done so we would have tried hard to have stopped them. But they did not, so we missed all of the fun this time . . . How is it there this fall? How many potatoes was there? How does the hogs gain? And how many have you sold? How does Mr. Chipman get along? I would give most anything to see you all tonight, but we are a long ways apart, you in a shanty, and I in a tent. I want that you should write to me as often as you can. I have not heard a word from home since I left there . . ."

***

It was Alice's question that prompted the next letter to be written. "Why aren't we writing to Pa?"

The question was one Nerva had been asking herself, especially with regard to his pleadings for home news. She had been putting it off because she always felt so tired at the end of each day, what with having to keep everything going on her own. But now she knew she ought not delay any longer. "We'll write 'im tomorrow," she announced.

So, in the late afternoon of the next day, as the soup pot slowly simmered their evening's meal by the fire, the first letter to Brainard Griffin was written. Nerva did the actual writing, of course, but she readily incorporated her daughters' suggestions.

"You must tell Pa about getting lost in the buggy with Edgar." "Tell him we've gotten *four* letters from him, and we read them over and over." "But we haven't got his likeness yet, what he wrote about back from the fort." "What about our new neighbor, Mr. Gilman? I'll bet Pa don't know the Wallaces have moved." "He'll want to know how Edgar Lincoln's doing." "Say I said 'ouch!' about his toothache." "Do tell him I dream about him every night." "Me too, I do too." "And thank him for *our* letters!"

Nerva also included her own news, writing of managing the farm accounts at Peters' store, of all their garden harvesting, of preparing Alice for the start of school, of planning the spring crops with Mr. Chipman, and what she had set up for hog butchering, adding:

"So you can see you don't need to worry none about us, as we're getting' along all right. I must say, however, I sure will be glad to see you a'comin' home!"

They concluded the letter with final greetings from them all, and wishes for God's blessings to be upon him while he was gone. Sealed up, it was addressed as he had directed: *Pvt. D. Brainard Griffin, Company F, 2nd Minnesota Volunteers, Lebanon Junction, Kentucky.*

That letter, the first of many, would be posted at Alba on their next trip into town.

***

The following Thursday was the day before the hogs were scheduled to be turned into meat for their table. Minerva spent a good part of the day in the barn, readying the assortment of ropes and pulleys, knives and sharpeners, and trestle tables and buckets that would be required the next morning. She wasn't satisfied until she had checked over everything a third time. She felt she had to, for with Brainard away, the preparation was all up to her.

Instead of having the girls drive the hogs one last time up into the woods, Minerva set them to sweeping out the tiny smokehouse and stacking beside it plenty of cut hickory branches. The slow smoldering of the branches, along with the sugar-salt rub, would provide the desired sweet, smoky flavor to the sides of bacon and hams to be hung and cured inside the building over the next three to four weeks.

Supper as well as bedtime was early that night, for the mess and commotion of the next day would come all too soon for the Griffins. In fact, even the rooster was still asleep in the pre-dawn hour when Minerva woke the girls. She needed them to get breakfast ready and wake and dress their brother while she went out to milk their cow. This day there would be little time to do anything more with the milk than just carry the large container down into their cellar to cool. "*P'raps cheese next week,*" she thought to herself.

The four of them were still at table when they heard Mr. Chipman's wagon drive up. As they cleaned up their breakfast dishes, they watched him get right to work, off-loading the other new barrels, then turning his attention to the pigpen, where he began tying each hog's feet together. The trussed hogs' noisy complaints, as well as the confused snortings of the separated sows, were not enough to cover the cheerful sounds of the arrival of the wagonload of grandparents and cousins. With their mother's permission, both girls burst out the door and ran to meet the wagon, adding their affectionate greetings to those of their grandparents and cousins. Mr. Chipman chimed in his "helloos" as he finished hog-tying the hogs.

Everything was ready. Everyone was there. All that remained was for the squealing to begin.

Chapter Seven

Letters from Pa

The following week, Nerva brought home a small packet postmarked from Fort Snelling. It was addressed by a different hand than Brainard's, but bore no return address. Curious as to both its sender and contents, she started to open it as soon as she hung up her coat and hat.

"What is it, Ma?" Ida May had crowded under the crook of her mother's arm, equally curious about the packet.

They both gave an inhaled gasp of pleasure when the last string was cut and the wrapping removed, for inside lay the long-awaited "likeness" Brainard had had made before his regiment headed south. The two-by-three-inch tintype portrayed him in full dress uniform, seated in a plain wing chair, as he stared somewhat stiffly straight into the lens of the camera.

To protect it from scratches, it was mounted under glass in a small wooden frame, painted glossy black. The frame closed with a side latch made of the same shiny brass that surrounded the glass.

"Doesn't he look just grand?" Nerva passed the framed picture of her husband to an eager Ida May. "What do ya' think of your Pa, all dressed up like that?"

Alice looked up from her reading, having heard the excitement in their voices. At her sister's insistence, she walked across the room and was handed the small treasure. The girls then took turns holding it in both hands, and each let out soft sighs as gentle kisses were placed on the glass-covered image of their father. "Can we keep it right here on the table? It'll almost be like he's with us," asked Alice.

"Course we can," said Nerva as she leaned the opened frame against the painted porcelain bowl that centered their table. The bowl was special as it was one of the few nice things the family had brought with them from Vermont, and it usually had some dried fruit or nuts in it for snacking.

Three letters also arrived over the next weeks, all from Brainard, and all postmarked from Lebanon Junction, Kentucky. They contained colorful vignettes of camp life, and all of them begged Nerva to write with news of family and farm. Because their first letter had not yet gotten through to him, each of Brainard's letters grew more desperate in tone as the weeks piled up without a single word from home.

November 11-12:

"My dear children, I am well and I hope that you are well, for Pa would not like to have his little children sick in Minnesota and he be away down here in Kentucky. How I would like to come up there for this evening and go into the shanty and talk to my little ones, and laugh and play with them, but no, instead of that I am away down here in a tent, talking to them on a piece of paper, and instead of laughing and playing, I am crying. You must keep still and let Ma write a good long letter to me, and tell her what to write for you too. You must try and read Pa's letters if you can, and write to him too. Pa has to go out on guard once in a while. He has to stand out all alone in the woods with a gun and keep watch of everything that is a going on.

And if I should see anybody and should tell them to halt three times and they should not stop, then I have to shoot them if I can. But I hope I shant have to shoot anyone . . . I am well and hearty yet, and anxiously looking for a letter from you every day. I have written six letters to you but have not received one word from home yet. It would do me a great deal of good to hear from you and to know how you are getting along.

We are all anxious to go from here and get into some place where there will be something to do. All the Regiment has to do is to guard the railroad each way from here for two to four miles, and to keep a guard about the camp. The Rebels are fortifying themselves at Bowling Green, which is about 60 miles from here, and if we get into any battle this fall, it will probably be there.

Minerva, I want that you should write to me as often as you can, for we are far from each other and the only way we have of conversing is on paper. You do not know how much good it would do me to get a good long letter from you . . ."

November 15-18:

"I am well today and in good spirits. There is not but one thing lacking for me to be happy, and that is a good long letter from home with good news from you and about everything else. I think every morning that when the mail comes in, there will be a letter for me, but no. I have been away from home for seven weeks and not one word from you yet. You cannot tell how anxious a soldier is to get a letter from his home.

The Colonel of our Regiment says that we should not be surprised if we were all back in Minnesota in three months time. I hope that will be so. God knows I do. But I think we shall see some active service before we go home. If we do, it is not probable that all of us will escape the bullets of the enemy, but I hope so.

I want that you should tell me whether you get all my letters or not. This makes 8 that I have written to you. I look anxiously for a letter from you because I want to know how you are and how you get along this cold weather. I heard you had some snow in Minnesota. How do Grandpa and Grandma get along? Who is a going to keep the school this winter? Has there been anyone else enlisted from there since I came away? Have any of you been sick? How do you get along for wood? How much do the hogs you kept weigh? Now be sure and write to me . . ."

Then, finally, he was able to rejoice:

November 22:

"I have just received your first letter written to me, and you had better believe that I was glad to hear from you all and to hear that you all are well. I am well today. Better than I expected to be a few days ago. Last Monday afternoon I had an ague chill and a hard fever all night. The tent has been full all day, but when I read your letter, I could not keep back the tears in spite of the crowd. I am glad that you get along with your work first rate, and hope that you and Mr. Chipman will get everything fixed up for winter so that you will enjoy yourself as well as you can. I hope that you will look out and not get lost upon the prairies anymore. Mr. Gilman will make a good neighbor. You say that you would be glad to see me. I do not believe that you would give more to see me than what I would to see you and the children. God bless their little hearts, and may you never repent it for letting me go and leave you. Tell the children to dream away about their Pa, for he hopes that someday he will come home.

I shall not worry about you at all now, for I think that you will get along first rate, but I shall look for another letter from you all the time until I get one."

Chapter Eight

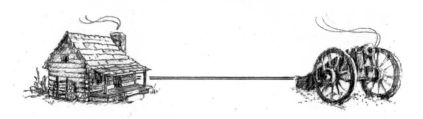

Family Times

The weather continued its dry but inescapable downward turn. Life on the farm and within the shanty settled into accomplishing the remaining prewinter chores. There was plenty for the girls and their mother to do, especially with school set to start soon, meaning Nerva would lose Alice's help each day.

"How long do I have to keep the little fire going in the smokehouse, Ma?" Alice's question at breakfast came a full week after the hog butchering day. She was responsible for tending the smoldering pile of hickory branches, contained for safety in a large rusted-out kettle on the smokehouse floor. The slight irritation in her voice was a result of the fact that her sister's job was already done.

Ida May had been responsible for taking care of the fire beneath their largest kettle, where the chunks of fat were rendered into lard. The whole process had only taken a single day to complete.

Alice even had to help Ida May ladle the rendered lard into bread pans to cool and harden, though her younger sister finished up the project alone. She wrapped the lard loaves in butcher paper and took them one by one down to the cool root cellar. There she stacked them neatly on the shelf next to the crocks of apple butter. Through the winter they would be needed for cooking, candles, and soap making.

"Till the smoke has fully cured them sides of bacon an' all of them hams we got hangin' in there. Not a day shorter, nor a day longer. But don't you fret none," her mother answered, "'cause I checked 'em this mornin' on my way out to milkin' an' they seem to be dryin' nicely ... maybe another week or so is all."

Alice buttoned a heavy cotton jacket over her warm woolen sweater and opened the door. Her relief was evident in the jollier tone of her voice as she said, "I'll let the chickens out to scratch, and bring in today's firewood while I watch the smokehouse fire." Then she pulled the door closed and skipped off the porch to do her chores.

"What's my morning chore, Ma?" asked Ida May. She hoped it wouldn't be much as she was looking forward to some time to play with the corn shuck dolls her father had made for her the week before he left.

"It'd help me most if you'd do up these here breakfast dishes whilst the milk cools a bit more. I've gotta toss down 'nough hay for the week for Rosie, Ol' Jim, an' the oxen, an' also grind up a couple bushel o' corn for the hogs an' chickens. That'll take up the rest of my mornin' I reckon."

"That's all I need to do?"

"Well, when the milk's cooled, you can scrape off the risen cream, add it to what I saved from yesterday, an' then churn it into butter, real careful, like you always do. Be sure an' take the buttermilk left behind out to the hogs. They'll love that! Oh, an' play with Edgar Lincoln a bit if you can. Keep him happy till I can come back inside."

Ida May's heart sank a little, as this was more than she had hoped to be responsible for. But she knew her help was needed, and she did enjoy the magic of white cream suddenly changing into yellow butter. Besides, she didn't mind playing with her brother at all, so she said, "You can count on me, Ma," and received a kiss on her forehead from her mother in reply.

Minerva headed out to the barn, dressed in her warmest wool against the chill. She was grateful that Brainard had worked so hard to lay by enough summer hay and leave standing the yellowed, but still nutritious, cornstalks to see their horse, milk cow, and oxen through the usually bitter cold months until spring. She knew there was also plenty of shucked corn from their two richest acres to keep her brown-eyed Jersey in milk and fatten the runt hogs remaining to be sold when they reached weight. There was plenty enough, too, to maintain the brood sows and chickens cooped up inside the small barn for protection from both winter cold and winter wolves. She and Brainard had agreed before he left to sell off the eight steers, rather than overwinter them, and Mr. Chipman had already taken care of that. Their price had been enough to pay not only the annual interest but also sixty dollars toward the balance owed on their farm, which was a great satisfaction to Minerva.

But the last of the firewood, cut and stacked to dry the previous summer up in the hillside woodlot, still needed to be brought down and restacked beside the shanty for easy use. Even with a dwindling supply available by the front porch, Minerva kept putting off that task until the first snow, wanting to make it easier for Ol' Jim to pull the loaded sled.

And the sorghum molasses still needed to be carted home from Hiram Winslow's blacksmith shop, where it was nearly boiled down to the right consistency for sweetening most of the family's cooking and baking. Nerva had paid four neighbor boys a dollar each to cut their acre of sorghum cane and haul the two wagonloads to his place in early November. There Winslow had run it through the small horse-powered mill he had made to service the surrounding community. With the girls and their little brother watching from their buggy, Nerva had helped by feeding in the five-foot to six-foot canes while Hiram kept the horse turning the mill. As the mill pressed out the cane juice, it was collected into a large, flat evaporating pan, and for the past week Mr. Winslow had kept a low fire burning under it to slowly boil the juice down to just the right thickness. His price for all his equipment and labor was half the finished molasses, but that would still leave the Griffins with plenty for the year to come.

***

With their chores all done, the afternoon was family time. Following a simple lunch of homemade bread, pickles, and cheese, Nerva took over caring for her son, while her daughters sat at the table together so Alice could continue helping Ida May get ready for when she would finally begin school.

"I'll say the letters, and you write them on the slate," Alice instructed. "We'll start with the alphabet again, and then I'll spell names and words for you."

"Don't go so fast as last time, Alice. I couldn't keep up. Sometimes the letters are hard," Ida May said petulantly, though she really was grateful for her sister's help.

"Aa . . . Bb . . . Cc . . . Dd . . ." Ida May carefully shaped each capital and lower case letter as Alice spoke them, and showed them for her sister's approval. Then they worked on the letters in names: "Ida May . . . Alice . . . Edgar . . . Ma . . . Pa." When she had spelled out the latter, Ida May paused to pick up his boxed tintype and say again, "Pa . . ." Practical words then followed, spoken and spelled by Alice, and written and shown by Ida May: "book . . . buggy . . . dress . . . shoes . . . lunch . . ."

Then they practiced counting out loud by ones, fives, and tens, and ended the session by Alice requiring Ida May to add up various combinations of fingers she held up using both her hands.

The afternoon finished as many of them did, with their mother rereading to them each of their father's, by then, seven letters. Edgar Lincoln, who had crawled up into Alice's lap, soon drifted off, content to be included in this family routine, even if it didn't seem playful in the least.

***

Thanksgiving had become a special time of family togetherness spent in the nearby home of Minerva's parents. Hellen and Eliza Churchill attended the same school as Alice, and the four cousins were often companions on adventures at either farmstead. Also included would be Allen, Minerva's brother, who shared the labor on his father's farm. Unfortunately, Nerva's sister, Mary, who was soon expecting her first child, would not be able to come down from her home in Spring Valley.

But the dinner in 1861 had a decidedly different mood, for the two young husbands, Brainard Griffin and Mary's spouse, Emery Durand, were not merely absent that unusually frigid November 28th, but off to war, with its accompanying threat of sickness and death.

A fairly quiet table followed the somber prayer of general thanksgiving and plea for protection offered by Grampa, for every heart seemed focused on the missing men. Still, two large roasted roosters, plus a variety of baked, steamed, and mashed fall vegetables went a long way toward keeping the day a celebration.

Thus the meal, topped off with generous slices of the apple and pumpkin pies Minerva had baked at home, was deemed a success despite its somewhat dampened beginning. At its conclusion, Alice's unexpected request puzzled everyone.

"Grampa," she began hesitantly, "Ida May and I have a wish for our Christmas..."

Almon, who loved his grandchildren dearly, raised his gray eyes to hers, giving her his full attention, though with a heavy heart. All conversation around the table ceased. Slowly stroking his stubbled chin, he asked, "What's the wish your little hearts have come up with, love?" He was guessing it would be something he couldn't possibly give them, like their father's return.

"We know it's prob'ly lots of money, maybe too much, but if we could have a map so's to follow along from his letters where Pa is, it sure would make us happy. And nothin' else from anybody... just that... it would be enough." With that, she glanced across the table at Ida May, who silently nodded as they had agreed. Then both girls dropped their eyes and folded their hands into their laps.

"A map, you say," their grandfather said thoughtfully, still fingering his stubble. "A United States map, I guess . . . to follow your Pa whilst he's gone to war . . . Well, I can't promise nothin' for sure, but p'raps I could stop in at Peter's an' see what they could do . . ."

The girls' eyes met in excited hope, and silent grins spread across both their faces. They then got up and, in an unusual show of affection, walked to the end of the table and kissed him simultaneously, one on each cheek.

***

Nerva set about saving up milk during the increasingly colder days that followed, planning to make a batch of her fresh farmer cheeses by the end of the week. Most of each morning's milking was added to the special five-gallon covered crock in the root cellar.

As a young girl, at Alice's age, Nerva had been carefully taught the art of cheese making by her mother on their farm in Vermont. Now she had begun passing on her knowledge and skill in the various steps involved to her own daughters.

"Ida May, how full's that crock now?" her mother asked as the young girl climbed back up into the kitchen, empty milk pail in hand.

"Way mor'an halfway, Ma. Tomorrow should about top it off."

"Tomorrow it is then," said Nerva. "I'd best get the cheesecloth cut into squares today. I've already checked an' we've got enough rennet. Oh, the kettle needs scalding yet. Would you fill it from the well, and make sure you get the well cover back on snug for me? Then build up the fire 'neath the kettle an' set it to boil."

"Yes, Ma," Ida May replied, and, trading the milking pail for the cast iron kettle, she hung the latter from the fireplace hook, put on her heavy coat to protect herself from the still-dry winter wind, and set off to the well with the water bucket.

The icy cold water she brought in was soon steaming, then finally boiling above the fire she had enlarged beneath the kettle. Nerva added to the boiling water the various knives and paddles they would need for cheese making to make sure they would be clean and ready, and Ida May kept the fire hot for another fifteen minutes.

Just before bedtime that evening, Nerva and Alice transferred the contents of the large crock into two smaller crocks set to either side of the fireplace where the milk would warm through the night.

Early the next morning, Nerva stirred a measured amount of rennet—the coagulating agent that causes the protein particles in milk to clump together—into the two crocks, and left them while she did her barn chores and fixed breakfast for all. By the time her work was done, the work of the rennet was also done. The milk in each crock seemed to be one solid mass.

"Ma! Look!" Ida May called to her mother, who was still hanging up her coat. Lightly tapping the top of one crock's contents with her finger, she added with wonder in her voice, "The milk's got . . . *hard*!"

"Leave it be, love," said Nerva. "That's called a curd now, an' we need to separate the watery part, called whey, from inside it."

Calling Alice down from the loft where she was reading, and urging Ida May to watch and learn, Nerva set about crisscrossing the single large curd in each crock into one-inch cubes with the knife, while Alice gently stirred the crocks' contents with a flattened wooden paddle, careful not to break up the cut curds too much. "Just right. Ever so gentle, my love," Nerva encouraged her. "See how she's doin' it, Ida May?"

As Alice stirred, the grayish whey began to separate out from the curd cubes, and Ida May, who had been too young the year before to care about cheese making, was totally fascinated at the changes happening to the milk. "It's changing just like when I make our butter, isn't it? Milk is *special*!"

"Now we need to cook these here curds and whey a bit. Ida May, you rehang that kettle for me so's I can pour this right in before we build up the fire." Both the hanging and the pouring were easily completed.

"Just a low fire," she cautioned Ida May, who was starting to feed small kindling to the post-breakfast embers. "This is the tricksiest part . . . heatin' it up very, very slow."

After an hour's slow rise in temperature, Nerva gave instructions for the next step: "Alice, set up the drain colander over the milk pail in the sink, and lay out the first square of cheesecloth in it. Watch how she does it, Ida May. I'll bring over sev'ral cupfuls, then you tie up the corners an' set it aside in the dishpan."

This process was repeated five times, and the whole sequence completed with the second batch, until eleven bundles of cheese curds were nestled in the pan. "Now we've got to salt 'em, girls. You watch how I do it, 'cause all of this'll soon be yours to do." Untying one bundle at a time, she instructed Alice, "Sprinkle the salt all over—not too much—whilst I stir the curds around a bit to get the salt everywhere." Turning to Ida May, she added, "Can you retie the bundles as we finish 'em, and take 'em over to the hooks on the front edge of the cupboard? You'll have to put one of them small bowls right under each one, so's they can drain into 'em overnight."

In the morning, six of the bundles were taken down and packed in a small crate to sell at Mr. Peters' store as fresh farmer's cheese the following day, for they had already planned a trip into Alba to cart home the sorghum molasses readied by Mr. Winslow. "I want two more for us to use as fresh," Nerva began, "an' the last three we'll salt again an' weight down to cure in the cellar for later."

***

That afternoon, when all the necessary chores were done and Edgar Lincoln was fast asleep, Nerva told the girls that Mr. Chipman had informed her he was to make a trip the next day down to McGregor in Iowa along the Mississippi River, and had offered to take with him and mail from there any message to her husband, as it would undoubtedly be delivered quicker. So on December 8th, the three females gathered themselves and their thoughts around the small family table with its kerosene lantern light to write a second letter. The girls passed Brainard's military tintype back and forth as they made suggestions for what to include.

"I'll start by tellin' him we're all well and a'gettin' along just first-rate with the farm work, even as freeze-eyed cold as it's been," their mother said, pen to paper as she spoke, struggling to write as carefully as possible. "We're not sufferin' any yet. An' he'll want to know how the butcherin' of them hogs went . . ."

"Tell him I did the smokehouse all by myself," added Alice, with Ida May chiming in, "And don't forget I did the lard." That reminded them all of the delicious "nut cakes" they had made using the fresh lard for deep-frying the nut-sized doughnuts the family always enjoyed so much, so Nerva added that bit of news to the letter.

Continuing to write, their mother noted, "Let's say we're ever so glad our letter finally got to him, and we hope this'n makes it too! And Thanksgivin' . . . I'll tell him how we all missed him, an' about all the fixin's we had. An' I don't want him to worry about us none, but I ought to let him know our wood supply is gettin' purty low . . ."

"And school starting soon, Ma. Think he'll be proud of me?"

"Oh, pshaw, Alice Jane. *Course* he will. But I'll write that too. He'll be right proud of you both, 'specially the way you've been a'helpin' Ida May get herself ready to begin next year."

When she had gotten all that down, and looked up for more ideas, Alice reminded her, "Tell him about Edgar Lincoln sayin' 'Pa! Pa!' all the time," which was immediately followed by Ida May's "And your cheese that's ever so good, Ma. The way you make it, bet he'll wish he had some."

"Just to be home is prob'bly his biggest wish . . . but with some of my cheese too, I reckon," laughed her mother as she added that also. "I think his sweet tooth will be glad to know 'bout all that molasses we'll be a'bringin' home tomorrow, so I'd better say that."

Then, with further expressions of affection for him and concerns for his welfare from them all, they closed this long, newsy letter, ready for Mr. Chipman to start it on its way in the morning.

Chapter Nine

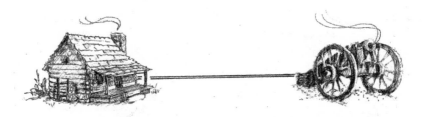

First Snow for Play and Work

"Ma," shouted Ida May as her mother returned to the shanty with the results of the morning milking in a half-filled bucket. "Ma, it *snowed* last night!"

The excitement and wonder in her voice was all of a child's world. But Nerva, glancing back at the snow her boots had tracked in, was more aware of the work that nature's change would make for them. Still, she treasured her young daughter's joy, and wished again that her husband was there to share it.

That long-awaited snow, which fell during the second week of December, was not much by Minnesota prairie standards. It was thin and dry, consistent with the prevailing cold dry spell. Yet enough settled to coat the ground sufficiently for easy movement of the sled. With dawn's arrival, the clouds continued their eastward movement, so that the thin blanket of crystals sparkled under a clear blue sky.

"Snow?" she joked. "Is *that* what this cold stuff stickin' to my boots is called?" They both laughed heartily enough to bring Alice down from the girls' sleeping loft. She was already warmly dressed, like Ida May, ready for some winter horseplay right after breakfast.

"Now you two wake your brother, an' get him bundled up like yourselves so's he can go out too. We'll just have toast for now, but I'll have some nice warm cider an' a boiled egg ready for you when you've worn out that new snow. Then I'm afraid it's trips to the woodlot all day for us, 'cause we gotta bring home the rest of that wood your pa cut last summer. 'Tain't much use to us unless we get it sledded down here, handy stacked next to the shanty."

"Yes, Ma," they said together. Soon all three children were out the door, with his sisters introducing Edgar Lincoln to his very first snow. By that time, the day had already warmed enough to make it too wet for sliding, but just right for slipping, and great for mittened fingers to gather up and shape into snowballs.

Their playtime didn't last long, however, as all three were quickly soaked through and exhausted, and needed to come in to escape the danger of getting seriously chilled. Nerva, her broad smile an indication of the pleasure she took in her children, helped them unwrap and hang their wet coats and mittens on the wall pegs next to the door. She picked up her son to nurse him as she handed the girls the mugs of cider she had already warmed on the new dual-purpose cookstove a neighbor, Mr. Holman, had finally installed the week before.

Brainard had always meant to get one, but somehow had never gotten it done. Just before leaving, he had made a barter with Holman, trading the help he had given during haying, some fence repairs, plus two of their feeder pigs, for this wonderful addition to their comfort and convenience.

Mr. Holman had set it into the fireplace so that its back stovepipe could run right up inside the chimney. The firebox itself, with its cooking surface above, jutted out into the room, providing significantly more room heat from considerably less wood than the original fireplace. It even had a side "oven" for baking, which Nerva was still learning how to use, adjusting the fire in the firebox according to the temperature she desired.

The only hitch was, when Mr. Holman finished, he demanded that Nerva pay him an additional dollar fifty for the stove, an amount she simply could not spare. All she could do, she told him, was promise to write Brainard about it and see what he was able to do. Apparently satisfied for the time being, Mr. Holman went home, leaving Nerva with a hollow feeling of vulnerability, which she would communicate to her husband in her next letter.

"Now," Nerva began, nodding thoughtfully, when everyone was warm and dry again, and had breakfasted on boiled eggs and more toast. "Now," she repeated, "it's work time. I'll hitch up Ol' Jim to the haulin' sled whilst you girls make sure you an' little Edgar Lincoln are dressed warm enough for a couple o' hours outside." Feeling their still-wet clothes on the pegs, she added, "You'll need your other coats, your old ones. An' work gloves too. These ain't close to dry."

It took all of twenty minutes to hitch the horse to the sled in the barn, her fingers fumbling in the cold with all the harness connections. The children had waited the while on the porch, lightly tossing the small balls they were able to make with the snow close by its edge. "Here's Ma," Alice called gaily to her siblings as she watched her mother approach.

Nerva was standing, feet wide apart, at the front of the seatless sled, holding Ol' Jim's reins as she leaned against a front railing. The girls clambered aboard behind her and pulled their brother up to snuggle between them for the short, unloaded run up the woodlot hill. The youngest, ever one for something new, jabbered his nine-month-old baby talk to the delight of all as they slid along on this new adventure.

When they arrived at the top beside the large woodpile, Nerva set out her instructions: "Girls, we'll all stack wood for the trip down, but you two can take turns mindin' Edgar Lincoln. That way he'll be safe, an' you won't be a'gettin' tired too soon. We'll lay the pieces crossways, side to side, so they won't shift none on the way down. Got that?"

"How high shall we stack 'em?" inquired Ida May.

"Let's try three high, see how that goes. We don't want too much for Ol' Jim to hafta pull, but we don't want to waste a trip neither."

So they set to work, Alice offering to tend to Edgar Lincoln first, and taking him off a ways into the woods. The other two began moving the woodpile onto the sled, two or three split pieces at a time. Slowly the sled was filled across, front to back, three rows deep, the split triangular shapes snuggling into each other firmly. Then a second and finally a third layer was added.

"Well, let's try that," Nerva said to her daughter. "Why don't you rest yourself there a bit on the side whilst I track down your sister an' brother?" Ida May smiled up in response as her mother left, calling, "Alice . . . Edgar Lincoln . . ."

In only a few minutes, Ida May watched the three coming back. Her little brother was in his mother's arms while her sister ran ahead to jump out from behind trees as they approached. Edgar Lincoln was issuing peals of laughter with each "Boo!" Ida May thought to herself, *If only Pa were here, this would be a perfect day!*

With Nerva standing again holding the reins, and Edgar braced safely between her legs, the girls walked down the hill beside the sled in case the wood load shifted. But Ol' Jim pulled slowly, steadily, and safely back to the tiny farmhouse. There Alice and her mother transferred the firewood to the stack just off the porch while Ida May took her turn entertaining her brother.

It was on the third repetition of this process that the accident occurred. Alice had once again been minding Edgar Lincoln, keeping him safely occupied away from the work, but had brought him back so Nerva could take care of his midmorning hunger. Temporarily replacing her mother, she was loading behind Ida May, who unexpectedly reached back to straighten the piece she had just added to the sled. Alice wasn't even looking when she dropped her three split pieces smack onto her younger sister's left hand.

"Owweee!" The wail burst out of Ida May as she yanked her hand from beneath the wood and pressed it to her chest with her right hand.

Alice's hand flew to her mouth in despair at what had just happened. "Ida May," she gasped.

Nerva was there in an instant, thrusting her bewildered son into Alice's arms, and encircling Ida May with her own. "Oh, my baby, let me see what's happened. Let's see how bad it is . . ." Turning the hand over and back and gently wiping the oozing blood onto her work apron, she continued, "Nothing feels broken. Ida May, show me you can move each finger . . ."

Though wincing as she did so, Ida May's finger flexing confirmed it would just be a deep bruise beneath the numerous scratches from the wood's sharp edges. "I wish Pa was here," she said softly.

"I know, love," her mother replied. "So do I . . ."

It was a more solemn family that trooped back to the shanty with this third load. What they had brought that day was hardly a start on how much they needed to bring down, but it would be enough for a while. Nerva announced: "We'll be needin' to ride into Peters' 'cause I *know* we ain't got the ointment Ida May is a'needin' for them cuts on her hand. Your Pa took it all with him when he left."

"I'll stay home with Edgar Lincoln, so's he can keep warm, if that'll help," Alice offered, still feeling quite badly for her carelessness. She was standing before her mother, head slightly down.

"That'd be right helpful, Alice dear," Nerva answered. But noting her daughter's demeanor, she added, "Now, don't you go a'blamin' yourself none. 'Twas an accident. Accidents happen. You just have to *go on*."

"Yes, Ma. But I'll try bein' more careful too."

Turning to her youngest two, warming themselves at the stove with its newly built-up fire, Nerva said, "Edgar Lincoln, Alice is agoin' to take care of you whilst I'm gone. Ida May, you'll be a'comin' with me. Are you warm an' dry 'nough to go now?"

"I guess so, Ma."

71

"Then I'll fix us up some bread an' cheese to eat on the way after I hitch up Ol' Jim to the buggy. Good thing there wasn't much snow, so travellin' should be all right. Why don't you get the lap quilts out for us?"

Soon they were on their way, creating fresh wheel tracks along the lane to Alba and Mr. Peters' store the mile beyond, apparently the first ones passing that way that day. They spoke lightly of what they saw, and since they were assured the other two were safe, both expected the day not to end all that badly.

In that they were correct, for when they arrived at the general store after an uneventful journey, Mr. Peters greeted them by holding up another letter from Brainard. Before passing it to them, however, the friendly clerk clucked over Ida May when he saw the injured hand she extended. He turned and reached up on the shelf behind him for the requested healing salve and bandaging, then came around the counter so he could hold her arm steady while her mother applied the salve into the cuts and bruises and gently wrapped the bandaging around and around to protect the series of wounds. Only then did Nerva ask for the letter, which Mr. Peters gave them along with his well wishes for Ida May's recovery. As a comfort, Nerva allowed Ida May to carry it in her apron pocket for the journey home. Both were excited to open and read it together with Alice when they got there.

On the way, Ida May looked over at her mother, resettled her hurting hand in her lap, and said with both gladness and sadness in her voice, "I've been wishin' *all day* that Pa was here." She nearly choked as she lifted up the letter and added, "Now it seems like he is!"

The baby was asleep in his cradle when they returned, so Alice was able to join them around the small table for the reading, and picked up her father's tintype to look at while she listened. As Nerva unfolded the letter, five five-dollar bills slid out, along with a dozen or so magazine clippings of young girls dressed in fancy clothes. She began counting out the bills into a neat stack, announcing, "Twenty-five dollars . . . imagine that! How *ever* did he get *this* much money?"

72

The girls, in the meantime, had snatched up the pictorials, identified as pages from *Leslie's Magazine*, the current literary rage in the bigger cities. A chorus of exclamations of pleasure came from both as each showed the other what she had found. "Would you look at all the lace on this dress!" "Isn't she beautiful with her hair curled that way?" "I wonder where she's going, dressed up like that . . ." "Do you suppose we'll ever have clothes this pretty?"

Nerva hushed them, then began to read. Several times she had to pause in her reading for one or the other of the girls to question her about what their father had written.

November 26-27, 1861

My dear Affectionate Wife and Children,

I will write a few lines to you this evening although I have not got any news to write to you. I am well and in good spirits today. We were paid off yesterday, up to the 31st of October. My pay amounted to $14.30. I am going to borrow $15.00 and then send $25. to you in this letter. It will be 2 months before I shall get any more to send to you if I live and do not get wounded in any battle.

I hope that you will get all the letters that I write to you, and that you will answer all that you can of them. Tell me all you can think of, for I am glad to hear anything from home.

It has been quite cool here the last three or four days. What kind of weather is it there this fall? Cold or not?

I am a'going to send some of Leslie's *pictorials along with this letter, and direct them to Ida, for I think they will please her first rate. They have got some very pretty dresses. I hope they will both of them be good girls and mind their Ma, for I cannot tell when I shall come home to help her take care of them. Now if you get this letter safe with the money, I want that you should write just as soon as you get it and let me know.*

I guess my Edgar Lincoln is nine months old today. I would like to see you all this morning. Tomorrow is Thanksgiving Day, here and also in Minnesota. I wish that I could be there and help you eat up the old rooster! It rained very hard last night and a good deal of thunder and lightning, very heavy, and still raining some this morning. I have waited until the mail has got in, but no letter for me . . .

I will close with my best wishes to you and all the rest of the folks in Minnesota and especially yourself and the children,

   D. B. Griffin"

"I miss Pa," Ida May said quietly when her mother finished reading. She flexed her bandaged fingers to ease the still-throbbing cuts and bruises.

"Me too," agreed Alice, a slight catch in her voice as she continued to anguish over what her carelessness had caused. "Me too," she repeated.

"And so do I," sighed Nerva, the third to hint at sadness. It was obvious to her girls how burdened she was, both by her missing companion, their father, but also by the weight of the full responsibility she bore alone for their family and farm.

They spontaneously got up from the table and circled their arms around one another to comfort each other's pain. "Tomorrow, if the snow holds, we'll have to get the rest of that wood down," Nerva concluded. "But in the meantime, why don't we make us up a nice batch of nutcakes, fried in some of that lard Ida May laid down for us?"

"Oh, Ma, can we?" Ida May temporarily forgot the pain in her hand at the promise of such a treat. "I'll go get a loaf of lard right now!"

"Alice, you build up the stove fire an' set the fry pan on top, ready for the lard. I'll get out the fixin's for the batter. We'll be enjoyin' 'em in no time at all!"

Each one of them accomplished her task, "right smart" as Brainard would have said had he been there, and regathered around the table. The flour was measured, a few precious teaspoons of sugar, along with the right amount of salt and soda were added, a nutmeg was grated a dozen times or so above the bowl, a couple of fresh eggs were beaten, then all were combined with the buttermilk from yesterday that both activated the soda and gave the nutcakes their special flavor. Mixed, it made a rather stiff dough.

"Alice, sprinkle just a bit of that flour on the countertop, then roll handfuls of dough into snakes like you've done before for Ida to cut. Make 'em the size of walnuts, Ida May. Whilst you do that, I'll check the fat to make sure it's hot enough. An' won't your pa wish he was here? My, I reckon we oughta write your pa "bout all this."

Ida May nodded in agreement to both the question and the suggestion.

The balls of dough were soon sizzling in the cast-iron skillet filled with hot melted fat. They browned on all sides as Nerva expertly rolled them over with the same slotted wooden spoon they had used for the apple butter. "Watch how I do it, so's you can do it next time," she instructed Alice.

It took three 'fries' to cook all the dough they had made. The girls already knew how to shake a little more sugar over them when they were done. Then, still warm, they greedily began to stuff themselves with the first batch of nutcakes from the new lard – a special ending to a difficult day.

Chapter Ten

December Conversations

Even though Nerva had just written Brainard a few days before the accident, when the family received his letter with the money and pictorials to end that painful day, all knew they had to write him right away. With her daughters' help, Nerva penned this brief note and posted it the following day:

My Dearest Brainard,

Your welcome letter came yesterday, the one with the $25 and the magazine pictures. Were so glad to hear you are well. That money will sure help us a lot, I tell you. And the girls are a fussin over those pictures nearly all the time. I wish you could see them, and listen a bit to their chatter. Weather heres been cold some, but mostly dry yet. We expect the snow will set in any day now. Mr. Chipmans agreed to help us get all your firewood down from that upper lot. but not until after we had a little accident. But don't worry yourself none, for everythins alright now. With all our food laid by, and that wood close up to the shanty, we should be about as ready as we can be for Ol Man Winter to arrive. One job you missed for sure yesterday was eatin your share *of the nutcakes fry we had with the new lard. Each of us had to eat a few extra since you didnt show. But I reckon we wouldve rather had you than the extra treats. Dear Brainard, you were missed.*

We already wrote you about our Thanksgivin without you. Reckon you just aint got that letter yet. Ill take this here one into town in the mornin sos you can know for sure that money came though alright.

The children and I all wish you to please take care of yourself, and dont let yourself get hurt any. We all miss you badly, and caint hardly wait for you to return.

With love from your Wife and Children,

P. Minerva Griffin

Then, while she was merely grateful to trade some of Brainard's precious twenty-five dollars for much-needed supplies the next day at the Alba Store, Minerva was thrilled to trade her letter to him for one from him. And though the family's agreement was that letters were to be opened at home for all to read together, her heart compelled her to read this one immediately. So as soon as she was back in the buggy she broke the seal and unfolded the single sheet from her husband, and read:

"Camp Anderson, Lebanon Junction, Dec. 2nd, 1861

My dear companion and children,

I will again seat myself for the purpose of writing a few lines to you. I am not as well as I was when I last wrote. I was on guard last Friday night at the bridge which stood in the place of the one that the rebels burnt before we came here. It rained and snowed some and I caught a bad cold. I feel a good deal better this morning, and manage to keep away from the doctors. It has rained so much that we are camped right in the mud, and have no chance to dry the straw in our tents so it is damp all of the time.

There is some talk of our going to Louisville to winter. If we do, it is not any probability of our ever being in any engagement during this war, for I think that it will be ended before Spring by all accounts. The

Rebels are getting discouraged in some places. I hope that it will end without the shedding of much blood.

I must tell you what we had for Thanksgiving. I had some baked chicken, pumpkin pie, apples and cider, bread and coffee.

I have not had but one letter from you yet. I should think that you could write to me as often as once in four weeks. When I write to you every week, do you get them all? I want that you should write to me and tell me whether you received the money that I sent you, $25.00, and Leslie's papers for Ida, and if you did, tell me what she said. I will get one and send it to Alice next time.

It is pretty cold writing. I have got on my overcoat. We have got no fire in the tent. How do you get along this cold weather? Do you manage to keep warm? I hope that I shall get a letter from you before I write again.

D. B. Griffin"

But not hearing from them didn't stop him from writing, for Brainard mailed them at least seven more letters during the month of December alone. His mind was jumbled as he wrote, with both the anguish of lonely separation and a strong sense of duty to his country in conflict.

Following the mail wagon's semiweekly deliveries, each letter was anxiously received at home in what became routine trips to the post office in Peters' General Store. Each letter was then read repeatedly, questioned and discussed over meals, and safely put away into a beribboned bundle in Nerva's dresser drawer.

Answering them was a different matter, as writing was not always as easy for Minerva as it was for her husband. *I know I should write him more,* was a troubling phrase that passed through her mind often, and was hardly addressed by her own answer, *But it's so hard for me, an' I'm not so good with words as he is.*

It also seemed like Brainard had no trouble finding downtime on his hands when he wasn't drilling, just waiting for military movements to be ordered. Such was *not* the case back home. The unending list of chores—in the shanty, in the barn, and in the fields—for which she was now solely responsible, and which were made much more difficult by the bitter cold, scarcely allowed any free time to write.

***

Two letters, written only a day apart, arrived from Brainard in the next mail. Both of them created a good deal of conversation around the table as Nerva read them to the girls.

"Lebanon, Ky.   Dec. 10, 1861

Dear affectionate wife and companion,

I hear that you are having a hard winter in Minnesota. I hope that you do not suffer with the cold any, but I do not know as you do not write to me, or else I do not get them, for I have not received but one letter from you.

"But we have written him again," interrupted Ida May. "Why does he say he's only gotten one letter from us?"

Her mother laid a comforting hand over the much smaller hand of her young daughter. "I reckon it just didn't get there yet. He's a long ways from here, don't forget. Oh, listen to what he says next."

I am to now work in the cook shop. I am the second cook. I have got two meals for the whole company, and do not have to be on other duty.

"Pa, a cook? For all those men he's with? Do you suppose he wears an apron an' all?"

"Oh, pshaw, Alice Jane. Yo'r pa always helped a bit in the kitchen. I must say, though, that the thought of him a'cookin' an' a'washin' dishes every day is pretty funny. But not near so funny as what else he says."

I washed for myself last Saturday, and some of the boys wanted that I should wash for them, and so I washed 11 pieces at 5 cents apiece, and on Sunday I washed 14 shirts, 7 pairs of drawers, one coat, and one pair of pants and some other pieces, which came to $1.60 . . . and helped get three meals besides. Did I not do first rate? My fingers *got sore some. All that I have to do is just to wash them out in two waters, and rinse them. They are most all woolen clothes.*

As her daughters giggled at that unknown image of their pa, Nerva quipped, "Sounds like I'll be a'gettin' lots more help with my house chores when he gets himself home. But now he does get a bit serious."

We expect to make a grand advance towards the enemies lines in a few days. You must not worry about me at all, for I do not think I will be in any danger as long as I stay in the cook shop. I shall stay there as long as I can, for I don't think it is as hard upon me as it is to be on drill and guard duty.

It is the opinion of everyone that the war will be ended by Spring.

D. B. Griffin."

Laying the letter down on the table, she grasped one hand of both girls and concluded, "That's the two things we'll have to trust in, that your Pa will be safe, and that he'll come home to us soon."

Then, with the innocent faith of a five-year-old, Ida May added, "An' we'll be safe until then, won't we, Ma?"

"Yes, love, safe until then."

After a reflective pause, Nerva opened the second letter and began to read:

"Wednesday evening, December 11, 1861

I dream every little while of being at home, seeing you and the little ones, but when I wake up I find that it is nothing but a dream. I hope that it will soon be so that I can see you all, but I have enlisted for the war and am bound to see the end of it if I live.

She had to pause again, to take that thought in, but her daughters only looked at each other and didn't interrupt.

I hope that it will not last long, but whether it does or not, I wish that I could hear from you a little oftener than I have. I know it is hard work for you to write, but if you knew how anxious I watch the mail every day, you would send a few words to me often.

Before she spoke to the girls, a silent promise was made, *Oh Brainard, I'll try to do better.* "How 'bout we try to write yo'r Pa this week? You be a'thinkin' of all the things you want me to say, all right?"

Their affirming nods led to her final comment, "Well, I'll just finish up this letter, an' then fix us a bite o' supper."

Jerry's wife wrote that you had got my picture. How did you like the looks of it? Did the children know that it was mine? Are the children well all of this winter? I would like to pull their ears a little this evening, and give them a kiss too. Would you do that for me, "Nerve"?

I am too chilly to write any more, so I will bid you goodnight and go to bed. Now write soon, which is the wish of your best friend and companion.

D. B. Griffin."

***

"Wonder why this letter's so fat?" Nerva said to the girls when she returned to the shanty after her quick trip into Alba for supplies and the mail the following week. Handing it to them to examine while she hung up her winter wear, she asked, "Ida May, would you make me a pot of tea to warm me up whilst I feed yo'r brother? An' Alice, be a dear an' light the lantern so's we can find out what all yo'r pa has to report this time."

It only took a few brief minutes for her to feed and comfort Edgar Lincoln, and then he was on the floor again, freeing Nerva to complete the group at the lamp-lit table. Ida May was given the honor of opening the envelope after successfully reading its from and to addresses. She discovered two separate folded sheets of paper inside, and as she drew them out, announced "Here's why it's so fat. There's two letters inside."

"Law me," Nerva said as she unfolded them and read the two headings. "One's for me, an' t'other one's for you. Why don't I read mine, an' then Alice you can read yours?"

Both girls drew their heads in closer as she began to read her letter:

"Lebanon, Ky December 15, 1861

Dear and affectionate wife,

I received a letter from you last night. It was only 4 days coming from McGregors."

"That's the one Mr. Chipman took for us after the butchering," interrupted Ida May.

"and you had better believe that I was glad to hear from you all once more, and to hear that you were all well. It is the second one that I have had from you. I am glad that you are well and getting along first rate. I am glad to hear that you have a good lot of pork and lard laid down. I should like to be there and help you fry 'nutcakes,' and eat some of them too. Is the shanty fixed up so as to be comfortable this winter? Will you have enough wood?"

Ida May broke in again: "We already told him 'bout all those things. Right after my accident, remember? He must have got that letter by now."

"I must tell you of a little skirmish that the teamsters got into. They went to a man's house to see if they could get some food for their teams. The man told them to get off his premises or he would shoot them. They offered to pay him for some food, and he told them here was the kind of food he would give them and fired a double barrel shot gun at them. There was four buckshot hit one of the men. They took the man prisoner."

"But why would that man?"

At this third interruption, Nerva raised her left hand to shush her inquisitive daughter, adding, "Let me finish first."

"We are only 60 miles from the enemy's army. There was about 12,000 started from here two or three days ago, but when we go I cannot tell, nor anyone else. We had lots of ladies here last night to see us get supper. They said it looked so odd to see men a'cooking. We were a'baking pancakes. They call them batter cakes.

Have you got any of the papers that I sent to you, and how many of the letters have you got? This is the 13th, and have you got the one with the money in it?"

"Can we count 'em, Ma? To see if we got 'em all?"

This more practical interruption didn't seem to bother her mother. She stood and smiled. "I'll go get the bundle, then, yes, we can stop and count them out." Beside her bed was a small three-drawer dresser. In its top drawer lay the precious bundle of letters from her husband. These she brought back to the table for Ida May to count aloud as she turned them over one by one. They did indeed number thirteen.

"Now can we go on?" There was no impatience at all in her voice, for she was rejoicing at the strong family bond the request had revealed.

"Yes, Ma. What else did Pa write?"

"I should like to be at home and see you and the children, especially my boy. I should like to hear him call 'Pa! Pa!' but I shall have to wait until the war is over and then if I am alive you will see me as soon as I can get home. You must not worry at all about me, for we are all of us taken good care of. I must stop, so good night, Nerva.

D. B. Griffin."

Nerva handed the second note to Alice. "Now you read this one."

Alice's reading pace was even slower than her mother's, as she had to sound out a number of words, and even had to ask for help with a few she couldn't do herself.

Perhaps a simple awareness of how special this was for her sister kept Ida May quiet, only interrupting once during the reading.

"Lebanon, Ky. Dec. 16, 1861

My Dear Children,

Oh, how I would like to see you all today. The longer I am away from you, the more I think of you, and many a time does my nose tickle and the tear drops roll down my cheeks. I hope that it will not be a great many months before we shall all see each other again. If Pa does get home alive and well, he don't think that he will ever go away and leave his little girls and his little boy as long as he lives. don't suppose that you would know me now if you could see me, for I have got my hair cut short and have not cut off my "mustn't touch it" since I came from home.

Does Grandpa get down to see you any this winter, and do you get up there any? I hope that you are both good girls and mind your Ma. You must tell Ma what you want her to tell me, and what little Edgar Lincoln says for himself. This winter he don't slide down the hill does he? You tell him he had better wait until next winter.

There is a 'right smart of slaves' around here. All sorts. Would you like to be a slave and be sold from your Ma and Pa and never see them again? No, I guess not. I think that you would rather let your Pa go away from home for a little while. There is a good many slaves in here every day. They are all black folks.

Now I must tell you what our 'kitchen' looks like. Well, we have got a shed boarded up on three sides, and covered, and two crotches drove down in front with a pole across them to hang the kettles on. Then we fixed up a table in the shape of an L the length of two boards one way and one the other. When we get the table set, we holler out 'grab pile, Co. F' and then the boys all scamper for the table. We have about 70 now, with about 30 of the Company in the hospital.

Alice, I sent Ida one of Leslie's papers. When they come around again I will buy one and send it to you. I will send the letter to you for I want that you should learn to read my letters and then learn to write a letter to your Pa.

Now Alice, I tell you what to do, you have your Ma get a good supper on the 13th of January,[1] and then get Uncle Allen to come down there and eat my share of it. I will get as good a supper as I can wherever I will be at the time, and set down and eat it. I think of you and like enough to drop a tear or two. I hope that they will soon turn into tears of joy, and we shall be able to see one another face to face

---

[1]   That would be his 31st birthday and their 10th wedding anniversary.

and set down to the same table and eat out of the same dishes. I think that we should all be happy then if we ever could be on this earth.

It is getting rather late, so I guess I will let you go to bed. Good-night Alice, kiss, good-night Ida, kiss, good-night Edgar, double kiss, because you must both kiss him for me, and kiss Ma too. This from your Father who is in the American Army in the State of Kentucky.

David Brainard Griffin."

"Lebanon, Ky.   Dec. 20th, 1861

Dear wife and children,

As I have a few moments to spare this afternoon, I thought that I would commence a letter to you. I feel as well as ever I did in my life.

Today we have had a regular old Yankee dinner. Les' see, we had some boiled fresh beef, and some baked beef, some boiled pork and cabbage, some sweet potatoes boiled, some boiled onions, and cold slaw and some good bakers bread and butter. There, was that not a good dinner? Our company lives the best of any company in the Regiment, because we have the best cook.

There is a company of Artillery about ½ mile from here. They have six horses on each cannon and a rider on each high horse and six men to handle the cannon. They go through the motions of loading and firing very fast, and when they wheel or go from one place to another they go on a full run. They shot at a target the other day two miles off. I could see the ball strike the hill close to the target. There is also a Regiment of Infantry (the same as we are) camped upon the other side of us. They drill right in sight of us every day. Then there is a number of Regiments further off. Our Regiment drills twice a day, company drill in the forenoon and Battalion drill in the afternoon, and then dress parade just at sundown.

We have not got but a little piece of candle left and I must fix up our bed and go to bed, so I must bid you goodnight. I think of you all a great many times a day, but I hope that we shall all live to see one another again. I have got a paper for Alice and I will send it along with this letter. Kiss our babies often for me. This from your husband and friend in Ky.

D. B. Griffin

To Minerva Griffin Alba P.O. Fillmore Co. Minnesota."

Oftentimes the letters from home and those from the battlefield crossed each other, one bearing information still being asked for that was already answered in the other. On the same day that Brainard had written the letter above, his family had written him while on a buggy outing to Forestville, about halfway to the county seat at Preston, to visit friends before Christmas. Nerva had added a note that she had used a little more of the twenty-five dollars there in Forestville to purchase a few small gifts for the children so their Christmas would be a little less bleak without him. Nerva also included their joined expressed hope that he would be returning safely to them very soon.

Thus, a short week later, he was able to respond:

"Lebanon, Ky.   December 27, 1861

I received a letter from you today, dated the 20th at Forestville, and I was glad to hear from you all and to hear that you were all well and that you had received the money which I sent you. I had worried some about it for fear that you would not get it, but I shall feel easy now. I was glad to learn that you have had some good visits. I hope that you will continue to have them although I am not in your midst.

Gen. Buell was here this week and had a review of the troops in this place. I have heard it said that the Brigade in which we are in was the best Brigade in Ky. and that is saying a great deal for there is a good many troops in Ky. at the present time.

I wish that you would write how you get along for things in the house and for clothes. If you need anything, just let me know for I can borrow some money of most any of the boys after pay day. I am glad that Ida got her papers, and as I said before, I should like to be there to show the pictures to her. I have sent some to Alice, and directed a letter to her, too. Tell them Pa hopes that someday he will come home and then he will not have to write to them. I guess that Edgar is a

e way he goes about. If he should live it would not
efore he would be a great help to his Mother, and
oo.

I hope that you will see me in the Spring. I hope
will answer your prayers. There was one boy died
his week. He has been sick sometime. It is the first
in the company. I am well now, and I hope that I
ust bid you good-night and good-bye too. D. B.
in and the babies."

ecember 31, 1861

d companion,

day of the year, and I received a Christmas letter
y, I thought that I would write a few lines to you
this evening. I am glad that you are getting along well, and that it is
pleasant weather there. It is very pleasant here tonight. I am in our
tent this evening with my coat off and without any fire, yet my hands
sweat so that I can hardly hold my pen. But as we are expecting to go
from here tomorrow, I will try to write a few lines. It has been a very
busy day in camp today. We have been mustered for pay and have
been a fixing to move. We do not know where we are a going to go,
but expect to go towards Sommerset where Zollicoffer, the Rebel
General, is. We shall probably see some fun before a great many weeks,
but we cannot tell. I will write to you as often as I get a chance to.

Tell Alice that I dream about her and all of you often. I hope that
your sausages will keep good until I come home for I should like to
have a taste in the shanty, or do you keep it all there? It will soon be
time to sow wheat if it is as warm all the time as it is here. Time slips
away very fast. It does not seem as though it was three months since I
left home. The boys are talking in the tent about our going home. They
think that we shall be home by the time the corn will want to be hoed.
I hope so too.

I must stop for I want to put this in the office tonight, but I must wish you a Happy New Year and I think that you will have one. Tell Alice to remember the dinner on the 13th. Good bye, Nerva.

This from D. B. Griffin."

Chapter Eleven

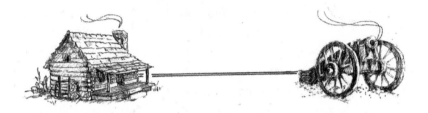

Christmas Without Pa

With loads of pent-up excitement edging her voice, Ida May needed one final assurance: "Tomorrow's Christmas, right?" Her mother nodded an affirmation, biting her lower lip as she began sewing the wooden buttons on the nearly finished infant gown for her sleeping son. So Ida May added, "But we haven't made our Christmas cookies yet..."

"I know, love. We'll be a'doin' that *all* afternoon, soon's I get this here gown done for your brother." Holding the simple cotton piece up with a shake, she asked, "What do you think? Wouldn't your Pa be proud of him, a'growin' up so fast?"

"Oh, Ma, you've made it perfect! That blue color is just right for his mop of blonde hair. And your stitching is so fine," she added, reaching out to finger the garment. "I'm *sure* he'll love runnin' around in it!"

All that week between their many chores, mother and daughters had been working alone or in pairs making gifts for each other. Nerva had helped Ida May design and sew a string-tied canvas book bag for Alice to use when school began in early January. She had also worked beside Alice, who was making a new dress-up pinafore apron for Ida May to wear to church. Alice was even at that moment up by the single small window of the girls' sleeping loft attaching the last of the lace ribbon along its shoulder straps.

The sisters, in turn, had been working together shaping a ball for Edgar Lincoln. They had found a nearly round pine knot in the woods while tending the pigs, and were smoothing off its rough edges. For sandpaper they were using handheld chunks of sandstone their father had collected from the nearby riverside bluffs. It was slow going, but by taking turns their project was not too tiring. They had already created pairs of quilted pot holders for both their mother and grandmother. Alice, more experienced at sewing, had carefully stitched their sets of initials in the bottom corners. And working together, they had created a lovely Christmas card for their grandfather out of a half sheet of good parchment paper they had gotten their mother to purchase from Mr. Peters.

Late evenings, by lamplight, after her daughters had finally dropped off to sleep, Nerva had made matching fully pleated dark blue skirts for them. They were made from the same fabric as her son's infant gown. She knew her mother had knitted winter mittens for all three, of wool dyed nearly an identical shade of blue.

"So . . . while you finish, Ma, can I get anything ready for the cookies?"

"Sure 'nough. Clear off the table first," her mother instructed as her needle poked back and forth through a sleeve button. "Then set out the flour tin, an' the large mixin' bowl an' that bowl of all them hickory nuts you two have been a'crackin' all week. An' don't forget the sorghum jug." She looked up to the shanty's raftered ceiling for a moment to ponder, then continued, "We'll also need some butter an' eggs brought up from the cellar."

"Do you want *me* to get 'em, Ma?"

"Yes, my Ida, but you be right careful on the ladder. Make it two trips so's your hands aren't full. Then you can stir up the fire some to a bakin' temper'ture. Surely by then I'll be done with these buttons. It'll be ready to tie up with a bit o' ribbon fer the little tyke."

Overhearing the cookie talk below her, Alice rehid her sewing project in her drawer of the small dresser the sisters shared and rushed down the ladder to join in. "I'll get the butter an' eggs, Ida May, and finish chopping up the nuts." She laughed lightly as she added, "Ma forgot the rolling pin and cookie cutters. I'll get them too. You do the rest like she said."

While their mother completed attaching the decorative buttons, the girls gathered the required ingredients and utensils. It wasn't long before flour had powdered all available surfaces, aprons, and hands, and the nutty sorghum-sweetened dough was mixed, rolled, and cut into stars and pony shapes.

"I'll finish 'em off with just a bit o' sugar on their tops," Nerva said. She used a cup-sized tin shaker to do the sprinkling, then the first cookie sheet was slipped into the side oven of the stove.

It was probably their delicious smell from baking that awakened Edgar Lincoln. His whimpered "Mama . . . Mama . . ." caused Nerva to temporarily excuse herself to clean, redress, and feed him.

The girls could overhear the mother-son morning conversation while they continued to roll out, cut, and sugar the second batch on their own. It was all ready to go in when the first tray came out. Four more trays of stars and ponies followed, and because Elgar Lincoln was content to play by himself on the floor, a small piece of pony cookie in each little fist, Nerva was able to return to the girls.

When the shaped cookies were all made, Ida May asked, "Can we do the apple nuts now?" She was referring to the family's other traditional Christmas cookie. These used chopped, dried apple slices instead of hickory nuts, with a small amount of purchased spices mixed in that replaced the sugar sprinkled on top.

"Of course we can," her mother replied. "An' we won't even have to clean the mixing bowls in between."

The apple nuts were rolled by hand into nut-sized balls and placed in neat rows on the baking trays. Making these treats completed the afternoon of baking.

Lots of laughter about the just-finished activity accompanied the sharing of warm cookies and cold milk that Christmas Eve, snug in their shanty on the Minnesota prairie. Everything was now ready for the family's expressions of mutual love, joy, and hope on the special morning to follow, which would happen over at the grandparents' farm.

All that was missing—and he would be deeply missed—was Pa.

Also absent from the Griffin family gathering would be Nerva's sister, Mary, along with her infant child. But she would not attend for the opposite reason. Her husband, Emery, had gotten home on holiday leave from the 8th Minnesota to his family in Spring Valley.

***

Even though it was Christmas Morning when they awoke, the farm chores still had to begin their day. After a round of brief cheerful wishes, and just a bit of complaining on Ida May's part, mother and daughters went their separate ways.

Nerva headed to the barn to milk the cow and feed the livestock. Although this was always a special time for her each day—a quiet time to ponder her situation—today she felt particularly overwhelmed. "Oh Lordy," she sighed over and over. "Can I make it till he gets back?"

Alice followed her only as far as the chicken coop, for her chores involved releasing the chickens from their night's safe confinement, scattering some cracked corn for them, and gathering their freshly laid eggs. This late in the season there were only a few each morning, but she couldn't leave them to freeze while the hens scratched for breakfast.

Ida May stayed inside to tend to Edgar Lincoln. He was by then awake and in need of washing and changing. He also needed something to temporarily satisfy his morning hunger until his mother's return. "Just you wait," Ida May lightly teased him as she shared a cookie with him.

"Won't tell you what it is, but you'll *love* your new toy!" The little round face grinned at his sister.

Finally the family was able to gather for a light breakfast of honeyed toast, fresh still-warm milk, and hard boiled eggs. Since the family's Christmas tree would be at their grandparents' house, their beribboned or plain brown paper wrapped gifts were brought to the table and proudly placed in front of each individual to be opened as soon as breakfast was eaten.

Ida May, the most excited, squealed with joy after tearing off the paper concealing her sister's gift to her. She jumped out of her chair, slipped the full apron over her head, and without even stopping to tie the sash around her still tiny waist, rushed to hug her sister. "Oh Alice, it's the most beautiful thing I've ever had! Thank you! Thank you!"

Alice beamed with pleasure. Then, with Ida May standing expectantly in front of her, Alice pulled her new book bag from its wrappings. Her eyes lit up, remembering the bedraggled shape of her old one. After testing the string's ability to close and reopen the bag, she stood and threw her arms around her sister. "Ida! You made this? Yourself? It's just perfect for school! I can carry *everything* in it!" Then remembering her sister's disappointment at not starting for another year yet, she added, "Tell you what, I'll make *you* one, just like this, for next year when you go with me!"

After seeing his sisters' actions and reactions, it didn't take Edgar Lincoln long to rip off the paper in which his hand-carved wooden ball had been concealed. Right to the floor he went from his mother's lap and began gleefully rolling and chasing it around the room with baby whoops of joy. He totally missed the fact that yet another present for him waited to be opened. His sisters had to do the honors for him. They held up the new, larger gown his mother had made and tried to coax him over to try it on. He was too entranced with his new ball to respond with more than an occasional glance.

As he played around and under their feet, his sisters urged Nerva to open their present. "Oh my, for me?" she feigned. "What *have* you two been up to, I wonder?" When the wrapping was undone and the matching pair of hot pads lay revealed, tears formed in the corners of her eyes. It was a confusion of ardent love and deep loneliness that suddenly swamped her. "My darlin's," she finally breathed, "how precious thoughtful of you! The onliest thing that could possibly make me happier would be for your pa to walk through that door right now!" With that, she reached across the table to them, shoving her love-gifts into their laps to open.

Eying each other's progress, the girls carefully opened the two packages together, drawing out the anticipation. Together then, they held up the twinned skirts to their young-girl waists, and twirled around to open out the pleats, their "Ohhs" and "Ahhs" filling the room.

Alice, closest to her mother, draped her new skirt over the back of her chair and turned to tightly hug her. "Ma, it's beautiful! I love it! I love you!"

Joining in the hug, Ida May added, "And they're the same as Edgar Lincoln's gown! Now we're all a pair, aren't we?"

"Yes, you're 'all a pair' as you say. How 'bout this? Why don't the both of you wear 'em to Grampa's today, an' I'll put Edgar Lincoln's new gown on him too? Now, if only your pa could see you, all dressed up alike!"

***

Without any new snow to hinder their progress, the three-mile buggy trip in the still-frosty air to the grandparents' home passed uneventfully. The ragged edges of the snow beside the lane reminded everyone of the next snowstorm surely yet to come. All bundled in together, and chattering away about the prospects for the rest of the day, they arrived half an hour later, still warm and in high spirits. Their cousins, Eliza and Hellen, rushed out to greet them, with Eliza excitedly shouting: "Grampa's tree! Grampa's tree! Wait till you see Grampa's Christmas tree!"

Nerva's daughters jumped down from the buggy, with their cousins chasing after them, and ran to the entryway of the house. There they were playfully prevented from viewing the heralded tree by their Uncle Allen, who kept dancing and dodging in front of them. Finally relenting, he allowed them to get past him and into the main room with its blazing open fireplace.

And there it was, at the center of their grandparents' kitchen table, this lovely tradition brought to America in recent years by newly arriving German immigrants: a small, fragrant pine tree— actually just the shapely top of a much larger tree—with more than a dozen candle stubs carefully attached at the ends of its branches. There were also bits of color scattered here and there by pieces of brightly colored paper, some cut into geometric shapes and others cleverly folded into tiny boxes, all hanging by short ribbons.

Almon Griffin was just finishing lighting them when they entered. "Just a couple more to light here to welcome you, Alice and Ida," he greeted them, as he hovered a taper lit from the fireplace over the last two candles.

"Oh-h-h . . . ," the sisters sighed again and again as they circled the table to see all sides of the wonderful tree.

"It's even prettier 'an last year, Grampa," Ida May said as she ran to hug him in the chair where he had sat down.

Alice noticed the four presents nestled beneath the tree's bottom branches, and silently slipped the wrapped hot pads for their grandmother from her apron pocket to add to the pile. With a gesture of her head, she encouraged Ida May to do the same thing with the Christmas card they had jointly made for their grandfather. In its creation, both had utilized their newly developing skills. Ida May had painstakingly copied the Bible verses about the birth of the Baby Jesus, after which Alice had surrounded them with tiny drawings of prairie plants and flowers.

"Law me, let me look at you young 'uns in your new clothes." This request of their grandmother, who had squeezed herself in between their mother and grandfather, made Alice and Ida May each grab one of their baby brother's hands so they could stand in a line before her. "Oh, your ma has made you look right purty, don't you think so, Almon?"

Their grandfather stroked his salt-and-pepper beard as he replied, "She sure 'nough did. Them's got to be the purtiest matchin' skirts an' gown I ever did see!"

"You're just carrying on, Grampa," Ida May said to him. "But read what we made you," she added, reaching under the Christmas tree and drawing out the card.

Removing it from the envelope that had been carefully folded, glued, and then lovingly addressed "To Our Grampa," he began to read, "I bring you good news of great joy which shall be for all the people . . ." Being a shortish man, he didn't have to bend over far for the girls to see the grateful twinkle in his eyes for what they had made him. "That there's the nicest card I ever got in all my years!"

"Now for you, Granma," Alice continued. "Merry Christmas from both of us."

Their grandmother's pursed lips broke to a full smile as she pulled the hot pads from their wrapper. "Hot pads! Just what I've been a'needin' 'cause my old ones are near done for. Don't hardly keep my hands safe no more. Oh, bless your dear lil' hearts!" As she said that, she swept both girls to her bosom, then pointed to two of the remaining packages. "Them's for you," she said.

Alice and Ida May found to their delight, as their mother had known they would, the mittens that not only matched each other but also matched the color of their new skirts. And when Nerva opened the present her mother put in her hands, she herself was truly surprised to find that she, too, had a matching pair of blue mittens, though hers had a much smaller pair for Edgar Lincoln tucked inside. Repeating Ida May's earlier observation, she turned to her daughters and said, "Now we're *all* a pair, aren't we?"

One gift remained. Alice and Ida May looked nervously at each other, remembering their extravagant request of their grandfather when they were here a month earlier. He picked it up and extended it toward them with a sorrowful smile. "'Tain't what you asked me for . . . 'Tain't what your hearts wanted . . . But maybe it'll help anyways . . ." He placed the flat package in Alice's outstretched hands, as both girls' upturned eyes already showed the gathering sense of disappointment their hearts couldn't hide.

Within the wrapping paper they found a dozen envelopes, each one with a three-penny stamp already attached. Under them, folded twice to size, were a dozen letter sheets. "So's you can write your pa every time he writes to you," began their grandfather. "I'm truly sorry, but I just couldn't get the wall map you asked for, no way. Too dear for the likes of me. From what your pa writes, he'll be home soon anyways, an' he can tell you himself where all he's been . . ." His voice trailed sadly off, for he was as disappointed as they were.

"That's all right, Grampa. We understand," Alice assured him, her arms quickly circling his neck. Ida May added her own arms and a suggestion that brightened everyone's heart: "Why don't we use the first one for *all* of us to write a bit to Pa!"

And so while the last of the meal was prepared, one by one they each gathered their greetings to Brainard that Christmas Day. From the youngest it was just a few words. Their elders added descriptions of the day, assurances of their well-being, and always the hope for his safe and soon return. Together they filled both sides of the page, and with the first envelope properly addressed by Nerva, it was ready to be sent on its way in the morning.

Following the sharing of these final gifts, the family sat together at their festive table. It had been enlarged by the addition of two sawhorses and several board planks cut to size for the purpose. Granma Polly had gotten up before dawn to start roasting the goose Grampa Almon had killed with a lucky shot two days before. As at their Thanksgiving meal, a variety of boiled and baked vegetables would complement the goose and freshly baked bread. The

Christmas cookies Nerva and her daughters had made the day before would be everyone's dessert.

***

The gifts were all given, the meal eaten, and a brief family time enjoyed in front of the fire before winter's approaching early darkness forced Nerva to announce it was time to head for home. Many more hugs, kisses, and expressions of thankfulness were exchanged while Uncle Allen hitched up Ol' Jim and brought his sister's buggy around to the porch for her. With a final round of well wishes, Nerva herded her daughters into the buggy. She received the sleeping Edgar Lincoln from the arms of her father and passed him to Alice beside her. Then "Hud Up!" she called, with a sharp shake of the harness, and started the return trek.

"I'm right sorry about you not gettin' that map you had your hearts set on," Nerva said after what seemed to her too long a period of silence. "Would've been special to trace your pa's journeying."

"It's all right, Ma," responded Alice quickly. "I've been thinking about it, and being able to write to Pa is probably more practical. Besides, there's a really large map on the schoolhouse wall. That's where I got the idea from. I reckon I can make a drawing from that, or something, and we can still follow where Pa goes. 'Course, I'd really rather that he just came home. Then we wouldn't need a map at all."

The buggy grew quiet again as the three who were still awake focused their thoughts on a faraway Union soldier, their David Brainard Griffin.

Chapter Twelve

Boots, Books, Birthdays, and Bullets

With the New Year, Alice started her third year of instruction at the community schoolhouse in Alba. Since the post office at Mr. Peters' general store was only a mile beyond, it became her responsibility to go there every Friday, before starting for home, to fetch any messages that might have arrived from her father that week. Most weeks there was at least one letter, and by Alice stopping for them, her mother was saved the extra buggy trips she had been making. It was the Griffins' routine then to sit together at the lamp-lit table as soon as Alice got home to devour Brainard's news.

And exciting news it was, for the Second Minnesota was finally on the move toward the Rebels. After three months of waiting, and now accompanied by seven other regiments, they were actively pursuing the Confederate troops who were under the command of General Felix Zollicoffer.

From Lebanon, Kentucky, they marched twenty-two miles to Campbellsville, as Brainard reported on January 6, 1862:

"We started on New Year's morning and marched 11 miles through as hilly a country as ever I saw. We camped that night near a creek and got along first rate. The cook and I was up the next morning by two o'clock to get breakfast, so that all were ready to start by sunrise. I have not seen any land in Ky. that I would exchange for mine. We are camped right in the middle of the secesh, and not but about 40 miles from the Rebel army.

There is two Regiments camped together here, 20 Companies, and they fetch in mutton, pork, and honey. The Col. of the Brigade tells our officers to let the boys go and get what they can, and if they get anything from a Union man they can pay him for it, and if from a secesh, he had better keep still.

You may not get as many letters from me as you have because I have not the chance to write when we are on the march that I have in camp, but I will write as often as I can. I hope that you will do the same."

When Nerva finished reading this letter, Ida May asked two questions. The first was easy to deal with: "What's this 'secesh' Pa keeps talking about?"

"Some folks are tryin' to break up our country, love. They want to leave, an' if they do, it's called 'secession.' So he's namin' the person 'a secesh' who wants to do that."

Her second question was harder to answer. "But isn't that stealing if they take stuff and don't pay for it?" That one required an evening's conversation to describe the confusing rights and wrongs about warfare.

Three days later, Brainard wrote again, much to the delight of his loved ones at home. By then the army had marched another twenty-one miles, all the way to Columbia, Ky, so that he could report:

"We are within 25 miles of the Rebel Gen. Zollicoffer. We expect to march towards him when we start again, and we may see some fun

before long. It may not be such fun to a great many of us, but we cannot tell who it will be."

"What's he talking about, Ma? What kind of fun are they having? And why won't some of them not get to have any?" It was Ida May again, innocent of the ways of war and the euphemisms of adults because of her tender age.

Nerva laid the letter down and reached across to grasp her younger daughter's hand. "Your pa's tryin' to make a little joke, love. He means there'll prob'bly be a terrible fight soon. An' if they can whup the Rebels, it'll be fun enough . . . But most likely, some folks are gonna get shot, or even kilt, and that won't be no fun . . ."

"Not Pa?"

"Like he wrote, 'We cannot tell who it will be.' We just got to go with that," her mother replied.

"But *not* Pa?" Ida insisted.

"No, I'm sure in my heart your Pa's comin' back to us, just like he said when he left us . . . Now, let me finish readin' this here letter."

"It is very likely that there will be some fighting before long. I cannot tell whether I shall be in the ranks or not, but if I am needed I shall not flinch a particle, but shoulder my gun and fight, even till the last drop of blood is shed. I have not the least desire to return home until the war is ended, for I think that I am in a good cause and that I am working for the good of my family and friends, as well as for my Country. If I die in the cause . . ."

At this, Nerva's voice faltered. She had to stop, take a deep breath, and looked with a mother's calm reassurance into the eyes of both her daughters, before continuing: *"If I die in the cause, I hope that my little family will never have to suffer for the want of the comforts of this world, and at the last, if we should not meet again in this world, we shall all meet in heaven. But I feel we shall all meet one another here again, and before many months too. Tell Chipman that he must have Duke and Dime broke first rate, for I expect that I shall have to use them some time."*

"See, your Pa is *sure* he's comin' home to us, comin' home to work again, and not too far off neither! We've just got to believe that with him. Can we do that, my Darlin's?" Their nodded assents, to their mother and to each other, strengthened her own resolve. "Listen how he finishes – can you picture this?"

"You must excuse my mistakes and bad writing, for I have had to sit down on a knapsack and take another one on my knees to write on that. Such is camp life."

"Let's write to Pa tonight, can we, Ma? We've got *lots* to tell him about!" Alice's earnest voice made it hard for her mother not to agree, though Nerva had planned to get everything ready for starting another batch of her cheese the following day. She knew it wasn't fair to her husband for them not to write more often than they did. Still, there was always *so much* for her to do around the farm with him gone.

"Yep, let's do that. What all should we tell 'im?"

Ida May quickly ticked off the first three things on her fingers: "Tell Pa about Baby Evelyn and Baby Julia born last week; and about how we read his letters over and over; and how Alice started school again."

"And don't forget the special birthday supper we had for him last week when Uncle Allen came, just like he asked," added Alice.

Nerva set the pen, ink pot, and writing paper out as the girls gathered on either side of her. The pale lamplight flickered a bit as she began, "I think I'll tell 'im first off that we're doin' first-rate, for that's what he'll be a'wantin' to know the most..."

She recorded the community and family news as her daughters had suggested, especially providing him full details of how she had prepared his favorite meal of boiled pork, potatoes, carrots, and onions on the thirteenth in honor of his thirty-first birthday and their tenth wedding anniversary. She wrote of the weather, particularly the minimal snow so far. And then from her heart she described how much they missed him and how proud they were of him.

"Won't this make Pa feel good when he gets it," Ida May said, holding the completed letter while her mother put his name and military address on the envelope.

"Yes, indeedy, it sure enough will," her mother replied.

***

The first few days of school had been hard on Alice. Her own insecurities about her father's safety were compounded by the accustomed companionship she knew she was missing at home. But that year there was a new teacher for the multigrade single-room school at Alba, Miss Rhoda Cray. New to teaching, as well as to the community, Miss Cray was one of those people who bubble over with enthusiasm, whatever the topic or task at hand, which is why Alice quickly grew fond of her. As time passed, she actually started looking forward to her days at school in a way she had never done before.

Alice also discovered that her fellow students seemed sincerely interested in her father's current absence. They were both curious and supportive. Their interest also increased her positive attitude toward school.

Besides her Churchill cousins, eighteen other children gathered from the surrounding farms for their annual four months of mixed-age education in the Alba schoolhouse. Reading, writing, and arithmetic (the proverbial 'Three Rs') filled most of each day, with a play break when the children ate their home-packed lunches. In addition, Miss Cray, who loved to study both nature and history, regularly enriched their curriculum by including natural science lessons and stories from the past. These history lessons spanned all the way from America's then-still brief history, to that of ancient Greece and Rome.

These children were in the midst, as they well knew, of their country's Civil War. And with the daughter of an actual Union soldier among them, those glimpses back at historical events became quite compelling for the community's students.

"Any news from Uncle Brainard?" The question was voiced one morning toward the end of January by Alice's cousin Eliza as the students were climbing the steps into the schoolhouse. Several friends stopped to echo the question and to listen to Alice's reply.

She lowered her new book bag to the unpainted wooden step where she stood. "We got two more letters last week. It was his birthday there, and he said he hopes he'll be home here for his next birthday. They're still marching closer nearly every day to the Rebel Army. I think they were only seven miles apart last he wrote. He says there'll probably be a battle any day now."

"How big's our army?" asked Ethan McCormick, whose father had lost an arm in a farming accident and could not serve in the war.

"Best I recall, he said they had eight regiments of infantry, like our Second Minnesota, and one of cavalry and one of artillery, and maybe some more to come. So . . . maybe ten thousand all together?"

"How 'bout the Rebels?" inquired Josephine Gates. Her father had the largest farm in the district, and therefore also hadn't enlisted.

"I don't remember he's said." Alice turned to continue into the schoolhouse. The others followed her, a light morning banter continuing between them.

"You afraid for him?" It was the McCormick boy again. A hushed silence fell at this blunt, almost invasive, question.

"I'm . . . Ma . . . He . . ." She stumbled with her words, then bravely blurted out: "He says we're not to worry none about him. Some'll get hurt or killed maybe, but we're to trust God for the future. And that's what I'm going to do!"

Her schoolmates, even Ethan, who was only curious, smiled in relief, and so the children moved on to start their day of learning. For Alice, it meant going right up to Miss Cray's desk and placing before her a small paper she drew out of her apron pocket and unfolded. On it she had copied out two lines from her father's last letter. She crossed her arms and waited as her teacher read:

"Tell Alice that I hope she will learn fast this winter so that when I come home she can read the papers to her Pa. I hope that she will be a good girl and mind what her teacher tells her."

Rhoda Cray handed the sheet of paper back and said, "You do what he says, Alice Jane Griffin, and I'll help you all the way!"

***

As January passed into February, the days and nights grew progressively colder and darker on the Minnesota prairie, though little snow had fallen as yet. Because Mr. Chipman had helped Nerva and the girls get the rest of the cordwood down to the shanty, that was no longer a bother. Yet it was so cold that even the new woodstove was not enough to keep the family comfortable, especially at night. A double layer of clothing was often needed, even inside.

But for Alice, even with an extra hour added as she walked to the post office and back after school, Fridays seemed less a drudgery because of the letters from her father she was able to bring to her family. Each one so far had been more than just news, but also messages of his love for them and of hope for their future together.

The unusually thick letter that Mr. Peters handed her the first week of February promised to be more of the same. With his last several letters focused on the impending battle, it was all Alice could do to keep from reading it right there in the store. But knowing her mother's insistence on opening all letters together, she politely thanked Mr. Peters and began hurrying home.

"Ma, we heard from Pa again!" Her announcement as she entered the shanty, with the last of the evening's light just beginning to change from pink to violet, brought both her mother and sister to their feet. They had been sitting opposite each other on two stools, encouraging Edgar Lincoln to take and retake the two steps between them.

"Then your Pa must still be all right," Nerva said, pressing her left palm over her heart. "Bein' Friday an' all, we've done up your chores, knowin' you'd be in late. So go ahead an' hang up all your winter wear whilst I pour you up a cup of fresh warm milk off the stove. Then we'll sit together an' see what he's got to say."

Ida May carried their single lamp over to the table and leaned her father's photograph against the base for the reading. Edgar Lincoln, rightly sensing the focus was no longer on him, retrieved his new ball from beside his cradle and began entertaining himself around the floor. Alice arrived at the same time as her warm milk and handed the letter to her mother.

As she always did, Nerva read aloud both addresses on the envelope, then opened it. She unfolded a double-sized sheet of heavier-than-normal writing paper. The girls then listened as read:

"Camp Hamilton, Ky January 22, 1862

My Dear and Affectionate Wife,

It is with a good deal of thankfulness towards my maker that I am spared to write to you once more. I am very happy to inform you that I have passed through the long wished for and long looked for battle without getting as much as a scratch. I have seen and heard so much in the last four days, that I am afraid I shall not begin to tell you the one half that I want to.

We had got breakfast about ready last Sunday morning, when a messenger came into camp with the report that the enemy was advancing with their whole force. We soon heard the guns cracking away at a fast rate. The regiment was called into line and started towards the scene of action on a 'double quick.' They went up within one fourth of a mile of the enemy when the 2nd Minnesota and the 9th Ohio formed into a battle line, and waited a few moments behind 'Finney's Battery' a'waiting orders. There was a cannon ball shot just over our heads and struck the ground about 30' behind us. It came through the air with a whistle and there was a good many heads that dodged, but your humble servant did not flinch. But before I say anything more, I will tell you how I came to be in the battle.

I was getting breakfast with the other cook when the company was called out. Our 'Orderly Sergeant' told us that we need not go out, but when I heard the cracking of the guns, I could not stand it. I told

Louis the cook that I did not enlist to cook, but to fight, and he could do just as he pleased, but I should take my gun and go with the company. So, I threw on my overcoat, for it was raining quite hard at the time, and buckled my cartridge belt around me, and bade the cook good-bye and started.

I ran about one mile and came up with the company after they had formed into line. We were then ordered to the field, to which we started through a thick piece of woods and came up to the enemy just as the 10th Indiana were retreating. The enemy was advancing with fixed bayonets, but the Minnesota boys came up to them with an Indian yell and such a volley as there was poured upon them for about 40 minutes, was never before heard. When the enemy gave way for us, we were so close to each other that some of our boys pulled their guns out of their hands. There was nothing but a fence between us.

There was 12 killed and 23 wounded in the Minnesota 2nd. There was not a man wounded in Co. F. The enemy had from 3,500 killed and over 300 taken prisoners. We followed them up for nine miles that day, but they did not make a stand at all. As we passed over the battlefield, we passed by the dead and dying, lying in all shapes and forms, and the wounded calling for water and begging us not to kill them. We told them that no man should be hurt for they were amongst friends.

As they ran they threw away everything that they could: blankets, guns (a good many of them flintlock muskets), knapsacks, coats, hats, and everything. Gen. Zollicoffer was killed on the field and a number of their officers killed and wounded or taken prisoners. It was a perfect Bull Run, only the 'Bull' run the other way.

Minerva, I have been in the most successful battle that has been fought in this campaign, and I shot off my gun at least 10 times at the enemy. We stood almost face to face, but I cannot realize nor does it seem to me that I have been in a battle at all. I did not feel the least bit excited, nor did I even think that I was in danger. Such is the case with most of the boys, but still I have seen enough. I have no desire to be in another battle, but if our Country calls me, I am ready to go.

This paper I got in a rebel's tent..."

"Well ..." It came out of Nerva as a breathy sigh. "He's still safe. His first battle, an' he's still safe!" She laid the letter down and smiled, but knew she'd be begged to read it again and again.

Alice and Ida May, more than just happy themselves, were thankful to see the relief on their mother's face, for they had watched the tension grow there each time their father had written about the battle that was coming. Now it had come. It was over. And he was still safe.

Chapter Thirteen

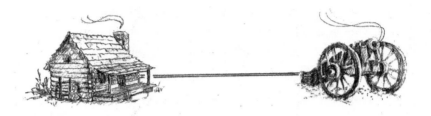

Candle Mold and Candles

The bitter but still dry cold deepened even more across the Minnesota prairie. It became ever harder to maintain a comfortable warmth in the shanty, though the woodstove was kept fully loaded day and night. Even when the family went to bed, multiple layers of clothing was the rule.

Chores became more difficult. Water had to be drawn two or even three times a day for the sheltered animals, for it quickly froze in their troughs and had to be chipped out before refilling. Many more armloads of firewood had to be carried into the house, and many more buckets of ashes had to be carried out and spread to enrich their kitchen garden. And there was always so much feed to grind for the animals, as they had to eat to keep warm, even inside the barn.

Brainard, learning from his family of their situation, commented on January 29th:

"I received a letter from you today which was mailed the 17th. I am sorry that you have such cold weather in Minn. And that you have not got a good home to live in. I hope that you will not suffer on

account of this cold weather. It will soon be spring, and then you will get along first rate . . . I think if I live to get home that I shall try to get us a house to live comfortable in, but there will be time enough to talk about that when I get there, and how soon that will be, you can tell just as well as I."

Finally it got so cold that Nerva announced one morning, "Alice, I don't want you to be a'goin' to school today. You'd best stay home with us, lest you freeze to death a'comin' or a'goin'."

"Ma—" Alice began, but was cut off by her mother.

"It's just too bad out there, somethin' bad could happen. There's also them German measles a'goin' around. You could catch them if you're already down sick."

"But Ma, I don't want to miss school. I'll get behind. Remember what Pa wrote in his letter last week about being so proud of me getting to the head of the class so much, and hoping the cold won't keep me from going to school? Besides, no one at my school has caught the measles yet."

"I know you don't want to miss any school, my love. But like I said, something bad could happen to you. I'm already so bushed out, tryin' to keep things a'goin' for your pa, I just don't know what I'd do . . . if . . ." Nerva sighed and slumped a bit as she finished her thought.

"At least you don't have to milk early mornings anymore. That's one good thing," observed Alice. That was true, for the prior week they had stopped milking Rosie, letting her dry up, as she was set to calve in another couple of months.

"That's one side of the coin, for sure, but t'other is that there's no fresh milk for you young'uns, nor butter neither, for that matter," her mother responded. "Anyways, I want you to stay home, at least today, until the weather breaks. Take some time for cipherin' an' readin' practice, but I'd like you also to help Ida May take care of Edgar Lincoln a bit." She put on her heavy wool sweater, work gloves, and long overcoat and headed out to the barn to begin her round of daily chores there.

It was that request that created the problem.

With Alice normally away at school all day, Ida May had been solely responsible for managing their little brother. She had been in the practice of getting out various household things for him to play with, which usually meant banging them around in his boyish way. This morning she had given Edgar Lincoln the family's candle mold. It was twelve joined tubes of tin in a two-by-six pattern, connected by a handle on each long side, and used in the making of their necessary supply of candles. Edgar Lincoln was, indeed, banging away on the floor with it.

"Ida May, he'll break it," scolded Alice, fists defiantly on hips.

"No he won't. He hasn't broken anything. He just has fun with things."

Giving her sister a hard look, Alice grabbed the candle-making tool out of Edgar Lincoln's pudgy hands, setting him into an immediate howl. "I said he'll *break* it," she repeated, turning away from her protesting brother to face her sister again.

"I'm here with him every day by myself. You think just because you're older'an me you know everything better'an me. Well, it's *not so.* I know how to keep little Edgar occupied," and with that, Ida May snatched the mold back and returned it to their brother, who was still crying nonstop on the floor. With the implement back in his possession, he immediately began banging it around again.

"Ma *told* me to help you!" Alice took a step toward her brother to remove the candle mold from him once more.

"Well, I don't *want* your help," was Ida May's sharp retort as she blocked her sister's movement. "Leave us be!"

"No, he's going to break it," Alice said a third time, this time slowly and deliberately for emphasis. She brushed past Ida May, reached down and retook the candle-making tool from Edgar Lincoln by one of its handles.

It happened quickly. Ida May spun around and grabbed the other handle. Both girls pulled. Hard. Hard enough for the soldered joints to shatter. Nearly a dozen pieces clattered to the floor between them, with each girl left holding a now useless handle.

Alice, horrified, cried, "Oh, no!" Ida May simply added her tears to those of her brother's, though for a very different reason.

It was just this scene that Nerva saw when she opened the door to come in for a warming break from her chores. She looked in dismay at the broken tool, and in consternation at her children. "What in *tarnation* is a'goin' on?" she demanded. Such strong language was unusual for her, but the situation seemed to justify it.

Each girl dropped her head and lowered her hand that still held one of the handles. "I'm sorry, Ma," Ida May blubbered between continuing sobs. "It's all my fault."

"No, it's my fault," corrected Alice as she put her arm around her younger sister and drew her in. "I shouldn't have insisted so . . ."

They all sat on the floor together and began fingering the broken pieces. With everyone now down on his level, Edgar Lincoln incorrectly sensed they were ready for play again, so he climbed up into his mother's lap and began exploring the contents of her apron pockets. Nerva ran her open hand through his curls, but was more intent on finding out what had happened.

Once the incident was explained, the real focus turned to what to do about it. "Alice, we'll put all these pieces in a carryin' sack, an' you can take them with you to Hiram Winslow next time you go to school. You remember where his blacksmith shop is, where we made our molasses, just out of town?"

"Yes, Ma, I do. I can do that. You really think he can fix it back right?" As Alice asked that, Ida May looked up imploringly as well.

"I reckon he can. That's what smiths do—fix up broken things. An' if he's not too busy, it won't take him too long either. That'll sure help us a lot 'cause I was plannin' on making candles sometime soon on account of us bein' most about out. That stub we used to light up little Edgar Lincoln's first birthday cake last night was nearly the last one left. What with all the other chores lined up for me to do, I just never got to it."

***

By the end of the following week the weather had eased enough for Alice to resume her daily trips to school. Although it had begun to snow a bit each night, with small drifts beginning to form along the lane, it wasn't nearly as cold as before. So Tuesday morning she set out half an hour earlier than usual, to give herself time to stop at the blacksmith shop on the way.

"Here's a dollar to pay Mr. Winslow," her mother added to the chorus of "good-byes" as Alice prepared to step down from the porch. She put the four coins safely in her apron pocket, joining her wrapped lunch sandwich, then waved one last time and set out. Book bag in one hand, the sack containing the various candle mold pieces in the other, and both swinging gently to the rhythm of her walking pace, Alice soon disappeared beyond the hill at the bottom of the lane that led to Alba.

Upon arriving, she tentatively approached the low, slope-roofed, double-chimneyed, rough-log shop where the community's resident blacksmith worked his trade. Short and burly, and blackened by charcoal dust from the twin bellowed furnaces within, Hiram Winslow was hammering away at a new pair of horseshoes. His face was glistening as red as the hot iron he was shaping when Alice stepped to his open doorway. Even at that distance she could feel on her frostbitten face the comforting warmth of his smithy fire.

"Why, hello there, Missy Griffin," he said, looking up in mid-swing. "How be you this fine Feb'wary day?" Despite his immense strength garnered from his years of labor, he was a kindly, jovial man, beloved by all the area children. They gladly took any opportunity to watch him at work, magically pounding various useful shapes out of iron.

"Just fine, thank you, Mr. Winslow. And you and your missus?" she asked politely. As she did so, she set down her book bag and

113

transferred the other sack to both hands, holding it right in front of her.

"We're fine too, though Martha's been a mite slow these past cold days . . . Say, what's that 'ere you've got in the sack? Somethin' for me?"

"Yes, sir, it's our candle mold. It got accidentally broken." Her cheeks began to grow hot as she relived her shame at the useless way it had happened. "And Ma was a'wondering if you could fix it up for us?" She stepped forward, close enough to show him the contents of the sack.

"Broken, huh? Well, lemme just see . . ." he said as he dumped the pile of pieces unto his workbench. "Why, that's an *easy* solderin' job! On your way to school, are you?" he observed, noticing her book bag. "You jus' leave it all here with me, and soon as I've finished up these here horseshoes for Mr. Gates, I'll put it back together good as new. You stop by after school to fetch it, 'cause I'll have it ready to go!"

"Oh, thank you, Mr. Winslow! I'll be back, but I have to check for mail from Pa first at Mr. Peters' store, so it won't be right after school."

"Won't matter none," the blacksmith replied as he set to hammering again. "It'll be ready whenever you get here. Hope you hear from your Pa today!"

***

At the end of the day, with winter's early evening not too far away, Alice arrived back at Mr. Winslow's shop, breathless from hurrying. She had been rewarded on her trip to the post office by *two* letters from her father, and she showed them to the blacksmith.

"Two letters . . . glory be," he said. "That should make your ma happy. And so'll this," he added, turning to his workbench behind him and offering her the restored candle mold. "What'd I tell you, good as new!" The carefully reconstructed implement showed he had good reason to be proud of his work. It was proof again that his customers, as well, had good reason to be pleased with his workmanship.

Taking it with pleasure, Alice reached into her apron pocket and drew out the four precious quarters her mother had given her that morning. "Here. Ma said I was to give you this. She hoped it'd be enough." She extended them in her palm-up hand to him.

"Ho, I'll only take *two* of them quawrters off'n you. Didn't have to remake anything, just soldered it back together." He plucked two of the coins from her palm and slipped them into the front pouch of his leather apron. "Take the rest back to your ma. Reckon she's got better things to do with 'em than give 'em to me." With that, he laughed wholeheartedly at his own joke.

Alice turned away, with her "Thanks, Mr. Winslow" thrown over her shoulder, and headed for home. She now had *five* prized possessions to deliver. And arriving home just before dark, she burst into the warm, lamp-lit shanty and announced: "Got the candle mold fixed . . . and got *two* letters from Pa!"

All the barn chores had already been completed for the evening. All the animals were safely shut in and fed for the night. So Nerva and Ida May were able to join Alice at the table, where she plopped down with her treasures. Edgar Lincoln crawled over, delighted to see his other playmate, and Alice lifted him up into her lap.

Nerva picked up the candle mold to examine its reconstruction and said, "Looks like he's done a right smart job . . . yep, looks ready to use!" She smiled lovingly at her elder daughter to show her appreciation.

"And he only charged us fifty cents," Alice said proudly, handing back the other two quarters.

Ida May, lifting from the table one letter in each hand, added, "*Two* letters from Pa! That makes . . . twenty-three all together, doesn't it? Can we read 'em before supper, Ma? Please, Ma?"

The latest two or three letters were always kept handy on the table by Brainard's propped-up photograph, to be reread many times before Nerva added them to the growing pile, tied with a ribbon and safely put away in her top dresser drawer. "Of course, love. Let's see what he has to say for himself this time." She reached for the two letters, opened them both, and, on the basis of checking which one had the earlier date, began to read:

"Thursday Morning, January 30th.

Good morning, Nerva,

I am well this morning and I hope you are the same. It rained hard all night, and as I lay in bed and heard it fall upon our tent, it made me think of home and how it sounded like falling upon the roof of our shanty..."

The rest of that letter briefly addressed their family finances, and reiterated his hope for a return home soon. The only item that required clarification for the girls was his statement: *"There is a good many slaves around here, but not any contraband in our camp yet."*

"What's he mean by 'contraband,' Ma?" Alice asked the question for both girls.

Nerva thought for a bit about how to make the concept meaningful to them. Nodding finally, she explained: "You know when you play checkers with Grampa? Well, when you get jumped, you lose yo'r playin' piece. The other'n takes it, right? That's somewhat the way it works out in war, too."

"The Rebels get jumped?" interrupted Ida May.

"No, I mean the Rebels call their slaves their property. Whenever they lose to our Union troops, like your Pa, they lose their property. That's kinda *like* getting jumped in checkers."

"When Pa writes us about how they've been a'foraging for food stuffs – hams, chickens, and the like – is that the same thing?" Alice asked, trying to help Ida May understand.

"Yep. Our soldiers move in, some slaves reckon they can just leave their owners, not work for 'em anymore, an' they run away. They run to where our Union boys are. That's when they become contraband. It's part of the spoils of war . . . unfortunate for 'em, 'cause they're a'losin' workers..."

"So Pa's just saying they don't have any runaway slaves with them yet?"

"That's about it, my dear. But that prob'bly won't last long."

His second letter, dated ten days later, began with what seemed a discouraging announcement:

"I am well as usual this evening, but some tired for we have been pretty busy today for we have to march again tomorrow. We have got to go back to Lebanon again, but where we are a'going to go from there we do not know. There has been a great deal of rain here and the roads are awful bad, so the government is unable to get supplies through to us . . . It is about 80 miles from here to Lebanon. It will probably take us eight or ten days to go through, and I shall not have a chance to write to you until we get through."

Ida May broke into her mother's reading: "Are they going backward then, instead of forwards? And what happens if they run out of supplies?"

Her sister spoke up reassuringly, "It's just the bad roads because of the rain. Once the rain lets up, they'll go after the Rebels again, won't they, Ma?"

"That's surely so. Soon's they're all resupplied, they'll head out again. Now, listen to how nice he ends his letter."

"I dream of home very often lately, and of the dear ones that I have left behind. I hope that it will not be long before I shall see you all. Kiss the children for me, especially Edgar Lincoln. He will be one year old by the time you get this. It does not seem so, does it, but time flies. And now I will bid you all goodnight and go to bed. Goodnight, Nerva; goodnight, Alice; goodnight, Ida; goodnight, Edgar Lincoln.

D. B. Griffin."

***

Since the next day was a Saturday, it was set aside for candle making, for Alice would be home all day to help. Before Nerva left to do her morning chores in the barn, she reviewed with the girls the steps of the process so they could work together effectively on the project. Then she gave them their assignments while she was out.

"Ida May, I need you to bring up from the cellar all the beeswax we saved from that honey we harvested just a'fore yo'r pa left. Kinda eyeball it, an' bring up about the same amount of the steer tallow yo'r pa an' me made last summer. You remember? It's harder'n that lard you rendered from the hog butcherin'. Better for candles"

"I can do that, Ma. An' I'll be right careful on the ladder, too, like you always say."

"Good. Now, Alice, I need you to carry in enough wood for the whole day so we won't have to stop. Load up the stove an' set the kettle on to boil, 'bout half full. While it heats, measure and cut, let's see, four dozen wicks from our ball of twisted linen string. Do you 'member where I keep it?"

"Yes, Ma. In that chest by the end of your bed. Is that all?"

"No, after they're all cut, I need you to draw the first set through the tiny hole at the bottom end of each tube in the mold. Then you've got to tie the other ends on that bar that's soldered above the tops of the tubes. That's it."

"You can count on me, Ma," Alice said, putting on her coat to start bring in the firewood.

Turning to her youngest child, who was chasing his ball back and forth across the floor, Nerva added, "And as for you, Edgar Lincoln Griffin, yo'r job is to try to stay out of mischief!"

The four set about their various tasks, but the young boy's was by far the easiest to accomplish.

By the time Nerva was back, her daughters had almost everything ready.

"Ida, honey, you equal out the beeswax an' tallow on the balance scale I just set out for you, an' drop 'em into the kettle to melt. Alice, my love, bring me that candle mold you got ready, an' let's put it in this here shallow pan with some cold water in it so's the tips will cool fast an' the wax not leak out. Guess we'll need a bucket of cold water. Will you get that for me?"

With Alice's assent, Nerva turned back to her other daughter. "Ida May, here's the dipper. Use it to stir the bits in the kettle to help'em melt whilst I feed your brother. Don't let it get too hot now, an' let me know soon's it's all melted. An' be careful, for melted wax is unforgivable hot!"

A contented Edgar Lincoln went right off to sleep after his midmorning feeding, freeing Nerva for the work to follow. The melted wax and fat mixture, floating on top of the heated water in the kettle, was ladled into the tubes of the candle mold, where it cooled and set up into hardened candles. These were then gently pulled out, the mold restrung with more wicks, and the process repeated. The cooling and setting took about two hours, aided by taking the mold out onto the cold porch for ten to fifteen minutes. By using most of the day, they were able to make themselves four dozen candles – enough to get them well into spring.

Initially, the setting time between pourings was spent rereading the entire bundle of letters from Brainard. As always, the girls commented throughout the affair, mostly with exclamations at his descriptions, but occasionally asking for more clarification. Together they traced his progress to date on the hand-drawn copy of the wall map at school that Alice had made during her free time.

Eventually, Edgar Lincoln awoke again and required their combined attention to keep him clean, fed, and amused. The letters, all reread together, were once again carefully put away.

Chapter Fourteen

A Letter from Minerva

February 10, 1862

My Beloved Husband,

Your children, even the little one, are finally abed and hopefully dreamin of you. So I am now alone once more with my thoughts of you, dear Brainard, so far away from us still. We all miss you badly, talk about you each day, and cant hardly wait for this terrible war to be over sos you can come back to us again.

We were all sorry to hear that you have to march all the way back to Lebanon, like a retreat. The girls and I hope the weather will soon be such as to allow you to chase after them Rebels again, and get more of them to lay down their arms like you told us they did at Mill Springs.

All three young ones are as well as I am. The German measles is again round, but none of ours has got it yet. Jim Thorntons girl and both George Spauldings boys are down bad, and several others farther out the valley. I heard some children up towards Chatfield have even died from it. I hope to God we dont catch it here. But the hard news with the measles is theyve decided to close down Alba school because of it, so thats the end of this years schoolin for Alice. She already had to miss a couple days last week on account of it being so cold. So now Ive set her up a little study space at the table where she can read and cipher some each day sos to keep up. Ida May also works on her letters and numbers most every day, and complains that she has to wait another year yet. Edgar Lincoln is agrowin like a weed. You wont hardly know him. And he sure nough wont know you atall. We all laugh bout him astudyin mischief!

It has finally started to pile up the snow all around, and the little ones have been havin quite a time of it, asleddin down to the shanty from the wood lot above. The girls are good with their brother, and he cant ever get to much of that fun. But he and Alice did take a bad tumble a day or so ago when the sled tipped over with the little tyke underneath. No bruises or breaks, just scared him an me a mite.

We were busy today amakin enough candles to last us til spring. The girls were such a help, you would have been right proud of em. I reckon the four batches we made gave em enough practice to do it without me next time. Well see.

This room at night sure misses the light from the fireplace, but I dont think we mind much, tradin that bit of light for the extra heat we get from the wood stove. But theres hardly nough light for me to see my work or write to you, even with both the kerosene lamp and a couple of side candles. Most nights my eyes are plum tuckered out when I go to bed.

Mrs. Bender sure gave us a start last week. She stopped by on her way home from Alba to tell us her Andrew had reported your whole Company had let yourselves get captured by the Rebels during the battle, but that you all managed to break loose and get away that same night. I suppose you didnt write us about that sos not to scare us any. Brainard, you must tell us all the news, good and bad, so we know for sure how you are adoin!

Ol Mr. Kingsly also paid us a visit last week. Said by all accounts hes heard, he spects you to be home by May. Hes hopin youll give us all a speech or two about what youve seen and done. I showed him the tied up stack of all your letters and told him I was sure youd have plenty to say. He also told me about some secret societies coming out in Indiana and Illinois against the war. Says they're aworkin against Pres. Lincoln and tryin to get the war stopped. Have you heard of them? What do you think about such a thing?

When Alice picked up your last two letters, she said Mr. Peters told her he had written to you. Did you get his letter yet? Who else do you get letters from? Does any of your family in Vermont write? Im addin a note from Eliza in this letter. My parents helped her write it.

I am athinkin Ill go up to Spring Valley to visit Mary if the weather eases. Whilst there, I could get a likeness taken of Edgar Lincoln to send to you. Wouldnt you like to see how much hes grown? It should get there safe to you. Its kinda sad how he knows the Presidents name and face, but he doesnt remember who you are, even from your photograph.

This week Mr. Chapman helped me load up enough wheat to sell to Mr. Peters to pay off this years taxes, so thats one thing you dont need to worry about while youre away. We did get a very good price for it, cause wheats 'sky high' as they say. I dont know bout next year, though. How are we possibly going to get our crops in ifn youre not home yet? Perhaps Mr. Kingslys right, and you will be back here by May. I dearly hope so!

But the longer youre away, the more I worry about you becomin a rowdy with all the city boys, or even a tobacco user. Who will you be when you come home? I want you to come back to us just like you left us. Then we will all be a happy family again.

I must quit writin as I have filled up two sheets and have run out of news to tell. Besides, my eyes are particular weary tonight. So, good-night my husband, and accept the love of your devoted wife and children.

Minerva Griffin

Alba, Fillmore County, Minnesota

Chapter Fifteen

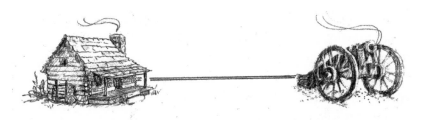

Connecting with Pa

"Ma, could we eat the same meal as Pa, like the one in his letter?"

Ida May's question was a bit of a surprise for Nerva. She continued kneading her bread dough on the other side of the table from where her daughter sat fingering their last letter from the battlefield. For clarification, she asked in response, "Why do you want to do that, love?"

"Well, he had to eat it with that stranger family. It was nice enough of them, I know, but still he *said* he wished he could have eaten it with us."

"So, if we fix the same meal . . . ?"

"We could pretend he *was* eating it with us instead!" As she finished her mother's sentence, Ida May stood up and rushed around the table to hug her and beg, "Oh, could we, Ma? It'd make me feel ever so much closer to him."

Nerva stopped working the dough and leaned back into her daughter's small, encircling arms. She then turned and placed her flour-coated hands on the girl's young shoulders and said, "O'course we can. We'll all feel closer to him. Why don't you find your sister, and she can come make a list for me off that letter so's I know what to make."

"I think she's doing her schoolwork up on our bed. Bet she'll like the idea, too."

And she did. Alice was very glad at the prospect of sharing her father's meal, and readily agreed to briefly leave what she was doing. But she hadn't been doing schoolwork. Spurred on by her Cousin Eliza's note that had been enclosed in her mother's last letter, she had begun writing her own first letter to her father. She figured it would only take a few minutes to copy out the supper list for Ma. Then she could come back and finish her letter to Pa.

Down the ladder both girls came, sharing the excitement of the moment. While Nerva continued kneading her bread dough, Alice quickly scanned her father's letter of February 20. Finding the passage, she read aloud as she wrote down the items for that evening's menu:

"I went off from the road, through the woods about two miles, and found a family there consisting of a man, three girls and two little boys. They said I was the first soldier that had ever been there. I went in and the old man had the girls go to work and get supper for me, which they did. It consisted of a piece of corn dodger, . . . a piece of cold pork, . . . some boiled eggs, . . . some butter, . . . and some sour milk. It was the first meal of victuals that I have eaten in a house since I left Minn. I think that I should have relished a meal of victuals at a table in our shanty with you and the children, better than I did that one."

Nerva ticked the items off with her floury fingers as she said, "Well, I've some fresh ground cornmeal for the cornbread, an' we had that pork roast last night, which I was a'savin' for sandwiches. Ida May can boil some eggs for us if she'll bring 'em up from the cellar, an' there's still plenty o' the last butter she made, I'm sure. But reckon we'll have to skip the milk as we've used it all up since Rosie dried up. That's close enough though, don't you think, Ida May? Four out of five?"

"It'll do, sure enough, Ma," her daughter replied. "I'll go down and get the eggs and butter right now."

"Ma," added Alice, distancing herself further from her writing project, "since you're still working that bread dough, how about I make the corn dodgers? I've watched you so many times, I'm sure I could do it myself."

"That'd be right nice, Alice Jane. I can talk you through the recipe whilst I finish up here. Then you'll be a part of his supper, too!"

Thus the small kitchen area of the single-room shanty soon became a beehive of activity. Nerva continued to fold and punch her dough, scattering flour on the table each time to keep the dough from sticking. Alice measured out and mixed the ingredients her mother called out from memory to her, then bacon-greased the cast-iron dodger pan to bake the small loaves of cornbread in. And Ida May tended the fire, set half a dozen eggs on to boil atop the wood stove, then turned her attention to the newly wakened Edgar Lincoln, who was calling for a playmate.

It took only a short time for the kneading to be completed and the bread dough safely tucked away into two covered loaf pans to slowly rise overnight and be baked in the morning. After cleaning up her scattered flour, Nerva sliced some of the cold pork and portioned it out onto their plates. During that same time, Ida May had timed the eggs by the mantle clock—twelve minutes—then placed them in a bowl of cold water to cool. And Alice had watched her dodgers rise and brown in the wood stove's side oven, by peeking several times, and eventually was able to put two pickle-shaped corn dodgers beside each serving of cold pork.

While Nerva tended to Edgar Lincoln's needs, Alice started to fill their drinking glasses with well water she had drawn and brought in. That's when she noticed something odd that Ida May had just done. A fourth chair had been brought to the table, and an empty fourth plate with eating utensils had been set before it. It was where their father always sat . . . She turned and saw that her sister had climbed up onto the sink counter and was just then reaching into the cupboard above for her father's favorite tea mug.

"What *are* you a'doing, Ida May?"

"I'm setting a place for Pa, just as if he was here."

Overhearing that exchange as she sat with her son on the settle by the stove, Nerva added, "So's we really can share the meal with him . . . my, my." A wistful look, both of overwhelming love for her children and the pain of separation from her husband, reigned upon her face. It changed into pure smile, however, as her gaze turned down to the boy child resting in her arms, so innocent, and so like his father, except for the blond color of his hair.

Supper that night was more fun than any time since Christmas. They included Brainard in all their table conversation, pretending to question him about his whereabouts, his health, and his daily activities. One of them would then answer for him, quoting from his multi-times read letters. Then the three would laugh in delight at the cleverness of the situation. Even Edgar Lincoln, though not understanding the cause of their mirth, joined in with gusto each time there was a burst of laughter.

"Tell us again about that snowball fight you had, Pa," began Ida May.

"On our way back to Lebanon, we camped in an old orchard. We got up the next morning and lo and behold it was a snowing very nice. It kept snowing until 10 o'clock, and the boys had a regular pitched battle with snowballs. We all enjoyed the sport first rate. We did not have to march any that day." That was Nerva.

"And when do you think you'll be comin' home to us?" inquired Ida May.

"The boys were all of them making calculations today when we should get our discharge and go back to Minnesota. We cannot see what there is now to hinder the Union men from gaining the day and of peace being declared before the first of April at the latest, but soldiers are not supposed to know anything in time of war so we cannot tell." It was Alice who answered for him this time.

Ida May kept the fun going with: "Please, Pa, tell us again about playing that new game you called 'baseball.' No one here knows what that is."

"I was on guard Monday, and Tuesday I played baseball all day. We had a good time of it, too. There was some 5 or 6 games played at the same time, both by the officers and men. We all enjoyed ourselves very much." Alice answered again.

"I must say, Brainard dear, I was a bit put out when Mr. Peters said I had to pay the three cents postage on your last letter. But when we opened it at home and found the five dollars. you sent, I was most glad you wrote."

"What did you do with the hair braids Alice and I sent you, Pa? Were you surprised? And have you taken any more 'contraband' from the Rebels?"

"Well, Alice, we started from Lebanon on the 22nd of February, and the first night we camped in Mr. Jackson's dooryard. The officers took possession of the house (a very nice one) and we soldiers took possession of the things out of doors, such as chickens, bacon, hams, and feed for the teams. We took his fence for firewood, too." Nerva had a hard time keeping a straight face as she spoke for her husband.

So it continued, long after Edgar Lincoln had tired of the play and drifted off to sleep in his mother's arms. When the others were equally tired of the amusement, Nerva put her son down in his crib at the end of her bed, then kissed both her daughters tenderly twice on behalf of both their parents, and sent them up the short ladder to their shared bed. She remained at the table a bit longer, lost in her own reflections of the evening's merriment. Finally, she stoked up the woodstove for the night, lowered the wick of the kerosene lantern to close off the flame, and lay down herself in the darkness, to sleep and dream of her faraway husband whose pretended presence they had all so much enjoyed.

Alice's letter writing would have to wait until morning . . .

***

By the following week, spring's reawakening had drawn close enough for the sap to begin to rise in the twenty or so sugar maples Brainard had carefully tended over the years on the ridge above the shanty. That meant it was time for Nerva to teach Alice how to tap them for the seemingly magical juices they would then reduce into the delicious maple syrup the whole family considered such a treat. Though the nights were still plenty cold, each day warmed enough for most of the snow to slowly melt and seep into the thawing ground beneath it. That, of course, meant mud.

"We'll be out traipsin' 'round up there all mornin' long. For that, we'll have to dress warm. So go put on sev'ral layers of your oldest clothes," Nerva instructed her elder daughter. Turning to her younger daughter, she continued, "Ida May, you'll need to stay behind an' play with Edgar Lincoln an' also have lunch ready for us when we return."

"Why'd you tell me to wear my old clothes, Ma?"

"Mud, that's why. We'll be trampin' in the mud the whole time. There's no two ways about it. So plan on getting' dirty. Now you get yourself dressed whilst I load up Ol' Jim's panniers with the drill an' taps, an' buckets."

"Yes, Ma," Alice called back as she climbed up again to the girls' sleeping loft to redress. Ida May sounded like an echo when she followed with her response.

Getting properly dressed only took Alice a couple of minutes, leaving her time for a bit of floor play with her brother until she heard Ol' Jim's familiar clip-clop as Nerva led him up to the shanty's porch. The trusty horse's load was light, even though his panniers were stuffed full with the supplies needed for the task: a hand drill and hammer, and several dozen each of the notched wooden tubes, called spiles, and cupped-hands-sized buckets to hang from them. All this equipment had been brought from Vermont, where both Griffin families had made maple syrup for generations.

The three children came out together as Alice joined her mother, who was holding Ol' Jim's lead for their walk up to the woodlot.

"We'll prob'ly be three or four hours, an' mighty cold an' hungry when we get back," Nerva informed Ida May. "Play with Edgar Lincoln till the little tyke tires for his nap, then fix us all some sandwiches. That cold pork from last night is ready to slice, 'long with the loaf of bread fresh yesterday. But mind you be careful with the big knife!"

"Yes, Ma, I'll be careful, and Edgar Lincoln an' I'll be just fine till you get back . . . count on it." As she finished, Ida May stooped to lift her brother up so they could wave good-bye together to their sister, their mother, and Ol' Jim, then they returned to the warmth of their little home.

With what they hoped was the last of winter's rosiness showing on their faces, mother and daughter's climb was uneventful. Nerva spent most of the time reviewing the "sugaring" details she had outlined to Alice as they sat before the woodstove after supper the evening before. "I'll drill the holes through the bark at the right spots, just like your pa always did. Soon's I'm done with a hole, you shove in the tap good an' tight, then hang one o' them collectin' buckets from the tap. That was always my part."

"And we have to come back out before supper?" asked Alice.

"Yep . . . ev'ry afternoon till the trees start to show a little green . . . a couple weeks at least. But after today it'll be you and Ida May who gather up the sap that's run and haul it back down to the house. If'n we can get forty gallons o' sap like last year, we can make us a whole gallon of syrup to enjoy!"

"Seems like a whole lot of work without Pa," Alice murmured with a bit of sadness in her voice.

"True," Nerva replied. "But the sweet reward at the end should make it all worthwhile, especially 'cause he's gone."

Mother and daughter made a good team as Alice was an eager learner and Nerva a patient teacher. Traipsing through the predicted muddy snow, they stopped at each of the maple trees for Nerva to drill two or three holes at a slightly up angle. Alice, working right behind her, slipped one of the handmade spiles into those holes, gave each a light tap with the hammer, then hung one of the small pails from the notch at the top for the sap to drip into.

The process took less than ten minutes for each tree, and the work was accompanied by an easy banter between them concerning the clear signs of spring they noticed, from the flickering birds above them to the squishy mud beneath their feet. Caught up in the moment, Alice threw her arms out wide and proclaimed: "It's so *good* to be out, an' *feel* spring a'comin' back!"

A little after noon they were headed back down to the shanty, slightly chilled but thrilled at what they had accomplished without Brainard. The promise of delicious maple syrup had begun . . .

True to her word, Ida May had the sandwiches set out and hot tea ready to brew to help warm her mother and sister when they arrived. Her morning with Edgar Lincoln had gone well, and she delighted in Alice's description of the process. That drew her in, for she knew that after this day it would be her job to go up with Alice to gather and bring home the contents of the numerous little pails for the next step.

Following lunch, they composed together a brief letter to Brainard, relating to him all the news they could think of, along with assurances of their well-being, which was shadowed only by their longing for his return. Since they had already answered his last letter, there was little else to say to him that day.

Their supper was later than usual that evening, for Nerva accompanied Alice for the first collecting to make sure everything was working correctly. Only one spile had slipped out so that the sap ran down the bark to the ground. Alice easily tapped it back in, and all the rest of the pails were nearly full. Between them they carried back nearly two gallons of the watery, almost tasteless liquid, the results of that first day's flow. Both girls, after dipping and licking their fingers, had a hard time believing that this could become the syrup they enjoyed so much on morning pancakes.

"I assure you," their mother said after pouring the first batch of sap into their largest cooking kettle and lifting it on to the woodstove to begin its long boiling-down process, "that this is exactly what your Pa always did, 'cepting we're gonna cook it down inside atop this here new stove 'stead of outside. Ev'ry day we'll add in what you two bring home, an' day by day it'll slowly get thicker an' sweeter. Just you wait an' see!"

Day after day for nearly three weeks the girls trudged up the hill, creating a clearly marked pathway through the retreating snow. Each time they dumped all the sap-filled pails into their collecting buckets, then carefully replaced each pail on its spile. Returning the way they had come was a slow process as they had to stop often to switch their carrying hands because of the weight of the sap. Once home, each day's flow was added to the ever-concentrating, ever-sweetening, ever-darkening and thickening contents of the kettle. Stirred regularly throughout each day to make sure it wasn't scorching on the bottom, the kettle was soon wafting the aroma of maple goodness throughout the shanty.

As the days grew longer and warmer, the first green leaf-buds began to appear, and the time to gather sap grew to a close. Nerva went up one last morning with Ol' Jim to pull all the pails and spiles. With no more daily liquid being added, the syrup boiled down to its promised amber-colored finish as well.

When the process was finally completed and the syrup allowed to cool, Nerva gave the following instructions to Alice and Ida May: "I want you to bring up all them narrow-necked half-gallon pottery jugs we've got stored down cellar. They're all stoppered tight, so's we won't need to clean 'em any. But you be careful not to drop 'em 'cause they'll break."

With ready hands to finish the project, Alice climbed the cellar ladder to hand them one by one to her sister. Just a thorough dusting was all they needed before the filling began, and this was quickly accomplished.

"Ida May, you steady this here funnel," Nerva said as she handed the tin tool to her, "whilst Alice dippers in the syrup." She said that as she passed the ladle with a demonstrating dip. "I need to tend to the little tyke, so's you'll be a'tidyin' it up without me. Now I'm sure I *don't* need to tell you to be careful, as you already *know* how much work it's taken to make, so I'll just trust it to you."

Working together, all the while imagining their father's face when he tasted his first pancake back at home, the sisters completed the transfer without spilling as much as a single drop. The wooden stoppers Brainard had whittled several years before were then reinserted and six of the jugs were ready to return to the cellar. The last one, not quite full, would remain in the kitchen for current use.

"Ma, could we have pancakes for supper tonight?" This Alice asked while her mother finished dressing Edgar Lincoln after his wooden-tub bath over near the stove. Ida May slipped in from behind Alice, a broad grin on her face in support of the request.

"I think that would be a perfect thing to do. We'll get our first reward for all our work. Hadn't decided yet on what to fix anyways." Saying this, she released her son down to the floor, and he immediately wobbledy-stepped across the room to his ball and plopped beside it to renew his playtime, so she moved to the cooking area to begin preparing the family's special supper.

Frying pancakes was so much easier on the top of the woodstove than it had always been in the fireplace, and the cakes even came out a lovelier shade of brown. With the first batch beginning to bubble, showing they were nearly ready to turn, she called the girls away from playing with their little brother to prepare the table. Plates, cups, and utensils were quickly set out. Butter and syrup were placed in the middle of the table beside their father's tintype, along with a fresh-drawn jug of water. Then Edgar Lincoln was plopped into his high chair.

Nerva slipped three pancakes onto each of the plates except Edgar's—he only got one—then sat down with her children for the grace that preceded every meal. Raising her bowed head, Ida May's glance turned to the place she had set for her absent father before saying, "I can't stop wishing Pa was here tonight for this first taste of our syrup."

"Well, love, the sooner he comes home, the more syrup there'll still be for him to enjoy. So, even if he's not with us tonight, let's wish him home as soon as can be," responded her mother.

***

It was during another late-winter snowfall —nearly the end of March—that Wesley Baldwin arrived at their door. Brainard had earlier written about a friend he had made, Private Baldwin, who was to be discharged for health reasons after a lengthy hospital stay, and who might stop by. But Minerva had not really expected to meet the Hamilton resident, as his home was some fifteen miles still further north.

She and her daughters were sitting around the table after morning chores talking about what they could write to the missing member of the family when they heard the unusual sound of loud knocking.

"Law me, now who could that be, out in weather like this? Must be bad news, or somethin'." Nerva rose and headed to unlatch the door. Both girls turned in their chairs to see who it could be.

"Are you Missus Griffin, Missus Brainard Griffin?" The tall and very thin stranger had a somewhat haggard look about him, even through the full-length blue Union coat he wore. But his smile appeared warm and genuine, and when Nerva nodded in answer to his question, he continued, "My name's Wesley Baldwin. I was serving with your husband in the Second Minnesota, but I took so bad sick they had to discharge me."

She could see he was very cold from traveling in the snow, and with that information she discarded her normal hesitation regarding strangers. With a further opening of the door and a gracious inward sweep of her arm she invited him into the warmth of their home. "Why Private Baldwin, Brainard wrote us you might be stopping in on your way back to family. How good of you. Set yourself down there by the fire," she said, pointing to the settle, "an' I'll find you a bite o' somethin' to eat."

"Much obliged, ma'am," he said as he brushed the gathered snow off his coat, then removed his infantry cap to her and held it over his heart. Acknowledging the girls, he added, "And you must be the two fine daughters he was always talking about."

Alice and Ida May both blushed with pleasure, hearing of their father's praise to his friends. "Yes, sir. I'm Alice, this here's my sister, Ida May, and over yonder sleepin' is our baby brother, Edgar Lincoln."

Nerva was handing him the last warm cup of tea from her morning pot, along with a buttered slice of yesterday's baked bread, when he began: "Like I said, I've been so poorly that they had to send me home. But Brainard hoped I would stop in passing to tell you how good he was doing."

Mother and daughters drew up their chairs in front of the settle to listen to his story. "We're very grateful indeed for any news we can get," Nerva replied.

"I don't know what kind of a cook he was before he left home, but he does a right smart job of it now, with Louis the cook teaching him, of course. Coffee for all of us in the morning. Soup nearly every day. Good soup, too! And he boils the meat and veg'tables most nights, plus cleans all the rabbits, turkeys, and chickens the boys bring in. Then he's hours ever after cleanin' up."

"Never much lifted a finger around this here kitchen," muttered Nerva. "Just wait till he gets back," she added with a wink to the girls.

"He prob'bly wrote you about our big battle at Mill Springs. Whoo-ee, that was a long day to remember. All the noise. Cannon shots blowing up everywhere. Men chasin' through the smoke and trees. Dead men . . . wounded . . . laying every whichaway. Face-to-face we were. Just a split rail fence between us. Rebels and us a'shootin' it out. And Brainard was always right in the thick of it. Yes, ma'am, you'd have been right proud of him."

All that talking set Private Baldwin to wheezing and coughing so hard his whole body was shaking. Concerned for his welfare, Nerva moved to him and placed a comforting hand on his shoulder until the spell passed.

"Well . . . that's why they're sendin' me home . . ."

"We surely don't want to tire you out any. An' you're prob'ly ready to set off again for your own folks and home. But is there anythin' else about the children's father? Is he sick much? How's his spirits, gener'ly? Does he ever have to work too hard?" Nerva sat back down, having expressed her earnest regard for both her husband and his friend now before her.

"Missus Griffin, I assure you Brainard is almost always of the best of spirits. All the boys love him like a brother. Oh, he gets a cold now and then, 'specially after night picket duty. All of us did that. But he enjoys hisself . . . has always done so with all we've been through. I'd have to say there's not a more happy man with army life than Brainard Griffin, 'cepting, of course, having to be separated from his family." He said the last with a sweep of his cap that took in all four of them, as well as the shanty that sheltered them. "And with General Grant capturin' Forts Henry and Donelson, with over fifteen thousand prisoners, too, maybe he'll have even *more* reason to be happy. And you will, too, when you hear him come a'knockin' at the door like I did this morning!"

With that, he stood to make his farewells. The three followed him to the door, wishing him well on the remainder of his trip home. They stood a long time watching from the porch as he strode away down the lane that headed to Alba, then Spring Valley, and on to his own loved ones awaiting him in Hamilton. The cold air and lightly falling snow ultimately drove them inside, but their hearts were fully warmed by their morning visitor.

Chapter Sixteen

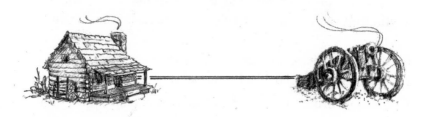

War Coats and War News

The last week of March was a busy one for the Griffins, including Eliza Churchill, who had returned for another short stay. For Minerva, it began with the annual township meeting, held in the community's schoolhouse. Before Brainard had left in September to volunteer as a soldier for the Union, many of his neighbors were suggesting that he should serve again as town clerk. He had been elected the very first town clerk for Beaver Township when they had arrived back in 1857, and apparently had done a good job. Some residents were now saying they would be willing to fill in for him with regards to the normal run of affairs should he be elected but not yet returned, for all still assumed his absence would be brief. That would be one of the decisions made at the meeting.

There wasn't much that Minerva could say to the local group gathered to conduct its annual business when she was asked about the man many obviously wanted to choose. "He writes regular, as most of you know, reports all the news he hears," she said. "An' he says they all of 'em expect to be home in a month or two. But who can tell in this terrible war? For him it's nothin' but guesswork."

When she sat down, Andrew Peters stood to speak next. "He's a good man, Brainard Griffin is, and he did a fine job for us the first time. Very professional like. So I think it's just a question of should we keep the job open for him till he returns, or move ahead without him."

"I agree he's done us good before." It was Jacob Leothold, the man then retiring from the position. "But supposin' we come back to him when soever he comes back to us, and elect someone else official in the meantime? Then nobody has to do fill in for him. Do you think he'd be offended by that, Missus Griffin?"

"When last he wrote, he gave as his opinion that the office might ought to go to someone who wouldn't be a'goin' off to war," Nerva clarified. "So's I don't think he'd be offended at all."

"Let's replace him then, at least for now . . . though I'd rather look for his speedy return," added Hiram Winslow. Nods of silent assent around the schoolroom conveyed the shared opinion of many of the other neighbors. "I nominate his father-in-law, Almon Griffin, if he'll do it," Winslow concluded.

"I'd be proud to try to live up to Brainard's reputation," Almon offered, "as well as pass it on to him when he's back among us." And with a round of "Ayes" from the small group when they voted, the matter was settled.

"I'll be sure to let Brainard know," said Nerva. "I think he'll be right pleased my pa was elected."

After the rest of the meeting's business was concluded, Nerva was chatting with two neighbor ladies when Mr. Peters approached with a somewhat flustered expression on his face. "Sakes alive, Minerva Griffin, I nearly plumb forgot I had a couple of things for you on the wagon. Almost took 'em back to the post office!"

"What ever could they be, Mr. Peters?"

"Don't rightly know—parcels of something. Lyman Case gave the first one to the post driver up in Chatfield to bring down to you. And didn't it turn out, on the way here, Mr. Colby up toward Spring Valley added another. I reckoned they must be from your husband

and you'd want 'em right away, so I brought 'em with me. Come out and I'll load 'em into your buggy." He headed out the school door, nodding farewell to the others as he passed them by.

"I'm *much* obliged to you, Mr. Peters," Nerva said excitedly to his back as she followed him out to his wagon.

"Here you be . . . two parcels. See, plainly addressed to you." After transferring them into her nearby buggy, he climbed back into his wagon, then remembered, "There's also a couple of other items for you, but you need to pay the postage on 'em, so I didn't bring 'em." Waving her a cheery "Farewell," he started off for home.

Nerva headed home, too, anticipating the prospect of viewing the things her husband had sent. Unlike Mr. Peters, she already knew what they were, for he had written about them several times: the Confederate officer's dress coat he had gotten during the Battle of Mill Springs, and his own winter dress coat and overcoat, no longer needed with the coming of spring down in Tennessee.

The three girls were as excited as she was when Nerva returned home with the parcels. They had been playing with Edgar Lincoln, who was just on the edge of taking his first real steps. Delighted to see his mother, he too became interested when she set both parcels before them on the floor.

"I'll get the knife to cut the string, an' we'll just see what's inside of 'em," Minerva said. She slid out of her overcoat, still necessary for traveling that spring in Minnesota, hung it with her hat and gloves on the peg by the door, got out her sharpest kitchen knife and returned to where the four children sat in a circle fingering the packages.

"Let's open the big one first," volunteered Ida May. It was the one sent down by Mr. Colby.

As soon as Minerva cut the four crossed strings that bundled it up, the girls opened out the crinkled brown wrapping paper, revealing Brainard's two Union Army coats. Each of his daughters grabbed one by the collar, stood up, and shook it out. The blue wool of both was a bit faded and soiled from daily wear in all kinds of weather, but their double rows of brass buttons down their fronts still gave an impression of military elegance.

"Those are Uncle Brainard's, right?" inquired Eliza as Alice shifted her hold on the longer overcoat to one hand at its collar, and gently brushed the folds out of it with her other hand. Ida May began copying her sister's brushing motion with the shorter dress coat she was holding up and admiring.

"Yes, these are your uncle's. Winter coats he won't need any longer 'cause it's already spring where he is, so far down South. Oh, wouldn't he look so grand in 'em if he was here! Now, let's open the other one ..."

Saying that, Nerva cut the strings that similarly bound up the smaller package. When its brown wrapper was opened, there was the Confederate officer's overcoat. It was gray instead of blue, with yellow piping at the seams, but when she picked it up they could all see it had the same double row of brass buttons as Brainard's coats.

"Now, this ain't your pa's, 'cause it's Rebel gray. Do you remember how he wrote 'bout pickin' this up after his first big battle? Well, here it is. It's kind of like a prize for him."

"Did the Rebel get killed?" asked Ida May.

"Law sakes, child, how would I know? Maybe, or maybe he just ran from his tent an' left it behind when your pa's Union troops were a'comin' after him. Guess we'll never know."

"Can we show them to Granma and Grampa when we take Eliza home?" Then Alice added: "Bet they'd like to see 'em, 'specially Pa's coats."

"Course we can, love. How about we take our things with us an' spend the night with 'em? Since I don't have to milk Rosie, all the stock can wait a bit for their breakfast till we get back home."

Her daughters would have clapped for joy at her response, like Eliza did, except for the fact they were still holding up the two coats.

"You girls go gather what you need, an' Eliza, you watch over Edgar Lincoln whilst I put together a few things to help some with supper."

As her daughters scampered up the ladder to their loft, Nerva called out once more: "Be sure an' dress warm enough for the drive over and back!"

"Yes, Ma," promised Alice as the sisters rushed to pack Alice's school bag with all they would need and laid out the second layer of woolen clothes to keep themselves warm. They then descended to help watch over their brother, while their mother packed for herself and her son. Eliza's warm things already hung by the door.

With Ol' Jim hitched up to the buggy, which was loaded with the rewrapped coats, some food supplies, four bundled up children, and all their overnight gear, Minerva started them out on their second adventure of that busy week.

"Thought we'd go the long ways, 'round by the post office, for Mr. Peters said there was mail for us to pay for there."

***

The two items she paid the postage for were a letter and a folded and tied Nashville newspaper, both mailed by Brainard. Neither were opened, however, until after they arrived at her parents' homestead, because another light snow began to fall and they wanted to hurry on.

Having seen the familiar buggy approaching, Almon and Polly were waiting together on the porch for their family to arrive, along with Allen and Hellen. All three girls in the buggy were waving gaily long before Ol' Jim drew up to a stop.

Allen moved forward to steady the horse for his sister as the girls jumped down and Alice was handed her little brother. Just meaning to set him down for a moment while hugs were shared around, Alice and all were startled and delighted to see Edgar Lincoln take his first actual steps – three of them – right into the waiting arms of his stooping grandmother. As exclamations of praise and encouragement from those around him acknowledged his accomplishment, he promptly plopped himself down on the ground, wondering what all the fuss was about.

When the greetings were completed, and everyone had moved inside, Nerva explained the reason for their visit. Alice and Ida May, each holding one of the rewrapped packages, approached their grandparents' table to open the bundles, then held up the three coats in turn.

"This is Pa's dress coat," began Ida May, holding it against her small body to show the gathered family. "Isn't it grand?"

"And this is his infantry overcoat for bad weather," continued Alice. "It isn't cold enough to need them anymore, so he sent them home."

Then together, each holding from its shoulder one side of the final coat, Alice announced, "And this here's a real Rebel officer's coat! Do you remember in Pa's letter how he said he got one after his battle and was sending it to us? Well, here it is!"

While the grandparents made comments examining the coats, Nerva stepped aside for some farm talk with her brother. "We hear the wolves circling around every night now, Allen. Haven't lost any stock yet, but others have already. Guess they're still a'feelin' us out."

"I better come out to shoot some of 'em for you, Min . . . that is, if there's enough moonlight to see 'em by."

"I was a'hopein' you'd offer. I surely would like you to, an' the moon's risin' early an' full right now, so's this would be a grand time if you could come."

Allen gave her a quick brotherly hug to reassure her, and promised, "We don't have much to do around here yet, so I'll just follow you home and spend a few days with you."

"Oh, thank you," she said, accepting his offer. "An' we can talk about spring work, too. I know it's not here yet, but it'll surely come soon, an' we need to decide how much more prairie land you can break for us if Brainard's not back in time for that."

Speaking his name reminded her of the things she had picked up from him at the post office and tucked away in the pocket of her long coat. As she went back to where it was hanging by the door, she announced to all: "An' there was a couple of things from him at the post office, too. Why don't you all find a place to sit, an' I'll read what he says."

The Griffin and Churchill girls barely had room to squeeze between their grandparents on the settle, while Allen took a chair on the other side of the fireplace and set a tired but willing Edgar Lincoln on his lap. Nerva stood in the middle between them and opened the letter first. A ten-dollar bill dropped to the floor when she unfolded the writing paper inside. "Oh, my goodness!" she said in surprise, and stooped to retrieve it and show the greenback around. In the process, she forgot all about being upset at having to pay the postage on the two items.

Instead, she began to read:

Camp near Nashville, Tenn.   March 13, 1862

My Dear Wife and Children,

I think that soldiering agrees with me first rate for I keep fat upon hard bread and coffee, with a little bacon and rice, which is the most of my living. We have beef, baker's bread, and potatoes once in a while. I have been a' frying some doughnuts this afternoon. It takes about a bushel to go around. We give them three apiece. They go like 'hot cakes' I tell you, after not having had any for some time. We cannot save fat enough, when we are on the march, to fry them in."

"Ma," interrupted Alice, "can you imagine frying a whole bushel full of nutcakes?" The three other adults readily agreed with her, sharing her amazement. Grampa Almon even held his thick arms out, forming the size and shape of a bushel basket, to everyone's delight.

"Nope. Can't picture it at all. Your pa is really havin' a time of it, isn't he?" she responded. "Now, listen as I read some more ..."

There is so many regiments around here that the fifes and drums and brass bands are playing from daylight until 9 o'clock at night. We have not received any marching orders yet but we have to be ready to march at a moment's warning. We have received good news from the Potomac and Arkansas and all of the other places of importance. I have bought a Louisville paper today which has got all the news in it that I have heard. I will send it to you."

Nerva reached down and picked up the other item he had sent, saying, "This must be the paper he's talking about." Putting it back on the floor in front of her, she continued reading.

Today the Captain called me into his tent and gave me $10.00 for doing extra duty as cook. He asked me if that was enough and I told him that I did not ask anything, but if the company gave me anything I would take it and be very thankful for it. I should send it all to my family, so I will send it to you in this letter.

"That explains this," Nerva said, lifting up the ten-dollar bill now resting in her lap. "There's just a bit more . . . umm . . . then he closes with . . ."

Now write as often as you can, for whenever I get a letter from you, it does me a great deal of good. I will write as often as I can so you may know where I am and how I am. I hope that I shall soon be where I shall not have to talk to you on paper, don't you? Give my best respects to all of our folks, and accept these few lines from your husband and companion in the Union Army in Tennessee. Goodnight.

D. B. Griffin

"He always writes such good letters, doesn't he, Almon?" Granma Polly reached across to nudge her husband, who had dozed off despite all the company.

"What's it?' sputtered Almon, shaking his head awake, to the delight of his granddaughters sitting between them.

"I said, Brainard always writes such good letters. Now, listen in to what else he says," she gently reprimanded him.

"This other's not a letter from him. It's a newspaper he sent us. A Louisville paper." Turning from them, Nerva extended the paper in her brother's direction, and added: "Allen, why don't *you* read us some of the headlines?"

Allen took the offered paper, unfolded it, and, checking his audience to make sure they were listening, began to read. "Here's a story about the Rebel General John B. Floyd blowing up two of the Cumberland River bridges into Nashville ahead of the approaching Union Army. That should be interesting. Or here's a report about our General Burnside getting his fleet of gunboats almost up to Richmond. Says they are part of General McClelland's Union advance against that rebellious city. Humm . . . And here's another about General Grant. You remember, the one who captured Forts Henry and Donelson? Well, he's moved all the way south into Alabama. So, which one do you want to hear me read first?"

***

After spending that night together all cozied up, Minerva and her children headed home again right after an early breakfast, as they had morning chores to do. They were accompanied by Allen on horseback.

His visit was both productive and fun. He and Nerva had two days to discuss the coming spring's farm work, but he also had plenty of playtime with the three young ones. Two nights of successful kills totaling three wolves and the possible wounding of two others had even driven the wolf pack away from the farm.

As Allen was finally preparing to return to his parent's farm, Nerva decided they should all accompany him part way, for she wanted to visit her good friend Sophrena Boynton over in Forestville. Missus Boynton had recently given birth to a new baby boy, and Minerva was anxious to see them both. So the children were packed up for another overnight away from home, and they all set off together again. The new snow on the road was still deep enough to show their tracks, but not enough to slow their progress.

They began with a quick loop into Alba to check for mail. There they were rewarded with *three* additional letters from Tennessee, two of them short ones Brainard sent in a single envelope, with postage paid on both this time. Resuming their trip, with Minerva guiding the buggy, and Uncle Allen keeping his horse as close as possible in order to hear, Alice read all three letters with a clear, strong voice.

His news was a mix of good and bad, but it was all of interest to them as they rode together. They were thrilled by the positive military news he relayed regarding the Union movement on Richmond, the capture of Memphis and New Orleans, and the expectation of a quick end to the conflict that kept him away from them. But they were equally disturbed by his reporting of inhumane punishment in the Union Army. It involved their own soldiers, hands tied with a rope tossed over a tree limb, being lifted to their toes for several hours.

Alice was personally disappointed by her father's explanation that, though he had been able to procure for her a *Leslie's Magazine*, which featured illustrations of his Battle of Mill Springs and the surrender of Fort Henry, he was not allowed at that time to send it. On the other hand, she was pleased when he mentioned he had received and enjoyed the note to him she had enclosed in her mother's last letter.

Everyone agreed when she read his comment:

"I cannot help thinking what a hard winter you have had. I think that you have had to fight with a harder enemy than I have had to, with the cold weather. I hope that you will not suffer so another winter."

There was also one passage they enjoyed so much they made Alice read it three times:

"I do not know which way we are a going to go from here, but it will be South somewhere. I hope that we will keep a going until we get the Rebels cornered up in some southern swamps where the mosquitoes will torment them day and night until they give up the ship and go home and learn war no more."

And one final passage, the last lines of the third letter, brought them near to tears:

"Tell the children that I think of them a great many times a day, and dream about you all very often. Tell them goodbye for me too.

Goodbye, Nerva. Once more I hope that I shall soon quit writing goodbye and be where I shall not have to leave you so long again.

D. B. Griffin"

When she finished her reading, they all rode along in silence for the final few minutes to the grandparents' place, pondering their own thoughts and emotions raised by their soldier's writing. Not wishing to go in to visit because of their long trip still ahead, Nerva simply patted Allen's leg as he remained mounted, thanking him again for his help with the wolves. They parted at the lane to the house, Allen calling his good-byes to all with assurances he'd take care of their chores the next day, and Nerva headed Ol' Jim east on the road to Forestville.

Once away, just their family again, Ida May announced: "I think we should make a list, right now, of all the things we want to tell Pa, like we done before." Turning, she added, "Then you could write it all for us, Ma, after we get to Missus Boynton's house."

"I'd be right glad to make that list," responded Alice.

Her mother chimed in, "First off, I need to tell him we haven't got *any* of that money from the state he keeps talkin' on about."

Other suggestions abounded, right up to their arrival in Forestville. And the list made it possible, during their visit with Sophrena and the new baby Boynton, for Minerva to write and send a good, long, newsy letter from them all, to her husband who had that week been off to war for six whole months.

With their eventual return home two days later, their busy week and the month of March drew to a close.

Chapter Seventeen

Spring News, Spring Growth, Spring Seeding

The following ten weeks were a combination of impatient waiting, hard marching, and more impatient waiting for Brainard. During that time his family received ten letters from him, although he had written eleven. He explained he had lost one somewhere along the Tennessee "hard tramp," as he called it, from Nashville to Pittsburg Landing.

The expected "orders from headquarters" he had written about earlier had finally come the beginning of April. Commanding General Ulysses S. Grant had decided to gather all his forces in the South (just as Brainard had also expected) to capture the highly important central railroad depot at Corinth, Mississippi. So all those regiments, which had been waiting for more than a month in the Nashville area, had obeyed and marched as rapidly as they could to join him. Brainard's regiment, because it had already fought and won earlier at Mill Springs, was at the tail end of that mass movement.

By the time the Second Minnesota Volunteers arrived at Pittsburg Landing as the final part of General Buell's forces, the bloodiest battle of the war to that date—the Battle of Shiloh, with 23,000 casualties—had already been fought over the two days before. All Minerva and the girls learned from Brainard when he wrote his April 20, 1862 *"short letter for the want of anything more to write about"* was:

"We are camped upon the ground where a battle was fought. It was a hard fought battle. As you have probably seen the accounts before, I will not try to describe it now. Our Regiment was not in the battle..."

But the harsh reality that he didn't tell them about was that the Second Minnesota had been assigned to burial duty. They had spent the next three days traversing the battlefield to find and bury the thousands of dead of both armies, singly if they could be identified, or in trenched mass graves if they could not. They also transported those who were wounded, often near death by that time, to field hospitals.

When that gruesome work was done, their camp was moved to where the other units had located, closer to the Rebel Army, which had retreated south to defend the railroad junction at Corinth. It was there the impatient waiting began again, and it would require more than a month before their victory was realized.

Minerva and her daughters read his weekly letters repeatedly, most often in their quiet evenings together before retiring for the night. Each one was welcomed as comforting proof that he was still alive and well. And each was answered as soon as possible, though usually responding to two or three of his at a time. Their letters were always a mix of family news, ongoing questions about running the farm and finances, and statements of unaltered affection as well as wishes for his speedy return to them.

Many of those letters sent to him also included notes from Alice. She wanted to take advantage of such opportunities to practice her writing and spelling. But she was also aware that these extra notes were especially treasured by her father. Occasionally bits of this or that from the other two children were also inserted—fingerprints, writing practice, lockets of hair, and the like.

All these letters eventually created a problem for Minerva, however, when young Ida May began insisting one early May morning that *she* be allowed to make the trip to the post office, too, either to mail their letter to her father, or to collect any letter from him. "Why does Alice get to do it and not me?" she questioned one morning as her sister was about to set off for Alba. "It isn't fair!"

"Because she's older than you are, love," her mother said softly, trying to soothe her youngest daughter's emotional outburst as she smoothed her tousled hair. Nerva reached to draw her even closer, but the young girl pulled away.

"But I'm old *enough*," she demanded, stomping a foot on the porch for emphasis. "Alice was going alone to school as old as I am now."

"That's true," her mother countered, "but . . ."

"But what?"

"But your Pa was here then, to help in case something happened. And he's not here now . . ." Minerva's voice trailed off with a sigh of inner regret as she looked into her daughter's intense dark eyes.

Ida May had already prepared her response: "That's *why* we have to make do without him for now. Besides, I know the way. I'm already as big as Alice, and I'm careful, too. You *know* I am!"

"Of course you are, but I need someone to stay here, to help me watch Edgar Lincoln so's I can go do your pa's chores. Who's going to do that?"

"I will when Alice goes, and Alice can when I go," Ida May answered triumphantly.

The best that Nerva could do at the time was to say she'd allow Ida May to accompany Alice for a few times, even though that meant she would have no help with her son. At least she could develop some assurance that her younger daughter wouldn't get lost. "After that," she said, "we'll see."

"May I go today, Ma?" she asked, with Alice still waiting at the start of their lane.

"Yes, yes, go along. I'll see to your brother for you."

Ida May rushed inside to get her coat, kissed her mother good-bye in passing while still buttoning it up, and raced down the short lane to tell her sister. Alice accepted the news, knowing it was then too late to complain. But she had always counted the time alone, going and coming, as a special time just for herself. She quickly made the best of it by asking her sister to tell all the things she remembered about their pa.

Beginning with her memory of his departure, Ida May counted off a list of images: his play with them on the floor, how dirty he looked washing up shirtless at the well after a full day at the field, reading to them evenings from the Bible before bedtime, the time the bees chased him home because he was taking their honey, how tickled proud he was holding his son for the first time. Alice, older and with earlier memories, added several of her own, much to the enjoyment of her sister, so they arrived at Mr. Peters' store in high spirits.

Their spirits were raised even higher when the storekeeper/postmaster gave them two more letters from the father they had been remembering together. Feeling very close to her sister over the shared memories, Alice immediately handed one of the letters to Ida May. That way both of them got to carry something home. She even allowed her sister the honor of announcing the news to their mother when they arrived at the shanty.

No one wanted to wait until after supper to read them, so Nerva gathered everyone at the table and opened the first envelope, dated April 25. Edgar Lincoln curled up in Ida May's lap, seeming to sense that no one would be paying attention to him. The girls were amazed to learn, as Nerva read, that there were now more than

150,000 Union troops in Brainard's vicinity. All three laughed at his self-description: *"I have not shaved yet, but I have my hair cut off short."* By way of contrast, the shared pain and growing disappointment was clear on all three faces as Nerva continued to read:

"You must not set any time for me to come home, for we cannot tell how long this war will last. The Union will carry the day sooner or later. It is seven months to the day since I left my little home and family. Will it be seven more months before I see them again? God forbid, but still many a loved one has left their home and friends never to return. I dreamed of seeing you all last night and talking to you about my adventures, but when I woke up I found myself in a tent down in Tenn., close to the Rebels, and close to the State line of Mississippi."

They could each sense his continuing frustration at their separation in his second letter, written only three days later:

"It takes a letter so long to go from here and to get an answer back from you again, that I do not know what to write about. I know that you cannot get along as well without me as you could with me, but you must try to look on the bright side of this world, and let the dark side pass by. If you cannot get along and have things just as you would like to have them, you must try and put up with them just as they are."

But as Nerva glanced ahead a bit, she exclaimed, "Oh no! No!" when she came to the next line. She put the letter down, paused for a moment with her fingers gathered to her lips, before picking it up to continue reading to the girls.

"Jerry's wife wrote that you had lost your calves, but you did not say anything about it in your letter of the 10th which I received last night. I was glad to hear that you were all well, but sorry to learn that you had to battle with the snow yet."

She hadn't planned to tell him this horrible news. Not only did she not want to give him more cause to worry about their welfare, she also just didn't want to have to, by the retelling, relive that terrible experience.

When the weather had changed enough to melt off all the snow the first week of April, Nerva had mistakenly assumed spring had finally arrived on the Minnesota prairie. On that basis she had led Rosie and her newborn calf twins, along with the yearling oxen, Duke and Dime, into the pasture for the first time since fall had changed to winter the year before. The reemerging prairie grass would be such a treat to them—a wonderful "spring tonic."

She had been so proud of herself, having helped with the successful birthing the week prior, and was hoping Brainard would be proud of her too. But she hadn't intended to leave them out there overnight. With everything else she had to remember, that one thing slipped her mind. And a fast-moving return of bitter winter weather that same night brought death in the pasture to both calves.

Nerva was devastated when she found them, frozen in a foot of new snow, the next morning. She had slept soundly through the entire change of weather and didn't know about it until she opened the shanty's front door. There at the pasture's fence she fell to her knees beside their lifeless bodies and wept—tears of loss, self-disappointment, and rage at her helpless situation.

"I wasn't a'going to tell your pa anything about that. Nothin' he could'a done anyways, just fret for us," she explained to the girls. "Reckon I'll have to lay it all out for him now . . ."

***

With the help of both Uncle Allen and Mr. Chipman, the spring fieldwork began. That last blast of winter was actually its last gasp, as the days did turn mostly sunny and warm, and the unspoken promise of a summer to follow quickened the spread of green across the gently undulating earth.

Back and forth across the rich prairie land Brainard had already opened, Duke and Dime pulled first the iron plow to reloosen the soil, then the spring-toothed harrow to smooth out the clods. Nerva took her turn as well when neither man was available, guiding the young oxen in their labor, but she could not have prepared the land without the men.

She and Alice then spent the following three days, which continued warm and dry, sowing crop seed—walking side-by-side, hour after hour, along the harrowed rows. In three separate fields they cast out handfuls of wheat, then oats, and finally sorghum, each saved from the previous year's crop. Both used the same repeated fluid motion of dipping and broadcasting in complementary arcs that doubled the amount a single person could sow. The shoulder sack each bore those days would grow lighter with every dip into its contents. Their hearts grew lighter, too, as much of their time was spent with Nerva answering questions about all that had happened in the family before Alice was born. Ever in her mind was the thought, *This'd be so much easier if'n we had the price o' one o' them newfangled planter machines to drag through these fields. M'be when Brainard gets back he can figure a way . . .*

Although she was tired at the end of each day, Nerva's day wasn't done. When they had returned to the shanty and taken care of the animals, she still needed to plant the seed potatoes, which had been stored in their cellar, as well as the seed packets of peas, carrots, onions, and turnips she had purchased from Mr. Peters. So, late each afternoon, Alice took her turn tending to her brother while she prepared the family's supper, and Nerva and Ida May together hoed and planted part of the large vegetable garden beside their home that would feed them through the coming year.

Just as they were finishing up the early garden planting the third day, Mr. Chipman drove his wagon up their lane, arriving from the direction of Alba. Still spry for his age, he jumped down and greeted Nerva and Ida May with the jovial question: "Ya' want news from the war?" He held up two more letters from Brainard as he said this, his eyes twinkling at his own joke.

"You *know* we do, Mr. Chipman," Ida May answered him. She threw down her hoe in her excitement and rushed to his side to take the precious messages from his outstretched hand. Almost forgetting her manners, she had to turn back and add, "Thank you, sir, for bringing them to us," before she returned to her mother, who was still leaning on her hoe. "Look, Ma, *two* letters!"

Nerva added her thanks and well wishes to Mr. Chipman as he climbed back into his wagon, turned a tight circle in the Griffin farmyard, and was about to start for home. She then called out, "Finished our seedin' today, an' our early kitchen garden as well. Won't be needin' your help again till first haying, but pr'aps you could open another acre or two for next year for us?"

"We'll see," he responded, a slight edge to his voice, but with a final friendly wave he headed down their lane.

Putting an arm around Ida May, Nerva said with a conspiratorial smile, "Why don't we hide these from Alice, an' surprise her with 'em after supper?" She slipped them into her daughter's apron pocket, raised her index finger to her lips, as they both laughed lightly.

"What did Mr. Chipman want?" asked Alice, stepping out onto the porch with Edgar Lincoln by the hand. She had noticed his brief presence through the small window beside the kitchen cabinet, but hadn't come out because her brother had just pulled a piece of firewood off the stack by the stove and it looked like trouble was brewing.

"He was just checkin' on our seedin' progress," her mother pretended. "Glad to know we finished it up today. Say, that soup you've made sure smells good clean out here, an' we're both mighty hungry, aren't we, Ida May?" It was a successful ploy to change the subject as they approached the porch.

"It's ready," Alice said, "Table's all set, and the biscuits only need a few more minutes. I just checked." She turned and led them all into the shanty.

"We'll wash up then," her mother replied, and herded her younger daughter toward the wash pan Alice had already set out on the counter for them. Nerva then took Edgar Lincoln aside and nursed him briefly. He would get some of Alice's soup broth as well, as he was beginning to switch to soft foods, but he still favored his mother's milk during the transition.

Conversation was minimal as they ate, for all were hungry and tired from the requirements of the last three long days in the sowing fields. So nothing seemed out of the ordinary when Ida May stood up after she finished eating, raised her arms over her head to stretch her weary muscles, then lowered them and gave a light pat to her apron pockets. With mock surprise she said, "What's this?" as she drew out the two secreted envelopes. "Why, they look like letters from Pa," she continued to pretend.

"Pa!" shouted Alice, jumping up from her seat. Her mother and sister began to laugh at their trick upon her. From that, Alice made the connection to their earlier visitor. "So *that's* why Mr. Chipman came! You *hid* them from me!"

"Now, now," quieted her mother, moving to Alice's side and lifting her pouting chin so she could look into her daughter's dark brown eyes. "We were just havin' a bit of fun with you. See, they're still not opened. We haven't read 'em yet. You haven't missed a thing."

Somewhat mollified, Alice sat back down as her mother continued, "To make up for it, why don't *you* do the reading, 'stead of me?"

Both letters were brief, a single paragraph each, and written only three days apart. Each was just a gathering of small bits of information and speculation. Alice almost glowed with pride as she translated her faraway father's written words to spoken ones. One part was of particular interest:

"I have quit the cook shop, and I intend to go with the boys until the war is ended, if I live, and we are confident that there will not be many more battles fought before it is ended."

Alice paused her reading, her brows furrowed in deepening concern, turned to her mother and said, "Pa used to say he wasn't in danger, being a cook and all. Now he says . . ." Locating what she wanted with her finger she continued, "*if I live . . .*"

"But finish what he wrote, love," prompted her mother. "He's sure this here terrible war is most about ended. He'll be home soon, just you wait an' see!"

Another part Alice had to read to them twice because it sounded so amazing:

"There is one Battery of six guns here that will shoot seven miles. They look like a big log. It takes 10-14 yoke of oxen to draw them."

When she read the good-byes to them at the end of the second letter, Alice asked, "It's not too late yet, Ma. Can we write Pa tonight and tell him about finishing the seeding?"

"*And* our early kitchen garden, too," Ida May chimed in.

"I think we'd better," concluded Nerva, "seein' as how he's wrote us *twice!*"

So the day and workweek ended with the girls making suggestions on bits to include. Nerva wrote the good news of their family's health and progress, while Edgar Lincoln drifted off to sleep in Alice's willing arms. One of them could take the finished letter to town in the morning.

As Nerva was milking Rosie early the next day, she began thinking about the eggs she had accumulated recently. With the chickens back in full production, there were already plenty to sell to Mr. Peters. So she decided to take the letter herself, along with four dozen of the eggs she had saved. That would give the girls a rest day from some of their chores, as she would take Edgar Lincoln with her. Besides, since she wanted to buy some flowered-print cloth to make her girls new spring bonnets as a surprise, she'd have to go without them sometime.

As asked, Alice carried a lit candle down into their cellar to light the three others in their wall holders to provide the illumination she needed. She then made several trips to bring up the eggs for her mother to take to town, as well as the risen cream from the last two days for Ida May to churn into butter. Alice's sole other responsibility would be to tend to their two sows, who had recently farrowed eight pink piglets apiece. After that, she planned on writing another note to her pa.

Ida May hoped to spend her free time outside beneath the late blossoming apple trees, looking again at the drawings of pretty dresses in the *Leslie's Magazine* sent by her father.

Chapter Eighteen

News from the Front

Life's pace picked up again in and around the Griffin shanty the following week. Two of their hens, obeying nature's call to reproduce, had gone broody some time before, hiding their clutches of eggs in the loft of the barn instead of the coop, then setting until they hatched. The proud mother hens had each marched out that week, followed by nearly two dozen fuzzy yellow chicks. That event so increased Ida May's responsibilities for providing watchful care to the henhouse that Alice had to take over her sister's twice-a-week butter-making chore, as well as tend to both the cattle and the expanded pen full of piglets.

Things got even more complicated when Mr. Chipman arrived to announce to Nerva: "Sorry to have to break this to you, Miz Griffin, but I ain't gonna be able to help you here no more. Just got too much at my own place to do, an' I'm alone same as you. I was right glad to be a help and all to start, 'specially since your Brainard was always such a help to me. But I didn't think he'd be gone this long, and I . . ." As he paused, his head dropped from looking at her eyes to looking at her feet.

Nerva responded as kindly as her trembling heart allowed. "Don't you be a'worryin' yourself none, Mr. Chipman. We're all right grateful for ever'thing you've done for us. We'll get along. An' you're right, none of us thought he'd be gone this long. Not even him."

Nerva only allowed her face and confidence to sag after Mr. Chipman had ridden away. *Lord, A'mighty. What'll I do now? That plowin' for next year needs doin' soon. I can't do it. Brainard . . . Oh, Lordy, how long are you goin' to be gone from us? Guess I'd best ride over to Father's an' see what he thinks. P'raps he can spare Allen a few more days . . .*

It did, indeed, work out that way. Allen came back for three days' worth of breaking the tall grass prairie sod for additional acres to plant into wheat the next year.

Of course, that meant the girls were needed to help their uncle with the oxen in the barnyard both morning and evening, as well as carry water and lunch out to him. Edgar Lincoln even spent a whole morning walking with Allen behind the plow, chattering constantly to his very patient uncle as he experienced his first lesson in prairie farming.

Meanwhile, Nerva took care of all the other barn chores, the cooking and washing, and most of the oversight of her son. Edgar Lincoln, growing quickly now that he was no longer crawling or nursing, was great fun to watch, for he was curious about everything. Of course, that meant he required constant observation, but he was a joy, and he seemed to be talking about something all the time.

Late evenings, with her children finally tucked in and her brother also asleep, Nerva would get out her sewing basket to work on the new bonnets for her growing daughters, and once she even penned a brief letter to her husband, which described how Mr. Chipman's decision worried her, not only for the lost help, but for any gossip people might make about it, as if it were somehow her fault.

The pace of Brainard's letters also picked up as May tended toward June. The girls agreed to take turns walking to Alba's post office, though one time they decided to walk together. Most of the time they carried a basket of some combination of eggs, butter, or fresh cheese to exchange for something needed, or for credit to their account. And most of the time they carried home a letter.

Ida May ran back all the way with one the last week of May, mailed from "Camp near Corinth, Miss" on May 14 that informed them:

"We have camped in a beautiful piece of timber, about 5 miles from Corinth, the last stronghold of the Rebels, I hope. We have been expecting a fight to come off every day now for over a week, but for some reason unknown to us, it has been delayed until now. We are advancing a little every day or two. We have to move slow on account of the swamps which we have to make roads through. I do not think the time is far distant when the Stars and Stripes will float triumphant over Corinth, and also over the whole South. We are now in the State of Miss. It is a pretty place of woods, quite large trees and no underbrush, and as green as any pasture. I think that it would be a good place for farmers to make good farms, but I, for one, do not want to live here as long as there is slavery . . .

I wish that you could see us today. I am sitting by the side of a tree in the shade, while I can look around me upon all sides and see the men, some under bough houses, some under shade of the trees, some writing, some reading, some playing cards, some cooking, some a washing their clothes, and others a loitering about the camp, while I can hear the sound of the bugle and drum. Such is camp life. All is joy, but who knows how soon we may be called forth to the battlefield amid the roar of the cannons and the muskets. I hope that it will soon cease. Then we will learn war no more . . ."

Nerva's sister, Mary Durand, came down from Spring Valley to spend a week with her parents, and while she was there she wrote a note to be included in the next letter to her brother-in-law. That prompted Nerva to write, but it had been long enough since her last letter that she already had plenty to write about.

My dear faraway husband,

Your welcome news from Miss. arrived this week, so we know again you are still safe and well. We are the same here, ever so busy always, but none sick, cept in missin you.

Everythins goin good round the farm, though it would sure be better if you were here. I think youd be a mite proud if you could see how well the crops is agrowin. The children all help with everythin I ask. Even your little boy walked along with his Uncle Allen and the team last week as he opened another 3 acres of prairie for next years wheat. He wants to be "big" faster than hes agrowin.

I aint got that money from Minnesota yet. You think I need to write somebody bout that? Were not in need any, but it sure would make things go easier for us if we had it.

I have walked the hay ground and it looks bout ready for the first cut. Who should I get to come? And how much should I offer?

Are you agoin to try to write again that letter you said you lost on the march down to Corinth? We want to know everything you do.

The children all send their love, as do I and sister Mary whose note to you Ill stick inside. Alice can take this in to Alba tomorrow.

From Nerva Griffin and your children,

P. Minerva Griffin

***

The next two letters arrived the same day in early June. One was brought home by Alice when she walked to Mr. Peters' store to trade their butter for his tea. The other, in a curious twist of fate, was delivered by a one-armed soldier Alice met on the way home, who asked her if she wasn't a Griffin.

"Yes, sir, I am," she answered, trying not to stare at his still-bandaged stump. "Alice Griffin," she added, wondering how he could possibly know her.

"Well, I'm George Spaulding, a friend of your Ma and Pa. Took a Reb bullet and lost half my arm," he said, lifting his left arm that now ended at his elbow. "Got a letter to deliver from your pa, and wanted to stop by to let you know he's all right."

"I got one too," she said, pulling hers from the basket. "Ma'll be right proud to see you, I'm sure, Mr. Spaulding. It's just a ways yet down this lane."

Together they walked the last mile, Alice asking one question after another regarding the welfare and activities of her father, and ex-Private Spaulding supplying a comforting response to each inquiry.

Much of the information had to be retold, as the same questions were asked by Nerva and Ida May after the walkers arrived at the shanty just a bit before noon: "Has Brainard been sick any?" "What does Pa do all day?" "Is he still happy?" "When's Pa coming home?"

Initially, Ida May couldn't get past the frightful thought that her own father might come home maimed like Mr. Spaulding, and she almost ran out of the room. But she wanted to know the details of her father's present situation, so she forced herself to stay and listen, despite the man's terrible wound.

"You'll stay and share dinner with us, won't you?" Nerva had been silently planning the meal she could quickly prepare for him and her family as she listened to his answers about Brainard.

"I'd be most obliged, Minerva," he answered, for he still had miles to travel to his parent's home place further north.

Conversation during the meal that followed continued to center on Brainard, but by now most of the questions came from Nerva. The girls, instead, focused their attention on the two letters that lay beside their mother's plate, still awaiting opening to reveal their personal content. Alice and Ida May would have to wait until Mr. Spaulding left, their mother had informed them.

When dinner was finally done, and George Spaulding resumed his journey home, uplifted by countless expressions of gratitude for his visit, the girls raced back to the table and each one picked up one of the letters. They returned just as quickly to their mother, who had stayed, waving good-bye, on the porch with Edgar Lincoln.

Plopping down on either side of her on the top step, they pulled her down between them and presented the letters for reading.

Opening the one hand-delivered by Mr. Spaulding, Minerva was surprised to also open a folded five-dollar bill. Placing that with a pat in her apron pocket, she began reading:

"Camp near Corinth, Miss. May 24th, 1862

My Dear Wife and Friends,

I will once more write a few lines to you. I am as well as usual this morning and I hope that this will find you all well. I received two letters from you this week and was glad to hear from you all. I have not written as soon as I should on account of the expectations of a battle every day. But there has not been one yet, only a few skirmishes with the pickets. We have to go out on picket duty every two or three days. We have built a good deal of breastworks and are prepared for an attack if the Rebels see fit to pitch in. We do not know why we do not attack them, but probably the Generals know the reasons."

Interrupted, Minerva had to stop and explain 'picket duty' and 'breastworks' to her daughters, increasing their ability to make mental pictures of their father's military activities.

Her question, "You remember how your pa wrote that sometimes he has to be out all night on guard duty?" brought head nods from both girls, so she continued, "Well, those boys are called pickets. It's kinda like our rooster, how he's forever a'struttin' around all the hens, an' settin' up a squawkin' as a warnin' whenever he sees somethin' that might be danger. So when your pa's on picket duty, he has to be out in front a'watchin' for the Rebel troops. And as for breastworks, I think they're the defenses the boys have to build to protect theirselves from gettin' shot. Seems like sometimes they dig a trench to hunker down in, or maybe even drag in some logs an' such to hide behind."

Alice thought to herself that she could use both terms when she next wrote to him so her pa would know she was with him, even back at home.

Nerva lifted again the letter she had let settle in her lap and continued reading:

"I was sorry to hear that Mr. Chipman had left you, but I hope that it will all turn out for the best. If anyone should see fit to talk about it, just let them go ahead and they will soon tire of it."

"We will get along all right, won't we, Ma?" asked Alice.

"Of course, dear, we'll manage. Some things'll be harder, no doubt, and some may not get done at all till your pa comes home, which is exactly what he wishes. Listen:"

"I hope that everything will be so shaped that I can be home in a few months, if alive and well. George Spaulding starts for home today or tomorrow. I am going to send this letter home by him, and I will send you five dollars in it."

As she read that, Nerva patted her apron pocket again, smiling and nodding, for she knew how much it would be a help to them. Then her tone and countenance sobered as she read further:

"There is a good deal of preparations made in expectations of the coming battle. Minn. has sent a boat down in order to carry the sick and wounded home. I hope that I shall not have to go home in it, but it would not be anything improbable for I intend to pitch in with the rest of the boys when the time comes. I hope that I shall be one of the lucky ones to come off unscathed."

With a discernable catch in her voice, Nerva whispered to him: "That's my hope too, my love ..."

And his affirmation of Alice that began his closing words brought actual tears to his eldest daughter's eyes: *"Tell Alice that I am glad that she can write such long letters to me."* She immediately determined that she would begin her next note to him that very night, and began making mental notes of the things she would tell him as she offered the second letter, the one she had brought home, to her mother to read.

"Why don't you read it instead, Alice, since you went and got it?"

Showing her excitement, which would only increase as she read aloud the news from her pa, she tore open the envelope and began to read:

"*Camp Beyond Corinth   June 1st, 1862*

My Dear Wife and Friends,

I am well today and in good spirits for the Stars and Stripes are now waving over Corinth. We have taken the place without a struggle. The Rebel Army evacuated it last Friday morning, leaving almost everything behind them. They tried to burn everything up, but 'skedaddled' so fast that there was a great deal of stuff saved from burning. Our Brigade was the first to go into their entrenchments. They met with no opposition except for a few pickets. We took a few prisoners that were left behind."

"Does that mean they won the battle and didn't even have to fight it?" a bewildered Ida May inquired.

"That's exactly what it sounds like, love," her mother affirmed. "Reckon we'll get him back safe yet!"

Chapter Nineteen

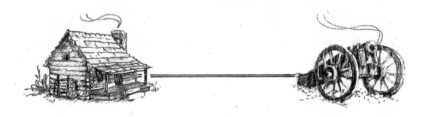

Good Seeding and Bad News

By the middle of June, the short spring on the Minnesota prairie already hinted at the summer soon to follow. The days were clearer, warmer, and longer, though rain showers still occasionally intruded upon the Griffin family's late afternoons or evenings.

The advancing season meant several things on the homestead needed to be accomplished in short order, as Nerva outlined to her young family while they all ate breakfast. "Now that your Uncle Allen has finished breakin' open the new acres for next year, as well as this year's spring plowin' and harrowin', we've got one more sowin' job to get done. With the weather cleared, we need to get the corn hill rows planted on the corner three acres. Alice, you'll have to help with that like before. Two, maybe three days. And Ida May, you get Edgar Lincoln again, an' there'll be enough milk to make us some fresh butter tomorrow whilst he naps."

Both girls exchanged glances, then nodded in assent. Their brother perked up in his mother's lap at the sound of his name, but since nothing seemed to come of it, he settled back down and continued to explore the pockets of the pants his mother had recently sewn for him.

"He'll be good, Ma," said Ida May. "I'll let him help me with my barn chores. He loves to be out there with the animals."

"That'll work fine then," her mother answered as she moved on down her mental list. "Long as you don't let him get too dirty." After another pause she continued, "Beyond that, we should get the rest of the kitchen garden in, an' I need to talk to Grampa about gettin' somebody to make our hay. I walked the field this mornin' while I drove the cattle out to pasture after milkin', an' it looks to be ready for its first cuttin' in another week or so. I also noticed some of the pasture fencin' looks weak from winter. Maybe Grampa can tend to that as well. Land sakes, I don't know how your pa gets all this done hisself ever' year!"

After loading the four one-bushel sacks of corn seed onto the wagon—the best of last year's crop saved for this year's sowing— along with the necessary hoes, poking sticks, and lunch sacks, and hitching up Ol' Jim to pull it, Nerva and Alice headed out to the far corner of the farm.

Soon after they were gone, Ida May led her brother around the farm as she gathered the eggs and fed cracked corn and table scraps to the chickens and pigs. While she was drawing fresh water to carry to both sets of animals, Edgar Lincoln had a great time chasing the hens until their frantic squawking called his sister to their defense. "They won't lay eggs for you if you scare 'em like that," she scolded, but with a laugh. Taking him back inside for some floor play with his wooden ball, it was eventually time for Edgar to take his morning nap.

As soon as he was down, Ida May grabbed the chance to make a surprise for her mother while he slept. She hoped for enough time to plant several short rows of beets, as well as several hills of string beans, both winter and summer squashes, and pumpkins. Having helped the year before, she remembered just how to do it and as rapidly as her young body was able, she was soon hoeing the rows for seeding the peas and making the small mounds for the beans, squashes, and pumpkins.

By noon, Edgar Lincoln was awake and as ready as she was for lunch. As they munched the pork roast sandwiches Nerva had made for them, Ida May told him all she had been doing while he slept, then offered the invitation, "Would you like to dig in the garden dirt while I plant all the seeds?" His enthusiastic reply settled her question of what to do with him while she finished her work. Clutching a large old stirring spoon, he followed her out to the garden, expecting a grand afternoon of play in the dirt.

The day was fading as fast as her energy when the hoeing and seeding were finally done. Though she was as covered with dirt as Edgar Lincoln, and her arms ached, Ida May was flooded with pride at all she had accomplished by the time her mother and sister rode back into their farmyard.

Nerva and Alice had had a full day as well, stopping only occasionally for refreshing drinks from their shared jug of cold water. Their brief rest for lunch sandwiches was spent sitting in the shade of the trees that edged one side of the field, while Ol' Jim continued to patiently nibble the grass verge as he waited to haul them back.

At the end of a row, late in the afternoon, Nerva laid down her hoe so she could arch her back. "We've pushed ourselves hard all day, Alice." She then sighed in the pleasure of the stretch.

Alice slipped the nearly empty seed bag off her shoulder, and steadying herself with her poking stick, turned back to survey the land they had planted. "Looks like we've done more than half the field already, Ma."

"Yep," her mother replied. "Reckon we'll be able to finish this up tomorrow, if'n somethin' doesn't turn up."

They both laughed, even though "things turning up" were an ever-present reality, often bad, on their farm—especially without Brainard there to help. They loaded their things on the wagon, and were quite content to sit together in reflective silence as they headed home.

As Ol' Jim brought them around the corner of the barn, both of them saw Ida May in the garden, working her hoe around the final hill, with more than a dozen others also planted, all neatly spaced around three edges of their garden so there would be plenty of room for both the climbers and the runners.

"Well, I declare, Ida May . . . are all those new hills in the garden patch what I think they are?" Her surprised mother pointed as she climbed down from the wagon.

Edgar Lincoln was plopped down on the far edge of the garden—an area not yet planted—sifting the fine dirt through both chubby hands. When he heard his mother's voice, he stood up and raised his arms and voice toward her, calling "Ma!"

"Yes, Ma, if you think you see three hills of string beans, and four hills each of squashes and pumpkins . . . plus," she beamed as she turned to point with her hoe, "three rows of beets!" A ring of happy triumph was in her voice as she answered.

Alice was as surprised as her mother and ran over to her sister to hug her, while Nerva went to pick up Edgar Lincoln and carry him inside, exclaiming over her shoulder, "You don't know how proud you've made me, Ida May!"

Together, then, the sisters washed at the well, playfully splashing each other from the drawn bucket since both were hot and tired and dirty from their day's work. But with afternoon chores still facing them before a late supper and bed, they headed into their beloved shanty to be whatever help their mother needed.

***

Soon after Nerva and Alice had left the following morning to finish planting the corn acres, Ida May heard a buggy-full of familiar voices helloing the house. "Come on, Edgar Lincoln, it's Grampa and Granma," she said, grabbing his arm and leading him to the door.

Sure enough, when they stepped out into the morning sunlight flooding the front porch, there were Almon and Polly, along with

Hellen and Eliza, just pulling up in front of the shanty. "Well, lookee there," Almon exclaimed, "two little 'uns come out to greet us!"

"Grampa! Granma! Hellen! Eliza!" shouted Ida May excitedly. She almost dragged her baby brother beside her as she rushed out to the buggy. "What brings you here?"

"Jus' stopped by to see if'n your Ma needs anything," her grandmother explained. "My, look how tall you are, Ida May! I declare, you're growin' like a weed! An' Edgar Lincoln, too. My word he's growed!"

Her granddaughter blushed a bit, but raised a smile to say, "Alice and Ma are out in the corn acres planting the rest of our corn. You can get there if you drive up that path," she indicated, pointing to the tracks that led past the barn. "She does need your help. Said so just last night."

"The girls don't need to come up with us, Almon." Polly turned and indicated with her hand that Hellen and Eliza should get down from the buggy. "Let's just leave 'em here to visit whilst we talk with Minerva."

"Sounds good to me," her husband responded, since the girls had already clambered down and were holding hands with their cousins, with excited words of greeting flowing between them. "We'll be back in a while. Have some fun till then," Almon said to them before calling to the horses and starting up the path in search of their daughter.

Past the barn and up a slight rise to the west, the well-used wagon ruts led the elderly pair out to the far corner of the family's homestead. They saw first Ol' Jim and the wagon, then Nerva, across the field, with Alice slightly behind, walking away from them along the harrowed rows Allen had prepared.

Each was repeating her half of the sowing process as they moved across the field. Nerva would hoe up a hill of dirt about eight inches across and four inches high, then step forward about a foot to hoe up the next one. Behind her, Alice used her poking stick to make two holes in the top of the hill, then squatted to finger two or

170

three kernels of corn drawn from the small shoulder sack she wore into each hole, and finally patted the holes closed on top of the seeds.

Coming to the far edge of the field, the two sowers moved over a measured distance to start their next pass back the other way. As they glanced up to confirm the direction of their destination, they saw the buggy with someone waiting for them.

"Look, Ma, someone's come. Wonder who it could be?" Alice said as she squinted across the distance.

"Reckon we'll find out soon enough, when we get to the other side," Nerva said lightly.

As they moved along closer, they could see there were two figures instead of one, and that they had both gotten down from their buggy to wave. Shading her eyes, Nerva said to her daughter, "I do believe that's my folks come to call. Why don't we just leave our stuff here and come back to finish after we've said hello?"

Even before she answered, Alice laid down her poking stick and removed the still-heavy seed sack slung over her shoulder. "Let's go see what they want. Hope it's not trouble," Alice said as she set off at a quick pace.

Her mother, not quite so nimble, arrived a bit after her daughter had greeted both grandparents with hugs and offered a sweep of her arm to show how much of the field they had already planted. "Ma, Pa," Nerva said, "how *good* to see you! What brings you way out here? Not bad news, I hope . . ."

"No, no," her father laughed. "Just came a'wonderin' if you needed help with things."

"Why, it was only yesterday I was tellin' the girls I needed to see you 'bout gettin' somebody to make our hay. It looks to be ready next week. Without Brainard, I don't know who to ask." As Nerva said this, Alice looked expectantly up at her grandfather, as sure as her mother that he'd know the answer.

"I reckon Daniel LeFevre might be the very one to ask," Almon replied. "Believe I saw a notice he put up in Peters' store last week.

He's offerin' his team an' equipment for hire on shares. If you want, we could swing by his place before we head for home to see if he's still interested. Small place, up by Bonsteele's, over in Section Twelve."

"Please, an' you can set it up with him if he is a'willing," answered Nerva. "Tell him we've got near forty acres of good prairie grass, an' he can have half for his wages."

"Sounds fair enough. I'll see what I can do for you. An' if he works out for you, well then he can do our place too. I just hadn't thought that far ahead."

Nerva had more to ask. "I also walked the pasture an' noticed some weak parts of the fencing. Wondered if'n you might have the time to fix 'em for me a'fore the cows break out? I hate to ask, but without Brainard . . ."

"Don't worry none about it, Minerva. I'd be right glad to tend to it next week, soon's I finish a couple breaks in my own pasture. Lucky, I'll have the tools all out. Glad to help." With that, her father helped his wife up into the buggy, then four voices filled the air with calls to "Take care!" as the horses were turned around and started back down the hill.

Nerva and Alice gaily waved at the retreating buggy as they walked back out to finish the corn field.

***

The Boynton's buggy pulled up to the shanty's front door early the next morning. It was so early that the night's gathered mist had not yet burned off. But, strangely, Sophrena just sat there without getting down.

Noticing her through the small kitchen window, Nerva moved to the door to welcome her neighbor, but when Sophrena *still* didn't get down, she walked out to the buggy to see what was the matter. "Mornin', Sophrena," Nerva hesitantly began. That was when she realized her visitor was crying. "What is it? What's wrong?" she asked, reaching caringly up to touch Sophrena's arm.

"Oh, Nerva, I can tell by your face you've not heard the news yet . . . an' I'm so sorry to be the one to bring it to you . . . but I heard last night that your man was killed . . . last week . . . in this terrible war!" At that, she burst into tears again.

Nerva was totally shocked by these words. At first she couldn't believe them simply because of the constant stream of letters from her husband. So she didn't know how to respond. She just stood there with a faraway look in her eyes, trying to take this news in. Her thoughts wildly raced: *It could be possible . . . but Brainard's too good a man for that to happen . . . but he is at war . . . but no one from the War Department has wrote me . . . no, I won't believe it unless they do . . . I won't say anything to the children . . . no one must say anything to them . . . I'll, I'll write him this very day so's he'll let me know he's all right . . . but what if . . . if . . . he can't? . . . All I can do is write and wait . . .*" Sophrena nervously watched her all the while.

Finally looking up, Nerva spoke: "That's hard news, Sophrena, mighty hard, but I won't say it's true till I hear it official like. I'm sure you came only because you care, but I'd be most grateful if you'd not pass it on to another soul just yet. So's the children don't hear what might not be true. Soon's I hear a thing, either way, I'll let you know . . ." She reached both arms in supplication to her friend and added the single word: "Please."

Sophrena nodded, gave a wistful smile to Nerva, nodded again and without even a word of farewell turned her buggy to start back for home.

Before Sophrena could possibly have completed her journey, Nerva had finished dashing off a quick, single-paragraphed plaintive note to her husband relating what she had heard, and begging most desperately for news from him as soon as humanly possible. She had also made arrangements with her children so that she could start her own unexplained trip into Alba. She would hold that rumor close to her heart for two weeks, without a word to her children.

Chapter Twenty

Haying and Praying and Happier News

Haying would be, by horse and hand, a four-step process in 1862 for the Griffins. First, a side-bar mower was drawn through the field by a pair of horses to cut the headed stalks of prairie grass that would nourish their cows and Ol' Jim through the next winter. A couple of days later, another piece of equipment—a mechanical rake—was pulled by the same horses over the cut swaths to turn over the hay and gather it into windrows so that the curing in the sun could continue. When it was sufficiently dry, ready to store without molding, a hay wagon was then slowly driven between the windrows while the hay was tossed by pitchfork from both sides onto the wagon's bed. Finally, the hay was transported back to the barn, where it was lifted up by a horse-drawn pulley system into the loft, from where it could easily be forked down to the mangers throughout the winter.

Daniel LeFevre was willing to do the cutting and stacking for them, so early Monday morning he arrived with his mower, bringing along his Pennsylvanian nephew, Jacob, to help with the team of horses. He told Nerva he expected it would take them four full days to cut all the knee-high prairie grass. Alice already knew Jacob from school, so whenever she and Ida May brought the LeFevres their noontime sandwiches and water that week, it was easy for them to sit and visit with him.

They were back three days later for the necessary turning of the cut hay, and with the warm summer days continuing unbroken, were finally able to begin the last two steps: loading the cured hay, and properly storing it.

Nerva's help was needed for the first of those tasks—handling the team while Daniel and Jacob, one on each side, pitched the hay onto the slow-moving wagon. They were able to get the loads safely into the barn without her. Although it meant her normal chores had to wait, it gave her precious time just to brood about what might or might not have happened to her beloved husband. Particularly distressing to her was an unusual break in the regular delivery of his letters.

All three children, meanwhile, enjoyed several hours each of those days, either watching from the woodlot above the field, or walking along holding hands whenever the workers and horses were close enough to an edge for them to see well.

The first four wagonloads were lifted without a hitch into the Griffin barn on Wednesday, and the last four transported home to the LeFevre barn on Saturday. In all, it was a hot, dusty, two-week-long process, but both families were pleased that this important part of the farming year was safely completed.

Young Ida May Griffin and Jacob LeFevre had no idea then how significant that week would turn out to be for them in their lives ahead ...

***

Sunday morning, June 29, promised another day as warm and dry as the prior week. That bode well for the church meeting announced for that day by the itinerant preacher, the Reverend J.M. Westfall. The gathering would be at the Alba schoolhouse, as usual, and was to be followed by a picnic lunch enjoyed together by each family who could stay.

"Wake up, my darlin's," Nerva called from the bottom of the sleeping loft ladder. "Time to rise an' shine with the sun." After reloading the firebox of the woodstove and setting a pan of four eggs on it to boil for their breakfast, she continued, "We'll be headin' into town for meetin' today, so your best Sunday-go-to-meetin' dresses, please."

The light sounds of movement above indicated to her that her daughters were responding, so she added one more instruction up the ladder: "Alice, love, you'll need to iron both best pinafores 'cause I haven't got to 'em since they was washed." Receiving no answer, she stepped back to the ladder and asked, "Alice, did you hear me?"

"Yes, Ma. I was still getting dressed. Be right down."

In just a few minutes she was there and had placed the flatiron on the stove to heat, padded the kitchen table with some toweling, and smoothed out her sister's pinafore, ready to iron. But because she didn't know how hot the stove's fire was, she didn't realize that she had let the flat iron heat too long. So as soon as she touched it to the pinafore, the white cotton fabric scorched dark brown in the shape of the iron. "Oh no, look what I've done!" she wailed. The flatiron clanked back onto the stove top in her desperation to get it away from the ruined pinafore.

Nerva swept across the room at once, fearing that Alice had burned herself. *What now? What more?* she repeated to herself until she saw that was not the case. Her relief, however, temporarily shifted to scolding Alice for her carelessness before it softened into, "We can fix it fine by just sewin' another pocket there."

The pinafore would have to wait for that repair on another day. This day, Ida May would have to wear second-best. Yet with the chance to go to town, she managed not to mind and told her sister not to worry. Even Edgar Lincoln was excited about the family outing and frolicked around the room in boyish anticipation.

Breakfast eaten and lunch basket packed, the children waited on the porch for their mother to hitch Ol' Jim to the buggy and circle out of the barn to get them. It seemed to be taking an extra-long time, and eventually Alice offered to go see if there was a problem. "You watch Edgar Lincoln," she instructed her sister, "an' I'll find out."

As soon as Alice entered the barn she heard her mother's distress. She found her outside the stall, leaning against Ol' Jim's neck, groaning and sobbing in the pain she could no longer keep within. "Ma, what's happened? Are you hurt?"

Nerva turned to face her, still overwhelmed by the mistaken images of her daughter burned and her husband dead. With a final sigh that indicated the comfort of Alice's presence, she revealed, "Oh, love, I was so scared for you, an' I miss your pa so much. Guess it just got the better of me for a moment. I'll be all right now."

"I'm so sorry I gave you such a fright this morning, Ma, to add to your worries. I'll try to be more careful." Then wishing to give her mother a bit more time alone, Alice added, "I'll tell 'em you're almost ready. You come when you can, Ma. We'll wait."

"Don't say nothing to the little ones about this, please, Alice. We've got to show 'em we're brave through all this, so's they can be too. Understand?"

"I do, Ma. And I think you're very brave."

Their eyes connected for a long moment in the cool darkness of the barn, then Alice turned and walked back to reassure her siblings.

After finally setting off to town, the sun continued to rise into the clear summer sky, and the early promise of a fine day seemed even more secure. That and the light chatter of the journey caused Nerva to think for just a moment her concerns for her family had melted away, even for the one from whom she had not heard, so far away in that dreadful war.

A mix of nearly twenty wagons and buggies was parked around the schoolhouse by the time the Griffin family arrived. At least half a dozen more were pulling in right behind them. It had been almost two months since the traveling preacher had come through Alba to encourage the local residents in their faith, so this looked to be a large gathering.

The early arrivers—Andrew Peters and Hiram Winslow—had already brought in the benches that were stored in the woodshed, and carried outside several of the two-student desks to serve as seats and tables for the picnic to follow. When the Griffins entered, they found the room filled with friendly gossip. All, young and old, were reporting their recent activities and farming progress. Nerva and her daughters gladly joined right in, contributing the war news they had learned from Brainard. Then Reverend Westfall stepped to the front, thumped his big black Bible down on the lectern by Miss Cray's desk, and raised his weathered right hand for silence to begin. Delighted to see her parents finally arrive, Allen, Hellen, and Eliza in tow, Nerva gathered her own family so all could sit together on a bench close to the front.

After leading the group through a couple of comforting hymns, sung from memory and without accompaniment, the preacher launched into his usual hour-long oration on the goodness of their God even in the midst of the human hardships and suffering they knew so well. This was followed by a moving prayer that the Almighty would protect and preserve His people, naming particularly the men from the area who were off to war, and that He would lead them all in the paths of eternal righteousness. The service ended with another hymn. As soon as it was sung, the restless children of all ages raced to the door, set free at last to laugh and play together.

Postmaster Peters stood at the door handing out letters to a few families as they exited. Two of them he extended to Nerva, who was deep in conversation with her mother as she was leaving. To her, as to each, he said, "These came late yesterday, and I reckoned I'd see you here today, so I brought 'em along." To her alone he added, "Good news as always, I hope, Miz Griffin."

"What a kind friend you are, Mr. Peters. Thank you. This will be a special surprise for the children when we get home," she said as she secreted them in her deep apron pocket, grinning in anticipation at both him and her mother. Inside herself she felt the release of her deeper secret—that unspoken fear—her Brainard could not be dead after all. He couldn't be, for she now held the written proof!

The neighbors had looked forward to a leisurely lunch and a rare afternoon of extended visiting. But by the time the lunch baskets were retrieved and the children reconnected with their parents, Reverend Westfall, still standing on the porch steps, called everyone's attention to storm clouds rapidly gathering in the west. This prompted their lunch to become a hurried affair instead, especially for those who had come some distance.

With the low rumblings of distant thunder already distinctly audible, the Griffins bade good-bye to all and started for home in hopes of reaching there before the summer storm unleashed itself on their part of the Minnesota prairie. But they had not gotten underway in time, for less than halfway home the sky darkened to a greenish black, the wind whipped in decidedly from the west, and huge raindrops and hailstones began pelting the buggy, the lane, and the woods around them. Even more frightening were the repeated flashing and booming of lightning strikes, though none of them near enough to endanger them.

Edgar Lincoln's whimpering quickly turned to outright wailing despite both sisters holding tightly onto him and shouting comforting words over the discomforting sounds surrounding them. But Ol' Jim never shied as he drew the family home—thoroughly wet and frightened, but safely home. Alice jumped down from the buggy and raced to open the barn door, and Nerva drove inside the sheltering structure.

She quickly unharnessed the horse and led him to his stall, where Alice was already forking in some hay while Ida May held her brother's hand. "All right, let's make for the house. Quickly now, so's we don't get any wetter'n we have to," instructed Nerva. Picking up her son, she led the dash to the shanty and inside, where it was both warm and dry.

"Let's all change out of our wet things," she said, "then I have a surprise for you. And Alice, would you please get the little tyke into some dry things whilst I put on a kettle for tea?"

"What's the surprise, Ma?" asked Ida May, struggling to get her drenched pinafore off.

"It's a surprise, that's what," was the only response she got as her mother added more wood to the firebox with a gay, gentle laugh.

Her own dress changed, Nerva shifted the settle closer to the woodstove and hung her apron on one end to dry. Checking first to make sure neither daughter was watching, she slipped the letters out of the apron's pocket and found them undamaged by the storm.

Soon Ida May came, followed shortly after by Alice and her little brother, and the three of them sat down with their mother to continue warming up. After a moment of silence, Ida May blurted out, "So, where's the surprise?"

"Right here, my love." There was extra joy in her voice as Nerva reached into the apron pocket hanging beside her and announced, "Two letters from your pa!"

Both girls jumped up, causing Edgar Lincoln to fall forward to the floor. More startled than hurt, the instant tears subsided when his mother picked him up. As soon as they were settled together again, Nerva opened the first letter and read:

"I have once more set myself down to write a few lines to you, so as to let you know how I am and what we are about. I am as well as usual and so are the rest of the boys, so far as heard from. We have been in pursuit of the enemy for the last week but could not get near enough to them to get in an engagement."

The letter continued to review the army's military news, then Brainard noted:

"The wheat is already out, but it is very light, not over 5 or 6 bushels to the acre. Some fields of corn look well, but generally the corn is very late. I have seen some as high as my head."

Nerva paused in her reading when Ida May observed, "There's no heads at all on our oats or wheat yet, and our corn's just barely peeking through the ground."

"Shows you how much earlier their season is than ours, for they don't have a hard winter down there like we do," Alice explained as her mother nodded in agreement, then started reading again.

The next part was all news Brainard had heard about old family friends and relatives and it held little interest for the girls as they didn't even know them, but their father got their full attention when he wrote:

"I received a letter from you yesterday and was glad to hear from you all again and from Mary, too. I see by your letter that you are a getting along with the farming first rate. You must not let Edgar drive the breaking team too much this summer. I am glad that he grows well and grows fast. I expect that he will be as smart as his "daddy" by the time I get home. I do not expect that I should know him now nor the other children either, but I could soon learn who they were if I could get there. I hope it will be before another winter. We are all very anxious to have the war close so that we can go home to our families and friends."

Alice and Ida May had laughed lightly between themselves at their father's references to their brother, but couldn't help interrupting when he wrote of coming home. "Oh, Ma, do you think it's possible?" began Alice, followed immediately by Ida May's breathless, "Before winter?"

"Well, we're just as anxious as he is to get him home to us, but I reckon we'll just have to wait an' see," their mother replied before reading the next part, which was of great interest to her.

"I wish that you would tell me how many acres of wheat, oats, and corn you have got in. ("I can do that easy enough," she said to no one in particular, before she continued reading.) *I think that you will get the necessary money from the Treasurer as soon as it gets there, so do not worry about it.* ("Hrumph," she muttered at his attempt at humor.) *We expect to get paid off again in a few days, and I shall stop*

the allotment then, and send the money by mail. You must tell me whether you get the money that I sent by Geo. Spaulding, also $5.00 before that. ("Done that already. Mail must not be getting' through to you," she said, as if he could hear her.) *I hardly know what you will do to get your hay cut, but I guess there is someone around there that will put up enough for you if they can have the money for doing it. If Father will see if he can get someone to cut some for you, I will try to do as much for him sometime, if I should live long enough. If you do not get enough put up, you can sell of the cattle this Fall if I am not there."* (That drew another chuckle from all of them as they realized they had already completed that task without him.)

"Well, let's finish this first one up," Nerva said when all had settled down again. "There's only a couple o' bits left."

"I believe that this would be a good country to live in if it were not for the curse to the American soil, African Slavery. Here it exists in its worst form. They are poorly fed and clothed, and hard worked."

The chunks of oak shifting within the woodstove broke the solemn silence that followed his dark observation. "My, my," Nerva sighed, and then, on a much lighter note, she finished the letter.

"How I wish that you could look out the window and see me a coming. I think that if you started on running, that I should meet you all half way, unless you run faster than I can. I must stop and bid you all goodbye, once more, so goodbye all

D. B. Griffin."

Nerva perused the brief letter one more time, then folded it and returned it to its envelope. As she laid it on the table, her hand settled on that message from Brainard momentarily, as if in lingering silent contact with him, then slid her hand over to the second letter. But instead of opening it, she held it out and asked, "Alice, would you like to read this other one to us?"

Nodding enthusiastically, Alice accepted the offered envelope, opened it with the same small penknife her mother had used, and after drawing out and unfolding the single page of her father's writing, she held it out for all to see. Then she began reading:

"I seat myself down this morning with a good will to write a few lines to you. I am as well as common this morning. We are a getting very hot weather just now. We have pitched our camp on a flat piece of timber land close to a fine creek so we have plenty of water and good spring water too. We have cleared out all of the underbrush and rubbage and fixed up shades around our tents so we are comfortable fixed as we can expect to be. We are not bothered any with mosquitoes, but the house flies are very thick during the day. We expect to stay here four or five weeks."

"Sounds like there won't be much marchin' for a while," observed Nerva, while Ida May squinched up her face at the mention of those troublesome flying insects.

As Alice continued to read the events her father related, they all had a good chuckle at his humorous description:

"The papers state that Gen Beauregard has gone to Charleston with his army. I know that they have not all gone there for I think that a good many of them have gone North as prisoners. It is reported that we have taken 20,000 prisoners."

"Twenty thousand, imagine that," commented Nerva.

The atmosphere got even better when Alice read her father's projections into his future. Ida May, in a burst of inner joy, began dancing around their small table, her hands tightly clenched at her chest, with young Edgar Lincoln following in imitation but not understanding the commotion.

"I do not expect that we shall ever have another chance to fire at them or to let them fire at us, for I think that this Regiment will never be in any more engagements with the Rebels. I believe that the long looked for time is not many months distant when we shall not be wanted to fight anymore."

But the youngsters' spontaneous celebration ended as her sister continued:

"Minerva, you think that it is hard for you to get along without someone to look to, but if you had been with me amongst some of the families left behind, you would say your lot was an easy one. Just

imagine yourself in the South with your little family of children with scarcely enough clothes to cover their nakedness, your husband taken and tied hand and foot and carried into the army, and the last mouthful of provisions taken from you, and not a mouthful of provisions a growing this summer. I have seen such and divided my rations with them. I feel thankful that your lot is as good as it is for you have a plenty to eat, drink and wear, and you can look forward to the time, if I am spared, when I will return to my home and family. My earnest prayer is that I may be spared to return and live a long and happy life with you and the babies. But I want to see the trouble between the North and South so effectively wiped out that it will never show itself again in my day nor anybody else's day, before I can go home contented."

With Edgar Lincoln now lost to slumber in his mother's arms, the other three, in silent contemplation of his words, looked back and forth amongst each other and the letter Alice held. Sighing heavily, Nerva broke the spell: "Yep, that's your pa all right."

It was a good thing that his concluding lines brought back a bit of their earlier joy:

"Tell Alice and Ida and Edgar that their Pa thinks of them a great many times a day and wishes that he could see them and have a fine play spell with them. Give my love to all of them and take a share of it yourself. From your husband in Mississippi,

D. B. Griffin."

Chapter Twenty-One

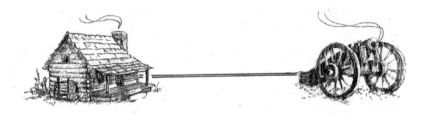

A Grand Fourth of July

With a grand sense of relief, Nerva arose early enough the next morning to write a quick note to her husband before the children woke up and required her attention. In a single sentence, she described the two weeks of inner pain she had secretly borne after being told the news of his death, during which time there were no letters from him or news about him to confirm or deny the report. She didn't use Sophrena's name, as she didn't want to create any personal tensions with the Boyntons, she just wrote she had been told he was dead. Then she concluded the brief missive with the words, *"You cant imagine the lump that left me when I finally heard from you and knew the story wasnt true. May it never be true, my dear Husband."*

The prior evening, before retiring, Alice had penned a note of her own. "Here, Ma," she said passing it to Nerva. "Next time you write Pa, put this in."

So Nerva folded the two half-page sheets together and slid them into the waiting envelope. When it was duly sealed and addressed, she gave it a kiss as Brainard often did, deeply thankful she could again write her man, who was still alive and well. As she sipped her morning cup of tea that followed, she decided two things: she could now tell her daughters what had occurred, since the news was obviously not true; and she would make a quick trip into Alba after her chores were done, not only to mail the letter, but also to see if Mr. Peters had any small flags the children could wave at the Fourth of July celebration planned in town for the following week.

Ida May arose first as usual, conscientious of her responsibility to free the chickens from their night's confinement. Still yawning and stretching as she descended the ladder, she arrived just in time to greet her mother, milk pail in hand, about to leave for her first daily chore.

"Morning, Ma. Off to tickle the milk outta Rosie?" This was her lively way of referring to the milking process, often observed, but not yet understood, she being only six.

"Yes, my love," Nerva said with a gay laugh, "while you set the chickens free from their prison." Her hand on the door latch, she added, "I told Alice last night to make us all some porridge for our breakfast when she comes down. You might need to remind her. In the meantime, there's a couple heels of bread for you an' your brother to gnaw on if'n he's awake when you come back in. Be a good girl an' look after him, won't you, till I'm done a'milkin'?" At her daughter's assenting nod, she headed for the barn.

Only moments behind her, Ida May approached the hen house, leaned down to unlatch and swing up the low door that kept their flock safe from night intruders like possums and raccoons. She then gave her childish imitation of a clucking hen to encourage their entrance into the new day. Dutifully, they crowded the doorway inside to oblige, and emerged flapping and cackling with a wide range of poultry vocabulary. The rooster, followed by his imitating cockerels, strutted around the edge of the flock, as if proud of possessing such fine-looking hens. All that commotion brought a daily joy to Ida May, for she understood how much the flock meant to the family's livelihood—and it was *her* responsibility. But since her mother had also made her responsible for tending to Edgar Lincoln, she knew she couldn't this day linger to watch.

He had already climbed out of his trundle bed by the time Ida May returned. When she entered the shanty she found him, still only half awake, standing at the window, where he had been watching her. "Good morning, little brother," she called to him, and his face lit up at the prospect of a play companion. "Ma said to get you dressed," she informed him as she moved to her mother's bed, where his day clothes were laid out, ready to replace his night clothes. "Phew. Smells like we need to get you out of that messy diaper an' get you cleaned up first." She didn't want him to think he had done something wrong, so it was said with a gay lilt in her voice as she unpinned it, but she found it hard to keep from gagging at the soiled smell.

The two of them were sitting out on the porch step watching the chickens scratch and peck, having started their own breakfasts with buttered bread heels, when Alice finally joined them in the fresh morning air. "Ma said you're s'posed to fix us all porridge," Ida May reminded her.

Alice had not forgotten. In fact, she was delayed because of a surprise. She had been quietly shelling hickory nuts up in the loft to add to their usual morning fare of cooked cracked oats. They were the last of the flavorful nuts she and her sister had gathered the prior fall.

"Already got the water on to boil," she responded, without giving away her surprise. "Just wanted to see if you two were all right." With a wave to Edgar Lincoln, she returned to her task inside.

She had added the cup of cracked oats to the boiling water, followed by the small bowl of nut meats and a couple tablespoons of their molasses for sweetening, and was slowly stirring the mixture when the rest of her family trooped in from the porch. Ida May and Edgar Lincoln came in holding hands. Behind them came Nerva, toting the pail of milk she had coaxed out of Rosie.

"Looks like you've got our porridge about ready, an' here's fresh milk to top it with." She put the pail down on the table, then peered into the kettle as Alice continued stirring with a wooden spoon to keep the contents from sticking. "Law me, what's them little brown pieces floatin' around in there?"

"They're my surprise, Ma. Thought I'd add the last of the hickory nuts Ida May an' I gathered after Pa left."

"A little bit of extra goodness. What a dear surprise," her mother praised.

When it was ready they all sat down together and held hands around for their table grace. Even though Ida May had said right away, "Oh, Alice, this is *so* good," it took a little coaxing to get Edgar Lincoln to try the porridge, since he had not had nuts in anything yet, but he too was soon enjoying Alice's treat.

Nerva then made an offer: "If you girls'll play with your brother, I'll clean up here an' take care of the milk. Then we can settle on some garden chores that need adoin' whilst it's still cool. Peas or taters, I'll let you choose."

"We could play hide-and-seek. He likes to do both of them," suggested Ida May.

"Hide-See! Hide-See!" Edgar Lincoln started shouting. "Me hide, an' you fine!" he squealed and started rolling under his mother's bed. And so they began. The three-person game, played inside and outside, lasted for most of an hour until interest waned, except for one final chase in from the barn. The young boy was now tired enough for a morning nap, and his sisters were now available for their morning chores.

"I'd like a fine mess o' peas picked and shelled. An' I wanna bowlful of new fingerling potatoes eased outta the ground," Nerva informed them when they sat down beside her. "They'll be our lunch today, 'long with the few bits o' roast left from last night. You two decide who does which, whilst I hitch up Ol' Jim for a quick trip into Alba to take care of some things."

The sisters eyed each other for a moment, then Alice volunteered, "I'll let her choose. I don't care which one." She knew they both loved to shell peas—to watch the little green globes pop into the bowl as their thumb slid down the opened pod—but she was feeling generous.

"I'll do the peas," announced Ida May. "Alice can dig potatoes better than I can." With that compliment returned, both were satisfied, and their mother was able to leave for town knowing all was well.

They picked pea pods together, since Ida May's task would take much longer. Then they parted, Ida May sitting on the porch step, the large bowl in her lap, separating the peas from their shells, while Alice went to the other end of the garden to complete her own task.

Nudging along on her knees from plant to plant, Alice wriggled her hands into the loose soil to find and pull out one or two of the thumb-sized tubers her mother called "fingerlings." It took her only halfway down the second row to fill her bowl, but by then her sister had finished her task as well.

Ida May gathered up the now empty pods and carried them out in her apron to the barn for the pigs to enjoy, while her sister started to carry both bowls inside the house. But with a bowl in each hand, and Ida May not yet returned, negotiating the doorway was more difficult than Alice expected. The result was she accidentally tipped the bowl of peas so much that half of them spilled out and rolled across the boards of the shanty floor in all directions. "Oh no," she wailed.

Luckily, Edgar Lincoln was still sleeping, for he would have found the situation another fun game set out for him. Even so, there was no way Alice could gather the hundreds of scattered peas before Ida May discovered what had happened. It got worse. As soon as her sister walked in, she started yelling in dismay, which awakened their brother into tears, and her mother returned. Taking in the entire commotion surrounding Alice's accident, Nerva then burst into laughter.

189

A confused Alice looked from her angry sister, to her frightened brother, to her laughing mother, and didn't know what to think until her mother composed herself enough to say, "Well, I *did* say I wanted a mess o' peas for lunch. It sure 'nough looks like that's *just* what I got!"

***

Their afternoon began by trying out the small American flags Nerva had purchased that morning at Mr. Peters. The girls held them high as they pretended to march around the room, while their brother mainly ran between and into them, waving his flag and yelling as if he were leading a charge. A great wave of love and pride—enough for two parents—swept over Nerva as she watched the scene and clapped. *Oh, if only their pa were here to see 'em. Wouldn't he be right proud?*

When the excitement seemed to wane a bit, Nerva pulled the children together around the table, her son on her lap, and told the girls her story of hearing the rumor of their father's death, her two-week-long quiet despair, and her total relief the day before upon the receipt of his two letters.

Following their initial reaction of shock at the news their mother had been given, Alice and Ida May listened intently, leaning in from either side. "I thought you seemed extra troubled, Ma. But I didn't know why. Now I understand." Those were Alice's words, but she really spoke for her sister as well, for Ida May was nodding her head beside her.

When the telling was done, both girls threw their arms around their mother's neck and shoulders, covered her cheeks with comforting kisses, and filled her heart with words of consolation. In the process, Edgar Lincoln was nearly smothered in their embrace, but he didn't struggle to escape this unusual display of affection. A renewed assurance that their family was still whole, even with Brainard away at war, bound them tightly together.

***

The following Friday was the Fourth of July. It dawned bright and warm, the cloudless summer sky a sure promise to be brighter and warmer by afternoon. A shared meal and some speeches at the schoolhouse had been planned by Beaver Township's leaders to mark the day, along with an undisclosed "Something Special." Many of the farm families were excited about attending, including both Griffin families, for this was to be a day to celebrate the Union their sons, fathers, and friends were away fighting for.

After breakfast, Nerva had roasted two of their largest cockerels for their family to bring for the feast. When these cooled, their platter topped off the large picnic basket that contained cups, plates, and utensils for the family, plus one of her cellar-aged farmer cheeses.

"Jackets for all," she ordered as she walked to the door.

"Jackets? But Ma, it's already hot outside," complained Ida May.

"It may be now, but it's sure to cool off a'fore we start for home in the dark. So we'll all need jackets. I'm out to hitch up Ol' Jim, an' I want you ready when I pull up."

"I'll see to it, Ma," Alice promised as her mother left for the barn, then Alice turned to Ida May. "Why don't you gather up our coats, an' I'll get Edgar Lincoln ready an' carry out the picnic basket? Oh, an' bring our flags too, okay?"

The family was soon on its way to the celebration, and they were not alone. Many "Hellos" were called to other families they encountered heading to the same destination. By the time they arrived, dozens of buggies were already parked around the schoolhouse, and their owners were milling about in small conversational groups.

Nerva spotted her parents, just climbing down from their buggy, so she guided Ol' Jim over to where they were parked, and as she pulled up, her sister Mary also arrived. The buggy had barely ceased its forward motion when Alice and Ida May jumped out and lifted Edgar Lincoln down between them. They waited for their mother to tie down their horse, then rushed to greet their family.

The four girl cousins ran off to find other friends, leaving all the adults behind.

Speeches were to be the first order of the day, but in order to gather and quiet the crowd, a local group of musicians struck up their rendition of the patriotic melody, "Battle Hymn of the Republic." That was all that was needed for the children to begin marching around as if they were in a parade, many of them waving small flags on sticks or gaily colored ribbons. But eventually the music worked, as families gradually assembled around the front porch of the school, where the three speakers were ready to begin. Many of the people simply sat on the ground, while others, especially around the edges, remained standing to better see and hear.

Almon Griffin, as township clerk, began with a brief welcome to all, followed by a recognition of the five area families with a father, son, or relative then serving in the war. "Would the following families please stand? We'd like to thank you all for the heavy contribution you're makin' toward keepin' our Union united: Baldwins, Barnes, Douglasses, Griffins, Lambs, Nichols, and Rutherfords." As they solemnly rose from their places, he added with an encompassing sweep of his arms, "Give 'em a hand folks. Show 'em we're grateful." With the crowd clapping heartily, the band lit into "When Johnnie Comes Marching Home Again," and the children repeated their flag-waving march around the gathering until the song ended.

The second speaker was Reverend Westfall. His was a lengthy retelling of the Union's history, from the early colonies, which struggled so hard to survive in their new homeland, up to the Continental Congress, which issued the Declaration of Independence. He then summarized the events of their Revolutionary War, the victory that ultimately led to the creation of the United States and the writing of the Constitution, both of which, he noted, were at that time being tested by the Civil War. His conclusion was a prayer to the Almighty for the return of peace to the land and its peoples.

By this time the crowd was a bit restless, so the final speaker, Mr. Peters, kept his remarks brief and to the point. His task, as their postmaster, was to encourage everyone to remain faithful in their support of the government's military efforts. The earnest plea he made caused the crowd to rise and cheer as the band lit into their rendition of "When Johnnie Comes Marching Home" again, and the children paraded one more time.

"That was mighty fine, mighty fine," Polly Griffin said to her daughters as the three of them walked back to their buggies to fetch their picnic baskets.

"Yep, made me feel good inside for what my Emery's a'doin'. Proud o' him—an' all the others o'course," Mary replied.

Nerva was slow to respond, and she did so quietly, with downcast eyes. "It still hurts, 'cause it's so hard with Brainard gone, an' everythin' we have to do without him. But it is a help our neighbors care."

The silence lasted until they approached the buggies and Mary asked, "Where should we set all our family down to eat?"

"I was a'thinkin' over in the shade of one of them chestnut trees," Polly pointed. "Not too many other folks there yet. An' we'll still be close 'nough to hear or see anythin' that's said or done."

"I see the Nichols over there, Ma. We could join them. Why don't we leave you there with our baskets, an' Mary an' I'll go round up the rest of our family?"

They soon returned with the others straggling behind. While they were gone, Polly had laid out the blankets and all their dinner things, so the meal was ready. Everyone sat around the blankets' edges and began helping themselves to cold chicken and vegetables, pickles and cheeses, bread and butter, and little nut cookies that Mary had brought.

The adults, except for Grampa Almon, lingered in conversation long after the food was gone. The children, however, freed from most parental constraints because of the occasion, happily leaped away into more youthful activities, racing, chasing, and hiding throughout the gathered families. As for Almon Griffin, he had walked away and disappeared without a word to anyone.

When the day had nearly worn itself out in this small community's celebration of the Union, Hiram Winslow climbed up on the schoolhouse porch and shouted for everyone's attention. "Hear, hear, neighbors and friends!" Most of the folks turned to him, stopping their chatter, as he continued. "We have one more thing for you. We promised somethin' special. But a'fore we bring it on, all o' you need to gather back with your famblies. An' that's especially the young'uns." He pointed to several small groups of children still at play. "When ever'one's ready, then we'll begin."

As the children obediently returned to their parents, a buzz of excitement ran through the crowd, speculating as to whatever the "Something Special" might be. It was already twilight, nearly time for all of them to begin heading home. So what could still be in store, they wondered to each other.

Suddenly, from the growing anticipatory silence broke Minerva Griffin's anguished scream, "Where's my baby? Where's Edgar Lincoln?" His sisters and cousins had returned without him, and none of them knew where he was, nor could they remember where they had last seen him. Frantic, she began shouting his name in all directions, and her searching cry was quickly taken up by other mothers throughout the crowd.

The fading light made it difficult to see clearly at any distance, so it was several minutes before Miss Cray called out, "Here he is! I've found him." He was curled up asleep by her schoolhouse steps—the exciting day had completely tuckered him out, and he had just collapsed. Rhoda Cray scooped him up and met Nerva halfway, Edgar Lincoln still fast asleep in her arms.

It was at that moment that Almon Griffin reappeared from behind the schoolhouse. "Everybody ready?" His booming voice quieted the still restless crowd, as he added: "Here we go!"

A whooshing sound broke the silence, immediately followed by a stream of light streaking up into the heavens. Then, to almost everyone's amazement, a burst of sparkling light filled most of the darkening sky. "Oohs" and "Ahs" echoed across the gathering as five more sky rockets burst in rapid succession above them. The children were especially delighted, as they had never seen such a thing. "So, fireworks was the special," Nerva concluded to Mary, while Polly observed with pleasure, "I wondered what it was Almon was up to. Been so secretive of late."

It was a wonderful finale to the day's festivities. Neighbors bade farewell before climbing into their buggies to disperse to their scattered homes. A nearly full moon provided a soft glow along the roads out of Alba, and many folks also lit candles in their carriage lanterns to help insure a safe trip home.

Chapter Twenty-Two

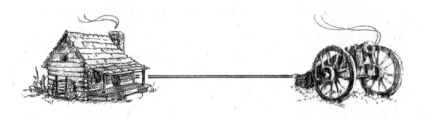

To the Creek and Post Office

"Now, who could that be, this early of a mornin'?" puzzled Nerva, startled by a repeated knocking at their shanty's door. The family's breakfast and morning chores were already done, and she and her daughters had just sat down to plan out their day when this interruption occurred.

"I'll see," offered Alice, stepping over to the door to open it.

Standing together on the porch, their fists raised to knock again, stood Molly Baldwin and Sarah McCormick, two of Alice's best school friends. Each had a homemade fishing pole resting on a shoulder, and Molly was also holding a rusty brown worm pail.

"Mornin' Alice," they said in unison, then Sarah continued, "we're off to Beaver Creek below Mr. Peters' store to catch us some fish. Care to come along?"

Alice turned an imploring look on her mother. She really enjoyed the times her father had taken her fishing, but with him gone, she hadn't been for nearly a year. On top of that, since school had been closed for the measles scare, she seldom got to see her friends. "Please, Ma, can I go? I've done my chores, an' I can finish up anything else you want when we get back."

Nerva bit her lip and turned away for a moment with a heaviness in her heart. She trusted the children, of course, but it was such a long way. Turning back, she started, "Well, love, I don't know . . ."

Alice quickly brought her mother to agreement with the pronouncement: "I'll bring us back a good string of fish for our supper."

"A mess o' fresh fish *would* be mighty tasty. Oh, all right, you can go if'n you promise—all of you—to be careful."

"We'll be careful, Miz Griffin, for sure," said Molly from the porch. Her "Count on that" was emphasized with a pointed finger.

"Thanks, Ma," Alice added, as she headed out to the barn to fetch the fishing pole her father had made for her, along with his small tin of store-bought hooks and lead sinkers.

Ida May had silently followed the exchange, and as soon as Alice had left for the barn she stood up and began to plead: "I wanna go too, Ma. Oh, please say yes."

Her mother wordlessly shook her head to deny the request.

"Why not, Ma? Why just Alice?"

"No, Ida May. I don't want you to go that far. You're too young without your pa."

The young girl stomped her foot and raised her voice in a petulant claim, "That's not fair! Alice always gets to do stuff, but not me!" In frustration, she turned away and began clambering up to their sleeping loft to escape.

"Ida May!" Now it was Nerva who raised her voice, and it was sharp enough for her daughter to pause halfway up the ladder and turn her defiant face back down to her mother. "You wipe that pout off'n your face this instant, do you hear?" Nerva's mouth was set and her eyes squinted from her slightly lowered head as she stared at Ida May, demanding her compliance.

But the slow tears that began spilling down her daughter's cheeks softened Nerva's manner. She stood, walked over to the base of the ladder, and reached both arms up to help Ida May come back down. "My dear, dear child," she began. "You remember what I told you last night about my fear for your pa?" Still sniffling and sighing, Ida May nodded.

"Guess that fear's still got the better o' me. Can't think straight at the chance of somethin' happenin' to one of you instead. Can you understand?"

Ida May nodded again and mumbled "Yes, Ma." Then in a flash she threw her arms around her mother's legs in resignation.

Stroking her daughter's dark hair with both hands, Nerva bent down to kiss the top of her head and whispered, "I still don't want you to go that far. But how 'bout instead you go with them as far as Mr. Peters an' fetch any mail back that's waitin' for us?"

"I could?" Ida May looked up at her mother's compassionate smile and wiped her cheeks dry with the backs of her hands.

"Yes, love. I'll tell Alice you'll be a'comin' along that far with 'em."

***

Upon reaching the store, the three older children waved good-bye to Ida May, ready to resume their way along the lane that continued southwest across the rolling prairie another two miles to Beaver Creek. Just then, Mr. Peters stepped out onto his porch and called to them. "Hey you young'uns, where you off to this fine mornin' with them fishin' poles?" They could tell from the broad smile on his face and the lilt in his voice that he wished he were going fishing, too.

"Down to Beaver Creek an' catch us some fish, Mr. Peters," Alice spoke for the three.

"What about Ida May here? She goin' too?"

"No, sir. She's to go home with any mail you've got for us. Ma needed her, I reckon."

Turning to Ida May, who by then was standing with him on the porch, the jolly man whispered only loud enough for her to hear, "Fact is, I've got four letters set by for you. Two from your pa, I believe, an' one from your Aunt Mary, an' one from Miz Boynton."

"Four? Two from Pa?" the young girl asked in pleased disbelief.

"Yep. Wondered when some one of you would be in for 'em. One of 'em from your pa had no postage, so I'll pay it an' just add that to your ma's bill. Say, won't she be excited when you bring 'em home?"

"Oh, Mr. Peters, sir, I can't wait to see Ma's face when I show her. Can I have 'em now?"

"Of course you can," he chuckled, "right after you pick out a penny candy for your way home."

As those two entered the store, Molly, Sarah, and Alice disappeared over a slight rise and continued the final two miles to their destination. Although named a creek, much of the year enough water ran between its tree-lined banks to create deep pools, regularly spaced, perfect for bass and crappie.

"There's a good spot," said Sarah after they reached their destination. "Shall we try there?"

Her suggestion sent all three to the creek's edge, and with much laughter, all soon had worm-baited lines tossed into the upstream end of the pool. They had come the right day, for the fish were in a mood to bite. Before the slow current had taken their lines to the downstream end of the pool, all three girls had snagged a fish—two good sized crappies and a bass that put up quite a struggle for Alice.

"That was a great start. Should we stay here and run our lines again?" asked Molly.

Holding up her two-pound bass, her thumb braced inside its gill as her father had taught her, Alice offered, "My pa always says to move on upstream 'cause we've prob'ly spooked the other fish here."

So they did, and their second attempt was as successful as their first, though Alice's was too small to keep. By repeating that process, after a little more than an hour each girl had a string of six or seven fish tied to a rock at the edge of the creek. It must have been their easy success, heightening their combined excitement, that spilled over into the frivolity that followed.

Alice started it by playfully splashing a handful of water on Sarah, who was kneeling beside the creek admiring her catch. "Hey, why'd you do that?" she demanded, jumping up to confront her provoker. There was no anger in her voice, but rather a hint of the laughter yet to come. Seeing what had just happened, Molly joined the fun by also shooting a cupped hand of water onto Sarah while her back was turned to address Alice. Sarah whirled around, and without thinking, pushed Molly down into the creek. "Take that!" she shouted in gleeful triumph, then turned with a menacing look to face her first tormentor.

Alice piggy-squealed and began retreating backward, but she tripped on the uneven ground as Sarah leaped forward. Her "Umph!" as she fell morphed into an escalating "No! No! No!" as Sarah grabbed her by the arm and wrestled her, too, into the water. The two wet girls each lunged for an arm and pulled Sarah face forward between them into the pool. As they continued laughing and thrashing, all three were soon choking on mouthfuls of water, and eventually had to simply plop down at the water's edge, exhausted.

So it was a thoroughly wet, somewhat muddied trio that began trooping home. "Ma won't even care about this," Alice said as she pointed to her disheveled condition. Then she held up her heavy string of fish in satisfaction, "Because of this!"

***

With four letters in her apron pocket and a penny candy to suck on while she walked, Ida May's spirits were bright as she hurried along the road homeward. Even her resentment over Alice's chance to go fishing was gone. All she thought about was how happy she would make her mother when she showed her the letters. She was so excited about that prospect that when she reached the lane up to their shanty she began to run, and arrived breathless, needing to bend forward and rest her hands on her knees for a moment.

"Gracious, child. What's your hurry?" Her mother was sitting on the porch step, Edgar Lincoln on her lap, combing out his long blond curls after a bath.

Still panting, Ida May answered by removing one letter at a time from her pocket, counting, "This, an' this, an' this, and this!"

"Glory be, is that *four* letters you brung home?" Nerva set aside her son and extended both arms to her daughter.

"Yes, Ma. Four letters. An' two of 'em are from Pa," and Ida May passed them into Nerva's waiting hands.

Nerva sorted through the letters and put two of them down in her lap. "Those are from your pa. They'll have to wait for Alice to get back. That's our 'greement. Them other two, let's see . . . They're from your Aunt Mary and Sophrena Boynton. We can read them now, I reckon. Alice won't mind."

Neither letter was important, the first a report of news from Spring Valley along with inquiries regarding the Griffin families, and the other a brief apology for the untrue rumor she had passed to Nerva and her relief that all was still well.

"Wonder what Pa's news is," Ida May murmured when her mother added the two read letters to the two unread ones in her lap.

"Me too, love. But we'd best wait for your sister. Then we'll all find out together."

***

The afternoon hadn't yet begun to fade when Molly, Sarah, and Alice returned. With the long walk home, the warm summer air had dried them out, but they still looked quite bedraggled as they trudged up the lane.

Nerva was sitting between her two younger children, Alice's *McGuffey Reader* in her lap, when she glanced up and saw the approaching mud-splattered trio. Ida May had been following with her finger, word for word, as her mother read, and when her mother gasped she too looked up.

"What in tarnation a'happened to you?" Nerva questioned Alice.

"I fell in the creek."

"*All* of you?" Nerva looked up and down at all three girls.

"Well . . . we were splashin' a bit, Ma, an' I guess we got carried away."

"Looks more like the creek *swept* you away," Nerva joked. "Anybody get hurt?"

"No, Ma. But we got these," Alice said as she held up her string of fish, followed by her two friends raising their catches too.

Nerva chuckled as she turned to Ida May while pointing to the line-up of crappie and bass Alice held. "Lookee there. Looks like supper to me. Does it you?" She then slapped the book on her thigh, saying with obvious joy, "If that don't beat all. Mercy, Alice Jane, wouldn't your pa be right proud of you now?"

While Alice then made her good-byes to the others, Nerva bent down to whisper to Ida May, "Let's not say anythin' about your pa's letters just yet. We'll surprise her like she done us."

Ida May pursed her lips and nodded, accepting the conspiracy.

***

The fish were delicious, fresh and crispy fried in saved bacon grease. Alice and Ida May had cleaned them together by the well, then let their mother carefully slice away the bones. To go with the fish, the girls boiled some of the garden's carrots and string beans, and their mother added a dried-apple pie. Edgar Lincoln was a bit hesitant at first, as he had never tasted fish before, but even he had gotten his fill when the meal was done.

Nerva pushed her chair back from the table, as if she were done. It was just enough to free the heavy apron pocket in her lap. "So . . . Alice . . . You surprised Ida May an' me with all those tasty fish you brought home." She glanced at Ida May, who nodded in agreement. "Well, Ida May's got a surprise for you, 'cause she brought some things home too." And with that said, she pulled the first two letters out. "Letters from your Aunt Mary and Sophrena Boynton." After only a slight pause for emphasis, she then drew out the other two. "An' *two* letters from your pa."

Alice jumped out of her chair, tipping it over backward. "Pa! Oh, this day is *perfect!*"

Ida May also stood, and moved beside her sister for a hug.

"Let's clean up our supper mess, an' then we'll read 'em," concluded Nerva.

By the time the dishes were cleaned and put away, the long summer day had begun to fade. It was dark enough that Nerva was able to put her son to bed, though not to sleep, as he continued to chatter softly to himself for a while. In the meantime, the girls had lit the lamp at the table and Alice had read the first two letters over again to her sister. So all three were ready to complete their day with news from husband/father Brainard.

Nerva picked up the first one and as she opened it Ida May informed them, "See, that's the one Pa didn't put postage on, an' Mr. Peters had to add it to our bill."

"Let's see here," Nerva said. As she unfolded the sheet of paper she discovered the five-dollar bill Brainard had tucked inside his letter. She laid it on the table with an audible "Thank you" spoken to him. Then she began to read.

His opening paragraph drew sighs from around the table as each remembered the issue he was referring to, and each considered his sobering reflections:

"In the first place I will assure you that I am alive and well, if it were not so, I should not be here a writing to you to day. Nerva, it made me feel bad to hear that it had been told to you that I, Brainard Griffin, of the 2nd Minn. reg. vol, was "dead." I wouldn't have cared anything about it if you had not have heard so... I should like to have called in and seen some of you before you had heard to the contrary. Would there not have been some staring done? I hope that I shall haunt the one who started the report, if it was done intentionally. I never thought that I should live long enough to hear the report of my death. But I am glad for your sake, and the little children. God bless

you all, that it is as well with me as it is to day, for I can say for one that I am well, and in camp, whilst thousands of our soldiers who started from their homes, with health and joy beaming in their faces, are now in their graves, or their constitutions shattered for life, and thousands more will be ere this war closes, I fear."

Then, after light bits of news about his company's activities, he turned sober again. Both girls listened with focused attention, and neither interrupted until their mother paused at the end of the passage.

"I hardly know what you will do this winter if I do not go home this fall, but I think that the best way for you to do will be to go ahead and get your hay cut, at least, and then if there is not any prospect of my getting home before winter, let the place out if you can, and if you cannot, then get the house fixed up so that you can live comfortable in it. You had better let out the cattle or sell them and rent a house in the Valley or somewhere where you can get your wood, and get it cut, &c. You must talk over the matter with your folks, and do the best that we can. It is different from what we expected when I came from home. Then we all thought that I should get back home before this time, but it has turned out differently, and there is no telling when I shall go home, if I live. But we all live in hopes that we shall see Minn. this fall..."

"Ma." It was Ida May. She had heard the catch in her mother's voice at the phrase *if I live.* "What if Pa . . . doesn't come home? What'll we do?"

That shared fear, so seldom spoken, weighted Nerva's letter-holding hand down to the table. It took her a moment to put away her own anxiety, that was asking the same question, so she could address the issue with some confidence. Taking a deep breath, she raised her eyes to her daughters and answered, "We've just got to keep the same hope your pa wrote about after that, that he'll be back home with us by fall."

"But . . ."

"No buts. That's what we've gotta do. That's all we *can* do." She then waited until both girls' hearts were with her before finishing his letter, as he did, on a much lighter note.

"You must tell Alice that Pa thinks a good deal of her letters. I think that she improves in writing. Tell Ida that she must write some to Pa too. Edgar will tell her what to write, I reckon. How much would I give if I could see you all this morning...money would not be of any value..."

"Sounds like it's time for all of us to write again. I reckon even little Edgar Lincoln could put somethin' down for his pa." With both girls expressing their agreement, Nerva added, "Let's make us a list, soon's we find out what else he's got to report. Alice, why don't you read this one? Maybe even let Ida May make out some o' the easy words if she can?"

Ida May was allowed to open the second envelope, and as she unfolded her father's letter a second five-dollar bill was revealed. She placed it on top of the first one, saying, "Five an' five makes ten, right?"

"Good for you," answered Alice. "Now help me read the letter."

With their chairs scooted together and the letter between them, Alice traced her reading with a finger, stopping for most of the short words for Ida May to sound out. It slowed the process down, but raised Ida May's confidence at recognizing some of the words her father regularly used.

This letter was briefer, but contained several lines that required commenting upon when they wrote next:

"We were called out night before last, in double quick time, for one of the guards had alarmed the camp by firing his gun. But we found out that it was not any thing attacking us but a few harmless cattle. So we laid down again, and slept as sound as ever until morning.

How did you spend the 4th...?

We have a plenty of apples, potatoes, milk, butter, and blackberries. We bag a few fish, and occasionally draw a porker by the heels, as we do the potatoes by the tops.

*There was a mail come in to day, but not any letter from "Nerva."
Yet I look very anxious for one, for I like to hear from you all, and hear
how you get along with the work on the farm, and how the crops
come out.*

*We are all very anxious to have the war end, so that we can go to
our homes. And I for one am as willing as any one to go home to my
little family and stay with them until death shall part us, and live in
peace the rest of our lives, for I have seen enough of war to last me for
a long time to come, as well as the effects of war."*

"Can we make up that list now?" asked Alice.

"I think we should," answered Nerva. "All that's happened to us,
an' all he tells us about sure give us plenty to include. You wanna
write 'em down for us?"

And thus their evening drew to a close. The listing of their
recent events, mixed with the things Brainard had written, filled
Alice's page—enough for *more* than a single letter.

Chapter Twenty-Three

Letters from Home

All four sat around the table to write their responses after a light supper of cold roast sandwiches and fresh carrots pulled that morning. Edgar Lincoln leaned forward on his mother's lap, prepared to do his part along with the rest. Nerva said she'd answer the questions Brainard had asked in his letter and update him on things around the farm. Alice wanted to write him about her fishing adventure. Ida May, still limited in her writing ability, wanted to try writing her first note to her father, with the Fourth of July as her theme. As for Edgar Lincoln, he had a half sheet of paper and a pencil stub to express himself like any year-and-a-half-old child would.

Nerva began her letter by assuring her husband that the family was well and also thanking him for the money he had sent, for it would cover their recent charges at Mr. Peters' store. Then she went to describe the good condition of the animals and crops, since that is what he wanted to know, adding it was almost time for the second cutting of hay. She concluded her part by asking Brainard to promise to take good care of himself, for they wanted and needed him healthy and home.

Alice's letter read:

Dear Pa, I miss you so much. I think about you every day. I always wonder what you are Doing. Your letters help a lot, but they're not the same as when you are really here.

I wish you had been home yesterday when I got back from Beaver Creek. I went fishing there with Molly Baldwin and Sarah McCormick. They are my friends from school. You know Their Pas. I caught 7 fish with the pole you made me. It was enough for the whole family to eat but I reckon if you had been here it would've done. They were very tasty. Even Edgar Lincoln liked the way Ma fried them.

Fishing was fun, I tell you, and I was very glad you had taught me how last year. I even remembered how you said to move up stream instead of down stream. I'm glad you're my Pa!

Pa, do you know yet when you can come home?

Me and Ida May, we show your likeness to Edgar Lincoln all the time. We tell him all about you, and what a good pa you are. He asks about you sometimes, but he doesn't know and love you like we do. Guess he was just too young when you left.

You wanted to know about my studies. School never started again after the measles went around. But I have my Reader here, and Ma helps with the Bible verses each day. I also do some numbers most every day so I'll still be pretty good when ever school starts up again. I do want you to be proud of me.

Ma will tell you all about the farm, but I think we're doing about the best we can with out You. Me and Ida May have to help Ma with all the chores. But we don't mind cause we want every thing to be just right when you come back.

I love you Pa.

Your daughter in Minnesota,

Alice Jane Griffin

Alice helped Ida May with some of her spelling, but the young girl wrote most of it herself. Her short note came out like this:

Pa, this is form Ida May.

Last week was 4TH July. We wint to Alba. Lots of every bodies was ther. We had speaches and musick. Grampa and Granma was ther. Aunt Mary and her babys to. Ma made good chickn. We had purdy fire works in the sky. Edgar Lincoln got lost and got found. He is all right now. What did you do for 4TH July?

I love you Pa. Please come home.

Ida May Griffin

And Edgar Lincoln's contribution looked like this:

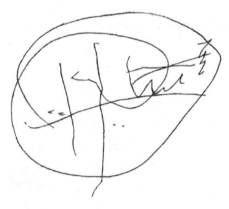

When the writing was done, the four pieces were folded together and stuffed into an envelope, which Nerva had already addressed. "Well, that sure 'nough makes a fat letter for your pa. Reckon he'll be tickled pink when he gets it. Now, which o' you two wants to be a'takin' it to town in the mornin'?"

Ida May's hand shot up, then she rushed around the table to her mother. "Oh, please, Ma, let me take it. I was the one who brung his letters home. It'd only be right."

Alice didn't mind because of all the walking she had done the day before, so it was agreed. And Ida May was thrilled that the letter she would carry to the post office this time would include a letter from her to her dear Pa.

Chapter Twenty-Four

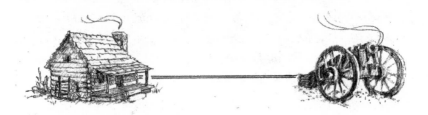

A Visitor from the Front

"So, now it needs to sit in the sun for a few days a'fore you come back?" Nerva asked Daniel LeFevre from her porch step.

The season had progressed far enough for the LeFevres to come back for the second cutting of hay. Daniel had stopped at the shanty to talk, as they had just completed raking the half-cured hay into windrows.

"That's right, Miz Griffin. How long depends on the weather. But I'll send Jacob over each day to check on it. He'll know by the feel. He's a good boy." As he said this, Mr. LeFevre turned to look at his nephew enjoying a dipper of water at the well with Nerva's daughters.

It was when she followed his gaze to the children that Nerva caught sight of a figure riding at a slow pace up their lane on horseback. He was dressed in blue, hat and all. But even at that distance, both he and the clothes he wore appeared thin and worn. She peered over Daniel's shoulder, shading her eyes from the summer sun for a better view. *Is it Brainard? Oh, dear God, is he home?* Her heart began to race, and she actually began to shiver despite the August heat.

As the man drew closer, Nerva was able to determine his body was too short and his hair too blond to be Brainard. Finally she recognized who it was, though the privations he had suffered since she had last seen him were obvious in his shrunken face and slightly emaciated physique. *Why, that's Jerry Nichols!* The visitor had become Brainard's best friend after they moved to Minnesota from Vermont. Now in the war he was also Brainard's closest companion in Company F.

Her husband had often mentioned in his letters how markedly their war experiences were affecting Jerry, and that he might even have to be sent home. *My, my. So this is what it's done to him. Dear Lord, does Brainard look the same?* He had also written that Jerry had told him how Mrs. Nichols regularly begged her husband in her letters to find some way—any way—to come home. *Well, I need my man too. But I know how much it means to him to settle this awful war. I'd never do that. I couldn't.*

Noticing her attention was diverted by the approaching soldier, Daniel made his good-byes, gathered his son and started up his raking team with a final, "Jacob'll be back tomorrow sometime, Miz Griffin." The LeFevres acknowledged the horseman as they passed him, though neither of them recognized him.

Jerry Nichols called to Nerva with a wave of his hand as he rode up to the shanty, where she stood. "Hello, Nerva. Haven't seen you around for quite a spell. Where you've been off to? Your husband about?" Always a jokester, his words flustered Nerva at first.

"Jerry Nichols, you know right well that *you're* the one's been gone, not me. An' with my Brainard to boot! Whatever are you a'gettin' at?"

With both hands, he lowered his cap to mid-chest and laughed, "Just a'teasin' you. You know me."

"Well, get yourself down off your high horse then, and come set a spell. Reckon you've got some news inside you we'd all love to hear." She stepped up on the porch so she could see the girls, still sitting by the well, and called, "Alice, Ida May, lookee here who's come back from the war to see us—Jerry Nichols! Come on in an' let's see what he's got to say."

The sisters jumped up and ran to the porch holding hands and chanting, "News about Pa! News about Pa!" They burst through the door and found Jerry seated at the table and entertaining Edgar Lincoln with a disappearing penny while their mother was stoking up the firebox to make a pot of tea. Surprised to see their father's friend so gaunt, they looked at each other in dismay, then approached him.

"Hello, Mr. Nichols. You were with Pa?"

"You must be Alice," Jerry responded to his questioner, "and that makes you Ida May, right?"

"Yes, sir, Mr. Nichols. But you've seen Pa?" Ida May's fully opened eyes and raised brows as she lowered her chin and bit her lip all indicated her excited anticipation.

"Yes, yes, I've seen your pa. Been with him nigh every day for the last nine months. Seen him; slept beside him; marched with him; washed mounds of clothes an' piles of dishes with him; drilled together in the rain, the snow, an' heat wors'en today; fought Rebels beside him . . ." Jerry paused with a faraway look in his eyes, remembering the sounds, the smells, and the dying. He shook his head, trying to rid himself of those memories so he could start again. "Guard duty, mail call, you name it. Yep, I've been with your pa."

Both girls were entranced by his listing of details, and respected him in their flow, for they could see on his face the inner pain that memory of battle drew up.

All the while, their mother had been fussing over the tea things with her back to them. But she had taken to her heart every word, every expression, confirming her image of Brainard's present condition. She, too, had caught the emotional content of his pause, and it caused her to wonder more about what her husband was thinking than what he was doing.

"Here's tea for us," she said, and brought to the table the tea pot, then four mugs along with a small jug of honey. "Dear me, I forgot the spoon," she confessed, turning back to the cupboard to fetch one. "I'll pour an' let you sweeten it yourself. Then I want to hear for sure everythin' about yourself an' about my Brainard."

As she walked around the table, filling their mugs with the steaming brown liquid, Jerry began his story. "Well, as I said to the young'uns here, we've been together every day since we rode out of Chatfield last September. And I must say, your Brainard has a way about him that allows him to enjoy himself wherever he is, whatever's happening. He's a real cracker, yes sir'ee. Never gets down. Nothing spoils it all for him. Well, that's not me. I know I'm always a'jokin' around, but I just get down sometimes. Like this here war we signed up for together. He's still in it. But it's taking too long for me. Couldn't stand being away from home any longer. Lost heart for the fight so bad it made me sick. Sick all over." He looked away from them again and hung his head, but wasn't through. "So sick they even put me into the hospital for a spell . . . with all the men who lost . . ."

The others watched him tremble and waited in silence.

Nerva was just about to try to draw him out of wherever he had gone when he began again. "That's not like your man, Nerva. He's as much for the war now as the day we signed up. Oh, it's not that he *loves* all the soldiering business. He just doesn't mind all the suffering it brings."

"Suffering? What do you mean?" asked Nerva.

"You wouldn't believe all they expect of us. Marching day after day, miles and miles. Don't make no difference whether it's sloshin' mud or face-freezing cold. Shelter tents? Only if they keep up. Rations? Half or less if the wagons don't arrive. Then sometimes turn around and march right back to where we started from. Don't make no sense."

He had similar things to report about the drudgery of river-water washing of clothes and bodies, daily drill, and all-night sentry duty. His descriptions of the military officers, camp sanitation, and the boredom of long periods just waiting somewhere were equally dim.

"What about when you had to fight the Rebels, Mr. Nichols?" Alice was wondering if he didn't like that part either. Her father had occasionally mentioned some of those other things, though never that harshly. *Does Pa think like Mr. Nichols about the fighting?*

"Now the fighting was a different thing. That's the only time it seemed like we were a'doing something. Know what I mean? Not just sitting around, or marching around, but man-to-man trying to settle this thing out. Course I wasn't too fond of the killing part, either of them or us. It was a hard thing even to see all the wounded. But I guess that's war. And I can do no more warring. That's why they allowed me to come home, at least for now. Still have to find out what a doc says before I report back."

"What about Pa, Mr. Nichols?" asked Ida May. "Is he all right?"

"Yep, he's all right. Stays well pretty much, even with the marching. Got a good job in the company kitchen, and likes it well enough."

That comment drew knowing smiles between mother and daughters.

"And everybody thinks the world of Mr. Griffin. Plain as day to see. Oh, I know he misses all of you. That's natural. Talks about you all the time, and reads your letters aloud. But the difference is, his heart's still in it. Mine isn't. I was just sick to come home . . ." His voice trailed away to a whisper as he spoke.

Nerva reached over to pat his hand, a gesture of the gratefulness she felt for his reassurance that her husband was as fine as his letters seemed to indicate. "That's okay, Jerry. We understand. I reckon all of us feel a mite better on Brainard, knowin' now what you've told us. So go back to makin' peace with Mrs. Nichols for doin' the best you could."

Jerry drained the last of his tea, stood with a wan smile to acknowledge each of them, then headed for the door. As he was untethering his horse, he looked back at the Griffin family, who had followed him out to the porch to wish him well on his way. "I'll be back," he assured them, and climbed up, ready to ride.

"You do that, Jerry Nichols. Welcome here anytime. At least until my Brainard gets hisself back," she joked. "Bring Mrs. Nichols with you next time if she's able to come."

Jerry nodded, gave a nudge to his horse, then pulled back on the reins and faced her once more. "I'd be obliged if you'd mention to Brainard when next you write that I stopped by. Let him know I kept my promise." With Nerva's affirming nod of her head, he turned his horse once more to return home.

Nerva stood watching as the girls reentered the house. *Just like Brainard wrote he'd be. Wonder what's in store for him? I do wonder . . .*

Chapter Twenty-Five

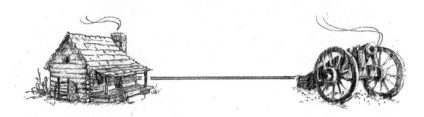

Terrible News

It was the last week of August, and the humid heat of late summer lay heavy across the Minnesota prairie. Ida May sat in the shade of the porch snapping string beans for the family's supper when Nerva returned from town. She watched her mother drive the buggy into the barn, expecting her to emerge momentarily, Edgar Lincoln in tow, for it never took long to settle Ol' Jim into his stall. When at least ten minutes had passed with still no sign of her, she began to worry.

Setting down her half-done bowl of beans, Ida May walked over to the barn to see if there was a problem. As she entered the barn, she barely had time to experience its comforting coolness when she heard the sound of her mother softly sobbing. "Ma, what is it? What's wrong? Are you hurt?" She rushed to the buggy and saw that Ol' Jim was still hitched up, Edgar Lincoln was asleep on the padded seat, and her mother, holding an opened letter in each hand, seemed to be suffering some kind of pain like Ida had never seen before.

"What is it, Ma?" she asked again after climbing up beside her. "Is it . . . is it about Pa?"

216

Nerva took a slow deep breath, then exhaled with a sigh as she stuffed the letters in her apron pocket. "It's from your pa, but not about your pa, Ida May. Yet it makes me fear for him nonetheless." She drew out her kerchief, dabbed her eyes first, then blew her nose, hard, as if to rid herself of her fears as well as her teary congestion. "Let's go in. Where's your sister?"

"She's inside, workin' on school stuff."

"How 'bout you fetch Ol' Jim some fresh hay whilst I unhitch him? Then we can carry this little tyke in an' I'll read to you an' Alice what your pa's wrote to us."

The horse tended to, they entered the shanty together, Nerva cradling the still-sleeping lad in her arms, and Ida May stooping to pick up the beans she needed to finish. After kissing her son's forehead as she laid him on her bed, Nerva walked over to the girls' ladder and called softly up to Alice. "Alice, I'm home. Come on down as I have news from your pa to read."

Alice had been laying on her bed, legs akimbo, enjoying a story in her *McGuffey's Reader*. She marked her place with a scrap of paper, then came right down to join her mother and sister. "News from Pa? What's . . . he . . . say?" The initial excitement in her voice faded when she noticed the two letters spread open on the table and guessed they had already been read without her.

Nerva's smile was more sad than happy as she responded, "You can see I didn't wait for you two this time. I just had a queer feelin' inside me 'bout 'em . . . had to look. I'll say right away, your pa's just fine. Couldn't be better 'less he was a'comin' home. But as much as we all trust that's exactly what he'll be a'doin' one day soon, these letters make me fear for him a bit."

"I found Ma cryin' in the barn after she read 'em. Not like I do when I stub my toe or somethin' but more like when the loneliness creeps over me." It was quite an insight for a girl of only six, but the unfairness of life was causing her to quickly grow beyond her years.

"That's it," her mother said. "That's it exactly. But I know you *want* to know, so let me read what he's wrote an' then you'll understand my tears." She then began to read, with Ida May, as quietly as possible, continuing to snap beans while Alice held and gazed at her father's picture.

The first thing that Brainard had written that frightened Nerva followed his questioning of their future: *"What will you do this winter?"* He had then, in stark terms, suggested, *"You had better plan as if I'll never come home..."*

Both girls gasped, their internal apprehensions clearly portrayed upon their young faces.

"Can you see how my heart stopped a moment when I read them words the first time?"

The next troubling thing was an incident Brainard had described in great detail—the killing of their Brigade Commander by a band of Southern guerillas. "When I read that part," Nerva explained to them, "I wondered . . . if they can kill a gen'ral that easy, how can anybody be safe down there?"

Then in the second letter he told them about the large number of family friends serving in the Third Minnesota Regiment who had been captured by Confederate forces less than fifty miles away from his own encampment. Two of the names were ones the girls recognized: Ellicutt Rundell and Edwin Rexford.

"What happens to a soldier if he gets captured?" Ida May was hoping it wouldn't be so bad, but suspected from the tears she had seen on her mother's face that reality pointed to a different outcome.

"Most are caged up in a prison, likely till the end of this terrible war. An' this is what I was imagining as I read it. What if your pa . . ." She looked away, unable to finish her sentence.

Finally she returned to them, picked up the letter again and said, "The onliest thing in all that he wrote that I could hold onto was this at the end . . . *If I should live to get home safe and be permitted to live in peace with my little family the remainder of my days is all that I can ask* . . . So let's go with that, shall we?"

Ida May nodded with her sister, but her father's letters and her mother's initial reaction to them burrowed deep into a corner of her memory, from where they often resurfaced over the next few weeks when her mind was not actively engaged elsewhere.

***

The children were long asleep and Nerva was sitting alone that night with worried thoughts of her faraway husband when she heard someone ride up in the pale moon darkness. Heavy bootsteps approached the shanty's door, alerting her to some kind of impending danger. Whoever it was outside began pounding on the door and calling her name in a hoarse, breathless voice.

Afraid to throw back the wooden locking bolt to open the door she called out, "Who's out there?"

"It's me, Chipman, Nerva. Got some terrible news."

Finally recognizing his voice, but with increasing dread because of his response, she opened the door to her highly agitated neighbor. "What is it, Mr. Chipman? What's happened?"

Instead of entering the lamp-lit room, he spoke quickly from where he stood. "It's the Injuns, Nerva. Up at Redwood. They're massacreein' settlers an' soldiers alike. A rider just came through with the news, an' he's on to Preston."

"Massacree? Indians?" she broke in. "Heaven help us, whatever for?"

"Who knows? Started up at the agency yesterday. Killed the soldiers there, then up an' down the river valley, burnin' ev'ry house an' settlement in their path, women an' children too. News is today they got all the way down to New Ulm. Got it surrounded . . ." His head dropped in grief and rage.

"New Ulm?" That can't be hardly more'n two or three days from here! Good Lord A'mighty, what'll happen to us?"

"Well, it's awful, o'course. But the militia'll step in. An' New Ulm's a long ways off. Don't worry none for now. There'll prob'ly be a town meetin' in a day or two. We're just spreadin' the word so's folks can start gettin' 'emselves prepared. So I'll be on my way, an' you take care."

He turned to go, but swung back around to ask, "Anythin' I can do for you, Nerva, seein's you're alone?" With the silent shake of her head, he tipped his hat, mounted and rode off.

Nerva shut and bolted the door as he disappeared down the lane, and stood with her hands and back pressed to the door as if that would help keep it shut. Her thoughts raced: *Brainard . . .We're alone . . . We need you here . . . I knew you shouldn't have gone, an' now it's come to this . . . What can I do . . . ? What can I tell the children . . . ? Anything . . . ? But how can we get ourselves ready if I don't tell 'em . . .? P'raps we should go to Father's place . . . ? Oh, Brainard . . .*

She returned to the table to ponder her options. And that's where Alice discovered her early the next morning when she came down, asleep, her head on her crossed arms.

"Ma, you didn't go to bed last night. What's wrong?"

Nerva woke with a start, momentarily confused about why she was there. Remembering her night visitor's message brought her right back to reality. To give herself time to think she simply said, "Oh, I must have dozed off. Goodness me, look at the time. I shoulda been out a'milkin' ages ago." She stood, brushed down her apron, and added, "Be a dear an' build up the fire to start us all a pan of porridge, would you? Then wake your sister. We'll talk when I get back in." Grabbing the milking pail, she hurried herself out the door so she wouldn't have to answer more questions from Alice just yet.

The gentle sloshing of Rosie's milk into the pail allowed her an undisturbed time to think. By the time she had finished, she had decided not to tell the girls just yet. *I'd best wait till after the town meetin'. Maybe I can get some help there on what to say. I don't want to frighten 'em. P'raps it'll all be over a'fore I have to tell 'em. For now, guess I'll just say I was still worried from the letters.*

***

Breakfast was eaten, but the girls remained at the table even though Edgar Lincoln kept calling them to come play with him.

"Alice says you didn't go to bed last night . . ."

It was all the opening Nerva needed. "After you two were off to sleep, I got to stewin' more 'bout your pa. I don't know . . . I just couldn't get the idea of him not comin' home outta my head."

"But, Ma, you said yourself we just need to hold onto Pa's plan to come home and live in peace."

"You're right, Alice. You're absolutely right. An' that's just what we're gonna do. Only it's so hard, him still gone and no answer 'bout *when* he'll be a'comin' back to us." She picked up his picture and held her gaze there a moment, then pulled herself together and continued, "Guess what I need to do is write him back today. Get it off my chest. Just talkin' to him that way might help ease my heart a mite." As she said that, she knew that what she really intended to write Brainard about was the new as yet unspoken Indian threat. She could tell him even if she couldn't tell them.

"We'll help you, Ma, won't we, Ida May? She already took care of the chickens while you were milkin' Rosie. I'll finish your barn chores for you, an' then we'll both play with Edgar Lincoln outside so it'll be nice an' peaceful in here for your writing."

Gratefully agreeing, Nerva got out the necessary paper, pen, ink, and stamped envelope as her daughters led their little brother outside. She began with a brief acknowledgment of his last two letters, along with an assurance of the well-being of the family and farm. Then she wrote in full detail regarding Mr. Chipman's message and her decision not to tell the children yet. She wrote with passion, resisting an urge to beg him to find some way to come home, as Mrs. Nichols had done. Instead, she simply reminded him how much he was needed and missed. In closing, she mentioned she was considering her sister Mary's invitation to move in with her up in Spring Valley, one answer to not having to face the coming winter alone out on the prairie.

When the letter was finished, she stepped to the door to call the children in. They weren't in view, so she walked out to the corner of the porch and called their names. With peals of laughter the three came running around the barn, the girls chasing Edgar Lincoln, pretending he was too fast to catch. Into his mother's arms he ran, and she swooped him up just as the girls arrived behind him. That little piece of joy was all she needed to restore her spirits.

"I want you young'uns to come inside for now. I'm headin' to town with this letter for your pa, and it'll be lunchtime a'fore I get back. Alice, I need you to take care of that for me."

"Yes, Ma, I will."

Ida May sidled up and took her mother's hand. "Are you feeling some better, now that you wrote Pa?"

"I am," Nerva assured her. "Yes indeed, I surely am."

Her caution to them about staying inside while she was gone was unusual, but the girls accepted it without question when she added, "I'll only be gone an hour or so. Maybe I can even bring us back a treat, somethin' good."

"Don't worry, Ma," her older daughter said. "I'll make sure we're all right. You just get that letter mailed to Pa."

***

Nerva pulled up in front of Mr. Peters' store, next to four other buggies already tied to his hitching post. She recognized two of them: her father's and the Gate's. Hurrying in, she found her father and Mrs. McCormick, along with the Widow Procious and Mr. Gates standing in a circle that included Mr. Peters. All of them were in a heated discussion about the Sioux uprising.

They all stopped when Nerva entered and welcomed her to join their circle. "We're all here 'cause of the Injun raids. S'pose that's why you've come too," offered Mrs. Procious.

"You've heard, of course?" asked Mr. Peters.

"Mr. Chipman was kind enough to stop by late last night with the terrible news. I was a'hopin' I could talk to somebody 'bout what best to say to my children. But what I really came for was to mail this letter to Brainard, lettin' him know what's happened."

"Mail goes out tomorra, Nerva, an' I'll get it on its way then. Meantime, we're here a'tryin' to figure out just what to do."

"I think we should be prepared to come together somewhere, then we can all help defend against them savages," began Thomas Gates.

"That's prob'ly right, an' here or the schoolhouse'd prob'ly be the prime place. But all in all we need to keep in mind that what's happenin' is at least a hundred miles from here. So we shouldn't be panicky," suggested Mr. Peters.

"An' Fort Ridgely is up there too, remember that. Militia there is strong. My own son-in-law's there. They'll stop 'em, sure," added Almon Griffin.

"Well, I ain't been able to decide what to tell my girls," Nerva inserted. "Don't want to scare 'em to pieces, but I want 'em ready to face whatever danger if'n it comes."

"I reckon what's best is to tell 'em a little bit about the trouble, so's they're aware, but keep saying how far away the trouble is, an' that the militia's already there a'takin' charge. That's what I'm a'goin' to do, anyways," advised Mrs. McCormick.

"How 'bout for now I work up a message system for passin' on all the news that comes in—who goes to tell who—so the word gets quickly spread?" That seemed a logical suggestion by Almon Griffin, since he was serving as town clerk that year.

"Sounds quite reasonable. You do that, Griffin, and we'll all be obliged to you." Mr. Gates checked the faces of the others as he said this, receiving their full confirmation.

They shook hands all around with words of encouragement, then they started drifting away for home, fortified that their cooperation would keep them safe. Nerva turned to her father before he departed, searching for any further reassurance.

"Maybe you oughta bring the children over an' stay with us a while," he said.

She was briefly tempted to accept this offer of her father's protection, but decided that unless things got worse, she was independently responsible for her own family. So she hugged him and whispered in his ear, "Thank you, Papa. If we need to, we'll come. But we should be all right for now." *We could also maybe head up to Mary's. Not all that happy 'bout facin' another winter alone either,* she thought.

He backed up a step holding both her hands. After lingering to look deep into her eyes, he nodded, turned and departed.

Nerva then followed Mr. Peters to his store to hand over her letter, request a pound of dried cherries for a party cake, and head home herself. She had decided she would wait as long as possible to tell the children. *P'raps I shant have to tell 'em at all if this all blows over in a day or two,* she resolved to herself as she drove into the yard, prepared now to face her children and get on with the day.

Chapter Twenty-Six

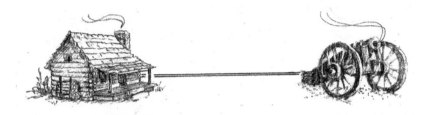

The News Revealed

It was only a few days after Nerva's trip to the Post Office that the network Almon Griffin organized to pass on any news had to be used. And the news the riders spread was alarming: soldiers had been sent out from Fort Ridgley to look for survivors and bury the dead, but these soldiers were attacked as well by the marauding Sioux, leaving many dead and wounded, and heightening fear among the nearby settlers. That area was still a long way off from Beaver Township, but the ability of the militia to defend the settlers now came into question.

Nerva took the news with grim determination to wait before she informed her girls, but the next letter from her husband forced her hand. Hoping he would not yet have heard about the Indian uprising, she had scanned the letter's contents at the post office. Unfortunately, he had already read an account in the Nashville newspaper, and mentioned it right away when he wrote. She started for home with a heaviness in her heart she couldn't dismiss.

I reckon it's time I told 'em, she mulled as she drove the buggy home. *Just what'll I say so they won't be scared to death? What'll they be thinkin' after I tell 'em? Oh Brainard, I need you here . . .*

With a final prayer for divine guidance in the words she must soon choose, she was unhitching Ol' Jim when the three children came bounding into the barn to greet her.

"Mama, Mama," Edgar Lincoln chanted as he reached up to be held.

"Saw you coming in, Ma. He just couldn't wait," Alice explained as she lifted her mother's small shopping satchel down from the buggy seat to make room for her brother to climb in.

"Any news from Pa?" queried Ida May, hope radiating across her face.

"Matter of fact, there is. But I've got some other news to tell you first, an' then we'll get to his letter."

Alice was halfway to the porch, but she had heard, and turned back to ask, "What is it, Ma?"

"Can't a body get in an' settled first?" Nerva laughed as she led Ida May and Edgar Lincoln inside, each by a hand.

Her youngest was soon distracted by his playthings on the floor, and Nerva was able to invite her daughters to sit with her at the table. "I'm gonna talk real soft to you, 'cause I want what I have to say for your ears," then indicating with her head, "an' not for his."

The girls scooted their chairs as close to their mother as possible, and each leaned in, allowing their mother to talk barely above a whisper.

"I need you to hear me through. An' I'll say right off, it's not about your pa. He's as fine as always. It's about us here . . . us bein' safe. If you listen careful, you'll see how if we just get scared it won't help us none. Instead, it's gettin' ourselves prepared that'll keep us safe." The bafflement on her daughters' faces contrasted greatly with the earnest pleading on her own, so she put the question to them directly: "Will you promise to listen as best you can to all I've got to say, an' leave the questions for after?"

"Yes, Ma," they said in unison, alternating looking at her and each other.

So she began. "A week or so ago, some of the Indians up at the Sioux Reservation began makin' a bit of trouble for some of the soldiers and settlers up by the agency. Mr. Chipman stopped by late one evening to tell me about how they'd gone all crazy over somethin' or other." She paused to let that sink in.

The girls looked at each other, then back to their mother, who continued: "They've been hurtin' people—a lot of people—down the river valley, an' the militia hasn't been able to stop 'em yet."

"Why would the Indians wanna do that?" an incredulous Alice asked.

"I don't know, dear. I don't think anybody knows yet."

"Will they hurt us too?"

This more pain-filled question from Ida May was the one Nerva had prayed wouldn't be asked. "Of course not, love. We'll be just fine," she tried to reassure her frightened daughter, though she considered it a promise she had no idea if she could keep.

"I want my Pa," Ida May whispered into her lap, the six-year-old feeling threatened.

"We all do," was the gentle response of her sister.

"But what if they *do* come here?"

"Ma's said they won't"

"If Pa was here I know we'd be all right. Why did he have to leave?"

Nerva spoke up: "Think about when he left us, Ida May. Remember how important he said it was for him to serve in the army, so's he could help President Lincoln save our Union?"

Ida May's question spoke to the heart of the matter: "Is servin' in the army more important than protectin' his own family?"

"But he couldn't know this would happen. If he thought so, I'm sure he'd have never left."

"Well, if he knew what's happenin' now he'd come right home, wouldn't he?" Ida May demanded, then said again, "I want my pa . . ."

"Listen to me careful now: all I can say is your pa's gone. And he *does* know, though I don't reckon he can do much about it . . . or us, way down there in Tennessee. Now, the soldiers up here at Fort Ridgley are set to move all the Indians back to their reservation, and quieten things down again. It may take some time. Still, for us, that's all a'happenin' a long, long ways away. And I didn't tell you yet, but your grampa has even fixed a way for all the folks around here to come together so's we'll have good protection if'n they'd ever somehow get close to here. But hear me out . . . that's *not* likely to happen. We'll just have to get ourselves prepared, stay alert to news, make sure we stay together safe, things like that."

She reached her hands out to grasp for a moment a hand of each daughter, then she took Brainard's letter from her pocket and opened it onto the table. "In his letter, your pa says he's already heard about this news. He's concerned, o'course, but he says he knows we're safe because it's not very close to us. He just wishes it wasn't happenin' 'cause he's not here to help us."

She thumbed down to the place she wanted and said, "Just listen to what he writes."

We have heard that the indians are murdering the inhabitants around Fort Ridgley, but we think that the reports are greatly exagerated. ("That means they make it sound badder than it really is," interspersed Nerva.) *If they are true, it is an awful butchery. It seems as though we are surrounded by enemies, both at home and away. I hope that the war with the South will speedily be put down, without counting the cost. And we think that it will be ended before another spring, but so we thought one year ago. I hope that you will get along this winter without any trouble.*"

"See how hopeful your pa is? An' then he writes like this in his next letter," she added as she turned to the second one and again found the place she wanted them to hear.

"I thought a good deal about you of late, and have wished a good many times that I could be home for a couple of weeks and get things fixed up for you. But I do not see but what you will get along first rate.

We hear pretty hard stories about the barbarity of the indians. It is awful to think of. I hope that they will not get down as far as you are. I think that this regiment had ought to go home and fight them, but I cannot tell. It is thought by our Colonel that we will go, so I was told just now and it come pretty straight too. If we do, I may get a chance to go home for a day or two, but I will not build any 'castles in the air' just yet."

"Oh, Ma, do you think Pa'll be coming home?" queried an excited Alice, as both girls looked longingly for their mother's response.

"He says it's just talk for now. An' you heard him say he might not even get to stop by to see us. But wouldn't that be grand?"

"So, what are we going to do, Ma?" Alice asked.

"I'll start with what we're not a'goin' to do, and that's cower down here, a'waitin' for somethin' bad to happen. No sir. We've got plenty to do with the garden an' such to keep us mighty busy. Just like your pa in the war—Rebels, half-rations, a'marchin' everywhere. But we'll need to be alert for news, kinda keep close track of each other, an' just be ready to move into town or to Grampa's if we need to—as farfetched as that might be. Agreed? In the meantime, listen to one more piece o' news he gives us." And once more she turned to his letter, this time to give her daughters something even better to think about.

"I have been into Louisville this afternoon, and I got my likeness taken. I thought that I would send it to you so you could see me once a year. It was a year yesterday since I enlisted, and you can see if I look any different than when I did then."

"Now *that's* what I'm gonna be thinkin' about, 'stead of them Indians as aren't gonna come here anyways!"

***

It wasn't long before there was reassuring news from the north, and Almon Griffin gladly spread the word that Governor Ramsey had brought together units from six Minnesota regiments. One of the units was the 7th Minnesota, Aunt Mary's husband's unit. They were all to be under the command of U.S. General John Pope, appointed by President Lincoln himself, with orders to quell the violence.

By the end of the month the Sioux had surrendered, all their captive settlers had been released, and nearly 1,500 warriors were being held for trial. That was an end to the threat, and Brainard was ultimately able to write to his family: *We hear that the indians want to settle the thing now, and that they have brought back the women that they took. I hope that they will make them pay dear for their bloody work.*

Chapter Twenty-Seven

One Year Gone

Their supper was done, the dishes washed and put away, and Edgar Lincoln was being put to bed by his mother. But the girls remained at the table, reflecting, in the soft lantern's glow, on the events of their day and the news from their father.

Ida May had been that day's courier – taking their latest letter to Brainard, written the night before, into Alba and returning with a new letter from him. Along the way home, under a sudden shower she really wasn't prepared for, she had lost her footing on one of the slippery rocks that normally provided a safe, dry passage across Beaver Creek. Into the water she had fallen, face down. She wasn't physically hurt, but not only had the tote bag of salt she had purchased been lost and all her clothes been splashed with mud, but the precious letter in her apron pocket had instantly become soaked.

She was quite a sight to behold when she arrived home twenty minutes later, by then even wetter than when she had fallen in. Although much of the stream's mud had been washed away by the continuing rain, Ida May was sure that the letter had suffered additional damage. That's what had brought on the flood of tears when she burst into the shanty and, without stopping, fled up the ladder to the loft and threw herself onto her bed – stream, mud, rain, and all – sobbing into her pillow.

Her sister and mother looked at each other in dismay. Nerva, hands and arms flour-covered as she kneaded today's bread baking, indicated with an upward swoop of her head to wordlessly direct Alice to go up and find out what had happened.

Standing on the top ladder rung, she whispered, "What is it, Ida May? What happened? Are you hurt?" As she waited for an answer, she surveyed her damp, distraught, and disheveled sister, and began to guess. "You got caught in the rain? Did you slip and fall?" She climbed up and sat down beside her, laying a calming hand on her back, and repeated, "What is it, Ida May?"

Her little sister's sobbing and shaking slowly began to subside. Finally, she turned over to face Alice and the anticipated consequences of her carelessness. After describing her misfortune-filled crossing of the creek, she drew out the letter. It was heavy and obviously as soaked as she was. "Losin' the salt was bad enough," she sniffed, "but this is the *worst* part," and she thrust the soggy envelope into her sister's hand, then buried her face in her pillow again.

"Oh, no!" escaped Alice's lips before realizing she might add to Ida May's distress. So she went on gently, "Well, let's see what we've got. P'raps it's not as bad inside as it looks from the outside." The envelope opened easily, and she pulled out a single large sheet of paper, folded in half, then again in thirds, and filled to the very end with the careful handwriting of their father. She opened it flat and laid it out on the quilt, saying, "Look, it's just damp, and the ink hasn't hardly run at all."

The excitement in her voice encouraged Ida May to rise up. "Really?" she sniffed.

"Truly. Listen, I'll read the start of it to show you, but then we've got to take it down to Ma."

Ida May sat up, wrapping her arms around her knees. After another sniff, she said, "What does Pa say?"

Focusing on the words of the damp letter, Alice began to read:

Camp in the mountains, near the middle gap, Aug 29, 1862

"My dear Wife and friends, as I have got a sheet of paper and a pen and ink, I will commence a letter to you, but I do not know when I can send it away as we are up in the Cumberland mountains. We have been without tents for about a week, but it has been very dry so we have got along very ..."

"Oh, the water's splotched the next word. It must be ... um ... 'well.' Yes, that's it." *"we have got along well so far. We are here for the purpose of preventing the rebel army from coming through the pass. We have a strong position here. We are camped upon a side hill in the woods, among the rocks. It is rumored that the rebels are making for Nashville, but if they undertake to come through here, we are ready to meet them ..."*

"He goes on, but see, the letter's fine. It's just the envelope that's ruined."

"You think Ma won't be mad?" asked Ida May.

"Course not, silly! She'll be glad you're not hurt ... and glad for the letter too. Say, I know a trick we can play that'll earn us a laugh. Maybe that'll help. See, I'll take down the envelope and explain how it got all wet and muddy. She'll start to get upset. Then you come down with the letter ... and when she sees it, she'll be so glad we'll *all* get to laugh about it. What do you say?"

The plan cheered her up, so she stayed behind for a moment while her sister took the envelope down to show their mother.

"Law me, what's that child gone and done now?" Nerva began when she laid eyes on the soggy mess Alice held out to her.

But before Alice could explain what had happened, Ida May appeared, carefully holding the top of the letter itself in her outstretched hands. Taking it, and turning it back and forth, Nerva could see immediately that it was not ruined after all. She set it down on the table and, laughing just as Alice had predicted, pulled her young daughter to her. "Looks like you an' that envelope got the worst of it, Ida May."

"And . . . the salt."

"Salt?"

Alice hadn't gotten that far in her telling, so she quickly finished the story.

"Well, never you mind, Ida May. At least you're all right, an' that's all that really counts. You can go back for more tomorrow if your heart wants to. For now, why don't you run up an' change, then let's sit together and read out this here letter from your pa. As for you, Alice Jane, next time you go fishin' maybe we won't have to salt your catch!"

***

The next morning, Nerva erupted with a "Land sakes alive!" and a slap to her forehead, as she and the children finished up their breakfast. The girls looked up puzzled. "Nearly got past me!" she continued. "Tomorrow's special. Know why?" She turned her glance back and forth between her daughters. The two girls looked blankly at each other. Both shrugged and raised their palms to indicate they didn't.

"Well, what was a'happenin' at this time a year ago?"

Alice had started taking a pile of breakfast dishes to the sink, but returned with them to stare in thought again at her sister. Ida May's exaggerated "I'm trying to remember" pose directed her left hand to her chin, fingers spread across her mouth.

"A year ago . . ." began Alice, then questioned, "Oh, is tomorrow the day Pa left us for the war?"

"That's it," her mother smiled. "Today's the twenty-fourth, an' tomorrow'll be one year to the day that he left us to walk up to Chatfield."

"Pa, Pa? Gone?" chimed in Edgar Lincoln.

"That's right, little brother. And I remember that day *real* clear," Ida May added with a wistful sigh generated by a flood of remembered images from the day.

The room grew quiet again for a moment, Nerva holding her husband's picture, and Alice staring out the kitchen window – both, like Ida May, lost in their memories of that day and what had transpired since.

Edgar looked from face to face, wondering what had happened to the three of them. Unable to understand, he left them to their quietude and headed for his floor toys.

It was their mother who broke the spell. "What a year it's been, both for him an' us. So, what should we do to kinda celebrate this anniversary tomorrow?"

Ida May's face brightened. "We could read all of his letters again, couldn't we, to remember all he's done . . . and . . . and . . ."

Alice supplied the other half of the plan: "And we could try to list out everything we've done, and the places we've gone, and the folks we've seen. It would sort of be like what Pa did in his letters to us."

"Sounds just right to me," Nerva affirmed. "Soon's all our chores 're done tomorrow, I'll get out that packet o' letters. We'll start back at the beginnin', and whilst we're a'readin' 'em, we'll try to remember all we were a'doin' when each letter came."

"How can we include Edgar Lincoln?" Alice's question brought him toddling over to the table, as he thought they were calling him.

Running her fingers through the long blond curls that covered his head, her mother replied, "We can tell some o' the things like stories to him. P'raps he'll remember 'em better that way. Won't stay interested for long, I s'pose, so we'll just haveta let 'im go. Well, if you young'uns can leave me be for a spell, I'd like to write your pa today, as it sounds like I won't have the time to do it tomorrow. So, Ida May, you take care of your brother whilst Alice does up the dishes an' sweeps out the shanty."

Ida May stood up, stomped a foot and burst out, "Why is it always *me* that takes care of him? Why can't Alice do it today?"

"If you want to do the dishes and sweep up as good as I can, I don't care," volunteered Alice. "I'll *gladly* switch with you."

Nerva was ready to affirm the change in chores when Ida May complained once more. "But I wanted to play with my doll, not my brother." The pout was plain in both the tone of her voice and the thrust of her chin.

"You can do that, my love, after my letter to your pa is done. But for now, you must choose Edgar Lincoln or dishes and sweepin'." Her words, though gentle, were tight with firmness and a bit of frustration.

Ida May reluctantly chose to take charge of her brother, and drug herself across the room to join him on the floor. As Alice busied herself with her two tasks, Nerva gathered paper, pen, inkwell, and envelope, and sat down at the table, her back to the children so she could concentrate on what she wanted to write.

***

September 25, 1862

Beloved Brainard,

Rec'd three letters from you since last I wrote. It does us all such good to hear from you each time, esp. to hear you are still alive and well. Were all well here, cept if you was here we would be better. And thank you for the money you send, for it all goes to Mr Peters for what we need to buy. The children have give me a bit of time to write. They are so good and grown up so fast you wouldnt believe.

It was right a year ago you left us. Were holdin on without you, but sometimes it seems only by a string. Course we know the marchin an battles an such are harder on you. A whole year now. How much longer do you think it will be?

Jery Nichols has stopped by to chat. Had lots of stories bout the war an all. Said you was holdin up purty good, but it was just to much for body an soul for him to be away. His missus is mighty happy, but I think I could beat her ifn it was you that was home.

Winter aint to far away now. Do you think theres things folks here should be makin to send for the soldiers? Praps mittens or socks or such like? Dont know what to do bout firewood. Piles almost gone. Who should I ask, and how much will it set me back? Otherwise Ive been studyin movin in with Mary for the winter. What do you think of that?

Last week I sold Rosy to Mr Partch she was dry anyway. Wont have her to worry bout this winter and her price covered almost half what you owed him, so thats good. Corns most about run out, but all the pigs are already plump. Im sure Mr Peters will buy em for butcherin, so that will ease up the barn chores. Oh, Mr Hill announced he will be aleavin us next month as hes to get married. Imagine that, Mr hill at his age. Onliest other news round here is Mary's Em got hisself promoted to Corp. She thinks thats just grand. Any chance of that for you?

One other thing I wanted to tell you, an this'll bust you right open. Last week I left the ladder up against the front porch as a small pine branch blew down on the roof in night wind. After getting it down an draggin it away, I came back to fetch the ladder and bless me there sat your Edgar Lincoln atop the roof! The little scamp had clumb up by hisself an was asittin up there so proud at what hed done. You better believe my heart stopped. Up I went as fast as ever I could to fetch him down safe. Gave him a right good scoldin but then I held him tight.

My papers full an the girls are astartin to ask when Ill be done, so I will close for now an seal this up with all our love. Please take good care of yourself cause we want you home.

Im sending you a letter I got from your sisters.

Minerva Griffin

As soon as Alice finished her assigned chores, she hurried up to the loft to pen a note to add to her mother's letter. It was short, but she hoped it would make her pa happy. She wanted him to know she had been thinking about all she could remember from the day he had left. Because her mother was still writing when Alice came down, she laid her folded note where her mother would see it, and joined her siblings on the floor.

***

The next morning was clear but cold, and it wasn't long before Ida May had tended to the chickens, Alice had done up the breakfast dishes and brought in enough stove wood for the day, and Nerva had taken care of the remaining barn animals. A happy anticipation for what lay ahead filled the household as mother retrieved the precious ribbon-wrapped bundle of letters from her dresser, and the children gathered around the table – Edgar Lincoln upon Alice's lap – for a special time of remembering.

Ida May started it by asking, "Alice, where did you find me a year ago today?"

Alice laughed. "Up in the hayloft, silly! Trying to hide from today! And what did we do with Pa before he left?"

Her answer was delayed a bit, as Ida May needed to think. "Oh, I remember. We walked arm-in-arm all 'round the farm, checkin' everything." She then turned to her brother, "Oh, Edgar Lincoln, you should have seen how fast I could run up to the top of the woodlot hill to be the last one to wave Pa goodbye!"

"Pa? He gone! To war!" she got in reply.

So it continued, and Nerva's eyes glowed with pleasure at the fun her daughters were having with that otherwise painful day. Finally she broke in, "Is it time for the first letter? I want both of you to remember what you did the day it arrived."

***

They spent the entire day – with a noontime sandwich break – reading all fifty-two letters they had received during the year past, and enjoying the retelling of all the adventures they could remember. There were a few tears now and then, some from exuberant laughter, others from reexperiencing painful things. Edgar Lincoln didn't last

238

long before becoming bored, but throughout the day he briefly left his floor play to rejoin his family's circle.

For supper, Nerva suggested they enjoy one of Brainard's favorite meals: vegetable soup with corn doggers, and apple pie for dessert. While Ida May entertained Edgar Lincoln by retelling a few of the day's stories, Alice helped her mother pare and cut the root vegetables brought up from their cellar. She also set the dried apple slices to soak while her mother mixed and rolled out the crusts for the pie.

The shanty soon was filled with both the savory aroma of the simmering herb-spiced soup and the cinnamon-sweet smell of the baking pie. Long before either was cooked, all four Griffins were very ready to eat.

The soup pot was eventually carried to the set table, and the previous day's baking of corn doggers brought out, along with a large pat of the last of their butter and glasses of freshly drawn water. They gathered their small circle of held hands, bowed their heads, and all that remained was the blessing.

"Dear Father in Heaven," Nerva began, "on this remembering day we give thee thanks, for this here food and for our family. Bless this food, and us together, but more 'specially bless the husband and father who isn't with us. Please keep him safe from all harm, wherever he is, and bring him back to us afore another year passes, for like he wrote to us, 'this war has been carried on about long enough.' This we all pray, amen."

A chorus of "amens" echoed her conclusion as they all sat down to eat the day's-end meal.

Chapter Twenty-Eight

Another Guest, Another Likeness

Ida May was breathless as she burst through the door of the shanty. "Ma, didn't Pa write somethin' about a Mr. Douglass acomin' home an' stoppin' by with some money for us?" She leaned her head forward in expectation.

"Why, yes, love. I believe he did. That letter we got last week. Why do you ask?"

"Cause there's a soldier acomin' up our lane, an' it might be him!"

"You don't say! Well, let's go see who 'tis." And with that, Nerva put down the stack of washed clothing she was putting away, and mother and daughter went out to the porch and shaded their eyes to peer at the approaching figure. They could readily tell by his mud-spattered blue uniform that he was, indeed, a Union soldier. But he was still too far down the pathway for them to recognize who he was.

The soldier noticed them on the porch's top step, so he stopped and raised his kepi cap in a friendly way, then called out, "Hello, Miz Griffin, it's me, Tom Douglass."

Those shouted words drew Alice and Edgar Lincoln out of the barn, where they had been playing up in the hayloft. With a gnawing fear of bad news, Alice led her brother across to the porch, joining Nerva and Ida May. "Is that Pa's friend?" she whispered.

"Appears to be," her mother replied. "Why don't you girls put the tea things out whilst your brother and I traipse down to meet him?" Taking Edgar Lincoln's hand, she started down the lane to welcome the son of their close neighbors. She knew he would have news of the war and of her beloved husband, which, for the moment, was far more important than the forty dollars Brainard had said Tom would be carrying to them.

Tom removed his cap again as they approached and presented them a wide, boyish grin. His face was tanned, his hair disheveled, and his uniform both worn and dirty, but Nerva knew the grin was sincere.

"Welcome home, Tom Douglass! Been to your folks yet?"

"No, ma'am. Headin' there now. But I promised Mr. Griffin I'd stop by on my way. Say, this here must be the young Edgar Lincoln he's always a'talkin' about. Proud, too, an' I can see why."

"Yep, this is his son," Nerva said as she reached her arm across the young boy's shoulders. "Well, you're most about home, but come in for a spell and rest yourself a bit afore you continue on." With that, she turned and led him up the path to their shanty.

The girls had returned to the porch, and they politely welcomed Tom when he finally arrived. They offered him tea, but he declined, explaining that he wanted to cover the remaining six miles to his parent's farm as quickly as he could.

"But I do have somethin' for you, Miz Griffin," he said, taking out the well-crumpled letter he had promised to deliver. "An' I can tell you straight out that your man is as well as a spring chicken. Loves what he's a'doin' and loves the boys he's a'doin' it with. Can't say the same for myself, but . . . guess that's why he's there an' I'm here."

"Lordy, Lordy, bless you, Tom Douglass, for stoppin' by with this here letter an' your welcome news 'bout my Brainard. Come back sometime, if you've a mind to, an' set awhile an' tell us stories of what's been happenin' in the war. An' be so kind, if you will, to give our best wishes to your ma an' pa when you get home."

"I'll do both, Miz Griffin. An' you take care, you hear? Mr. Griffin wouldn't want to come home to find you all run down or somethin' else bad."

Nerva drew the three children in close as he waved his good-bye, and together they watched as he resumed his long journey from the war's front to his boyhood home. After only a few moments, Ida May expressed the family's longing: "Let's go in and read the letter from Pa he brought!"

At their table, Nerva opened the envelope after reading aloud its address and slipped out the folded letter. Two twenty-dollar bills lay in the middle when she unfolded it, causing the three children to clap – Edgar Lincoln imitating the response of his sisters. "Forty dollars! Think o' that! Just like he promised. Oh, your pa, young'uns, is such a *fine* man."

Before reading it all to them, in case there were things she needed to edit, Nerva skimmed over its contents to highlight things for them they would find special. "Well, he says he's gettin' our letters all right, so that's good . . . an' glad to know we're a'gettin' along first-rate here . . . has some stuff I'll read you 'bout marchin' an' all with thousands o' troops . . . oh, your Uncle Henry from Vermont has now enlisted . . . other family news of folks you don't know back there . . . Mercy, he says he went into Nashville an' had his likeness taken, so's we could see what he looks like, now he's been gone a year!" She looked up at the children. "Won't that be grand to see! Wonder when we'll get it?" As she finished scanning the letter she added, "Oh, listen to how he closes."

"I cannot write any more tonight. It is past nine o'clock, and the wind flares the candle, for my "house" is not very tight. When I get up in the morning my blanket is wet through with the dew. Well, I must bid you all a good bye and go to bed again hoping that it will not be long before we shall see each other again."

They all sat in silence for a few moments, then Nerva returned to the letter's beginning and with a warmed heart read it all the way through to her listening children.

***

At the end of the week, Nerva sent Alice to Alba for some needed baking supplies. After making her purchase, Mr. Peters handed her a small, flat package. "'Tain't justa letter this time, Miss Alice," he said. "Must be somethin' special. My regards to your ma, please."

As she walked briskly home, Alice couldn't be sure what it was her father had sent them but she had a guess and a growing hope that it was his likeness. Several times she patted the package she had tucked in her apron pocket beside the starter yeast and seasonings requested by her mother, and each time she whispered to herself: *It's him . . . I know it's him!*

She drew the things out as soon as she entered the shanty, announcing, "Here's your baking things, Ma, and also something from Pa. It's a package of something."

Ida May left off playing with her brother and approached her sister with an enthusiastic "From Pa?"

"Wonder what it is this time," their mother said, remembering the mussel shell rings he had made and sent them the month before, but hoping it was what she really longed for. Taking the starter yeast and seasonings in one hand and the package in the other, she kissed Alice on the forehead and added, "Well, let's find out."

She let Alice cut the string and unwrap the heavy wrapping paper. Inside, a folded letter enclosed a very thick rectangular card. When Alice turned it over, she gasped and held up a picture of her father. He appeared long haired and fully bearded, wearing his dress Union jacket, and stared directly but somberly at them. It was printed on paper, instead of glass as his likeness the year before from Fort Snelling had been. She passed the picture to her sister and the letter to her mother.

After glancing over Ida May's shoulder at the image of the man she dearly loved and sorely missed, Nerva took it to study its details closer. Then she handed it back, unfolded his letter and read the narrative of his regimental skirmishes and the large gathering of Union forces around Nashville.

The girls listened intently to their father's words as he described being without a change of clothes for a long stretch, and not even being able to wash the ones they had, and how it seemed to him not much progress was being made toward ending the war, though the marching, picketing, and skirmishing continued for his regiment.

There were two passages, however, that elicited their response, requiring Nerva to read each one a second time, then allow them an opportunity to talk about what he had said.

The first was his observation:

"There is not a great deal of sickness in the regiment just now, but it is reduced down one half since we left Minn. one year ago. What will it be one year from now if the war lasts that long?"

"Why is Pa's regiment now only half?" Ida May asked. "What's happened to the rest of the soldiers?"

"Sickness, o'course. That's what he's talkin' about. You remember Jerry Nichols an' Tom Douglass, come home? Others I s'pose in hospitals nearby. And some . . . killed in battle or captured prisoners . . . you know that."

"Does that make Pa in more danger than before? With fewer men to fight . . ." Alice sought her mother's reassurance, to quell a new level of fear.

"Can't imagine why, Alice. You know how your pa's always talkin' about loads of new men getting added in. I do believe he's as safe now as he ever was. An' that's what all of us has gotta do— believe he's safe and comin' home one day."

The second passage they discussed was his emotional response to Nerva's last letter, written on the anniversary of his departure. He said:

"As I lay down to sleep that night, with the stars shining in my face, as clear as ever they did in a cold winter night, my thoughts turned homeward, to my wife and children, of the many happy hours we have spent together. I wondered whether we should ever spend any more happy days and hours together. I knew well that you were thinking of me that night. We shall probably long remember that night, if we are permitted to live in the enjoyment of each others presence and comforts on this earth again, and I believe that we shall, some time, but how soon we cannot tell.

As you wrote, it is a horrible thing (war), whether the rebels in the South, or the Indians in the North. I cannot bear to think of it!

"Why's there war everywhere, Ma, instead of the happy days together Pa writes about?"

"Can't answer that, Alice, any more'an I can tell you when things'll be back right again. Your pa believes – an' I believe – that time's ahead for us. War is just war, horrible like he says. But it ends. Count on that."

Later that evening, after the children were all asleep, Nerva picked up her husband's new photograph, moved the settle closer to the fire, and spent a few quiet moments ruminating: *He looks so sober . . . an' older. Wonder if he feels older? Bet he'd like to see what we look like, him a year gone. The children have all growed so much. Guess it's close to time to move in with Mary. Firewood's almost gone. Sorghum crop all dried up . . . lost, unlike my father's . . . so's there no molasses to have to make this year. Plenty o' hay an' oats for feed, but all them animals are such hard work 'thout him. Better to sell 'em all. An' there's still the Indians to worry 'bout too, us out here alone. We'll surely be a help an' comfort to each other. P'raps we could get our likenesses done there in Spring Valley to send to him. Wouldn't he love that! Yes, I should write her today, an' Brainard, too. See what they both think about us amovin . . .*

Minerva got out her writing supplies and spent the last hour of her day addressing her thoughts twice, to both her sister and her husband, and requested their responses to help her decide for sure.

Chapter Twenty-Nine

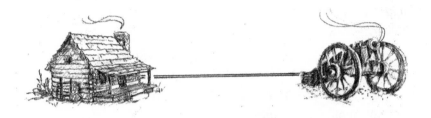

Move to Spring Valley

"Ma, are you still thinking about us all going up to Spring Valley to live with Aunt Mary?" Alice asked one early November afternoon when she arrived back from school.

"I'm still a'ponderin' it, yes. There a reason behind your question?"

"No, not really. I was just thinking about what it would be like, going to school up there. Wouldn't have any friends. Wouldn't even *know* anybody . . ."

The idea of moving to Spring Valley, at least for this second winter with Brainard away, had actually been mentioned several times in the correspondence between Nerva and Brainard, as well as between Nerva and her sister. There wasn't any disagreement between them because of the obvious advantages: shared housing during the deep-cold Minnesota winter; a safer place for the Griffins instead of being alone on the prairie; and at the town's larger school, Ida May would be able to start attending. The only question was when to make the move. They would have to sell off all their livestock, and her father or brother would need to stop by occasionally to check on the place, but the only real disadvantage concerned the probable toll the harsh winter would have on the abandoned shanty.

Winter's gettin' here fast, Nerva acknowledged to herself, as she thought about her answer to Alice's question. *Guess we'd better make our move a'fore it sets in. I'd best ask Allen if he can spare the time to help us.*

Turning back to her daughter, she consoled, "I'm sorry 'bout that, Alice dear. But you'll make friends fast enough. You *know* everybody likes you. That's nothin' for you to worry an' stew about. Let's talk about it over supper tonight."

"Oh, I'm not afraid about moving. It's all right with me. I was just wondering what it would be like."

***

During their evening meal the agreement to move was quickly made, and the conversation turned to talking through what all would need to be done.

"I'm writin' Aunt Mary tonight to tell her we're a'comin' for sure. Whilst I'm a'doin' that, I want you to start a'gatherin' up the clothes an' school things and such, all you'll need to take for the winter there. I'll start on that for little Edgar an' me soon's I'm done writin' Mary."

"What about the animals, Ma? What'll we do with them?" Alice inquired, standing with Ida May at the base of their loft ladder.

"Oh, well. What I've been a'thinkin' is I'll stop over to Grampa's on my way home from Alba. P'raps he'll take 'em all. I can also ask him an' Allen if they can help us move and then look in on our place whilst we're gone. We'll work somethin' out. I also should stop by Mr. Partch's place to see 'bout how to settle up what's left on that debt to him. Your pa bought some farm equipment from him just before he left. For now, I'll write Mary if one of you can look after your brother till it's bedtime."

The girls decided to take turns, one minding Edgar Lincoln while the other one began laying out things to pack. And Nerva got out her writing things to compose the letter she would take to the post office in the morning.

***

Nerva was feeling elated when she arrived back at the shanty early the next afternoon with everything settled. Not only had there been another letter from Brainard waiting for her, but Mr. Peters was eager to take charge of fattening the last of their pigs as he always had ready buyers for the meat. And when she got to her father's farm her luck doubled again, for while her mother wanted to take their full lot of chickens to add to her little flock, who should be visiting her father but Mr. Partch, and he was willing to take the young oxen pair, Dime and Duke, to cover that debt. To top it off, Allen had offered a farm wagon and his company as driver for their move up to Mary's. They even agreed on two days hence for the date, which would be time enough for the family to finish packing.

The children were playing in the barn when Ol' Jim pulled Nerva up the lane. She called to them and they stepped aside so she could drive her buggy right in. "Looks like you're a'havin' a heap o' fun," she laughed.

"We are, Ma," responded Alice. "We're taking turns hiding Ida May's cornhusk doll."

"Well, I've got some more fun for you here," Nerva said as she waved the letter. "Good news from your pa. An' more good news 'bout our move. Alice, would you help me unhitch Ol' Jim?"

"Come on, little brother, I'll race you into the shanty!" Ida May invited, and off they ran, though she was playful enough to let him win. It wasn't long before Nerva and Alice joined them around the woodstove, shedding jackets and warming their hands.

"What does Pa say?" inquired Ida May.

"And what's that news about our move?" added Alice.

"Land sakes, I'm gonna read the letter to you – I'll do that over supper – but he's safe and well, an' happy to hear from us. Says he wants to come home an' roll around on the floor with you young'uns again. Oh, isn't this perfect? Says he wants us to have our likenesses taken so's he can look at us now an' then to cheer hisself up, and says next time he'll write to us in Spring Valley 'cause he reckons that's where we'll be. Now, as for the rest of my day, everythin's set – ever last thing – animals, farm, an' Uncle Allen to drive us. An' you'd never guess who just happened to be a'visiting Grampa—Mr. Partch! Didn't even have to go to his place 'cause he was right there, and we worked it out for him to take young Duke an' Dime to cover the debt. Isn't that all good news?"

"All you didn't say was when." Alice's eyes swept the room, taking in all the things that still needed packing, whether for taking or for storage.

"Day after tomorrow, love," Nerva answered, "which means we've got a lot of work yet ahead of us to be ready by then. But I know both of you'll be a big help to me in that, startin' this very night." She was disheartened when she saw the petulant frown on Ida May's face. "What is it, Ida May?"

"Do we have to start tonight? I wanted to play with my doll . . . upstairs . . . alone . . ."

"You've had most of the day already to play!" It came out sharper than she intended, but Nerva needed both daughters' full cooperation. Softer this time, she explained: "Hard winter's almost here. We've got to get up there a'fore it comes. It'll be day after next, so all of us have gotta help as much as we can. That's you, too. Understand?"

Ida May hung her head and reluctantly nodded. "Yes, Ma," was all she answered before she turned and retreated up the loft ladder to finish gathering into one small pile the clothes she needed to take, while also putting all of her other things away in her dresser drawer.

Alice, meanwhile, was putting away in cupboards and drawers everything she didn't think they'd need to take to Spring Valley. She also kept up a watchful chatter with her brother, freeing her mother to prepare, and eventually serve, their evening meal.

By the time they sat down to eat, Ida May's mood had swung enough toward anticipating the move that she could actually enjoy her mother's letter reading and tale telling – which made the evening far more pleasant for all.

***

Packing up didn't turn out to be as hard as they expected, for they were only taking some bedding, their winter clothes, and half the edibles already harvested and stored. Mary had previously assured them she could provide everything else they would need, like furniture and cooking utensils. The rest of their things would stay behind for their return in the spring. So when Allen arrived a day later with the wagon, they were ready to load up and go.

"Ida May," Nerva called out, "were you able to bring down those two bundles of you girls's clothes?"

"Yes, Ma. Weren't heavy at all. There they are behind your dresser," she said, pointing to the back of her grandfather's farm wagon. "See 'em?"

"Oh, yes. And Alice, dear, did you finish bringing up all the cellar things I pointed out to you last night?"

"Almost done, Ma. Two more trips I think—the last of the jugs, if Uncle Allen still has room."

"Looks like it. Bring 'em up. Guess they'll fit right here by the tailgate just fine."

Allen walked back to the porch after securing the doors of the now-empty barn. He was carrying two wiggling tow sacks, which contained the chickens for his mother. "Are we 'bout ready?" he asked as he checked the harnesses of the wagon's pair of horses. He was to drive their load of things to Spring Valley, while his sister and her children traveled in their buggy drawn by Ol' Jim.

All of them were glad as they climbed aboard that the early November day was dry and not too cold, for bad weather would have made for a miserable trip. Ida May had already helped Edgar Lincoln into the buggy when Alice emerged with the final two jugs. Allen took them, placed them snug in the remaining corner, slapped

251

up the tailgate, and headed for the wagon seat as Alice climbed into her place on the other side of Edgar Lincoln. Nerva was securing the latch on the shanty's door when all of a sudden Ida May gave a cry of despair, jumped down from the buggy, and ran up to the porch.

"What'ers the matter, Ida May?"

"Oh, Ma, I forgot my doll! It's what Pa *made* me! It's still on the bed!"

"Sakes alive, child, go an' fetch it. We'll wait. An' then we'll be off."

Once inside, Ida May was up the ladder as quickly as a frightened cat. There in the middle of their bed sat her cornhusk doll, waiting to be remembered. She grabbed her father's parting gift, raced down the ladder, and arrived out of breath back to the buggy.

Nerva secured the door this time, then climbed in with her brood. Reins in hand, she nodded to her brother, and they set off.

Their first stop was at the post office. She had only intended to request that Mr. Peters forward their mail to Mary's house, but was pleased that he handed her another letter from Brainard as well. Mr. Peters wished them well, and promised to look in on their homestead whenever he happened to be close by. "Now, you take care, Minerva Griffin," he said in farewell. "An' we'll all plan on seein' you back come springtime."

A second stop, just as brief, was at her parents' farm to pick up the basket lunch her mother had promised to make for their day-long journey. Allen got down and carried the sacks of chickens over to release them among his mother's hens, and the three children got down to stretch their legs a bit. Nerva had barely reached the front door when her father threw it open to greet them. From behind him, Hellen and Eliza hurried out to see their cousins, and her mother emerged, napkin-covered basket in hand. "So, it's up to Mary's with you," Almon Griffin said, drawing his daughter into the house for a moment.

Taking the basket from Polly and smiling her thanks, Nerva collected her thoughts before answering. "Yes, Pa. Closed the shanty up as tight as we could. Got most of what we'll need packed into the wagon. Mary's house is small, but we'll make do. Girls'll be a great help with little Hattie. An' the boys'll keep each other . . . busy." She and her parents all laughed at her last word, then she finished, "Was so good of Mary to offer."

Her parents nodded through her recitation, then mother reached for daughter and whispered, "You won't be so far away. Come back to see us if'n winter permits. Just so's we can know all is well." Backing up, but still holding on, Polly smiled, nodded in her motherly way, then let go her daughter's hand to move beside her husband.

As Nerva turned to leave, her father added his own farewell. "Your ma an' me, we'll miss you. But with Mary, you'll be all right. So . . ." was all he could get out without choking.

The good-byes of the four girls went easier. Hugs around, mixed with the gaiety of this new adventure, and they were ready to part. Eliza kissed the wiggling Edgar Lincoln as she passed him up, and, even though he was still too young to understand the significance of what they were doing, urged his mother, "Le's go, Ma!" Allen remounted the loaded wagon, while Nerva climbed back aboard the buggy and settled in to concentrate on the journey ahead.

The miles passed uneventfully. The weather held clear, and their lunch stop was almost like a summer picnic. Along the way, Alice and Ida May played guessing games with each other, their brother mostly slept, and their mother and uncle, traveling side-by-side as often as possible, kept up a running conversation about Brainard's and Emory's war experiences. Thus they came that evening to their final stop, in front of the Jefferson Street home rented by the Durands.

***

Mary had prepared a single room for her sister's family – the only space she could spare – but it was large enough for them to sleep in. It had two beds to share, an extra dresser to make room for all their clothing, and a small desk by the window for writing, reading, and schoolwork. "This'll do just fine," Nerva assured Mary after Allen had helped her bring in all their things.

While the adult sisters unpacked, the young girls took over the care of ten-month-old Harriet, called Hattie; and the boys, Edgar Lincoln and his slightly older cousin Louis Lincoln, began the gleeful tumbling and chasing that would occupy most of their time together over the following months.

Chapter Thirty

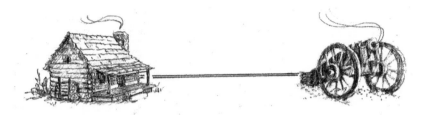

School and Images

"Have you got your school satchels ready? Let me see how you look." Nerva wanted one last check before she walked her girls to the town's school to enroll them.

Ida May had been particularly fidgety over breakfast. Her Aunt Mary, attempting to corral the young girl's hair into beribboned pigtails, had repeatedly fussed, "How can I get these ribbons into your hair if you don't sit still?" It would be, after all, her very first day of school.

And Alice had been complaining all morning about having to wear the same dress as her little sister. "We look like twins! Can't I have my *own* clothes sometime?"

"We can talk 'bout that when you get home tonight. Got a couple ideas already, but we don't have time now. Both of you, now, let me see you."

The two stood before her, each with her satchel in hand containing two pencils, a bound sheaf of paper, and a small lunch of bread, cheese, and an apple. Alice's also had a penknife for sharpening the pencils and her copy of *McGuffey's Reader*. They were wearing the matching new dark calico dresses with pocketed pinafores Nerva had recently sewn for them, and about which Alice had expressed her displeasure. Both were still rosy-cheeked from their early morning washing in Mary's tin bathtub. Fondly tucking in a few wispy curls that had escaped from Ida May's hair ribbons, their mother pronounced them "Perfect!"

Left unspoken was *How I wish their pa was here, though. He'd be mighty tickled to see his two girls off to school together. Oh, Brainard, we do miss you, an' you're a'missin' so much here!* What Nerva couldn't know was that those same longings were weighing in her daughters' hearts.

"We'll be off then, Mary," she said to her sister as she ushered the girls toward the door where their winter coats hung. "I'll be back soon to help you with little Hattie. An' thank you for watchin' over Edgar Lincoln whilst I'm gone."

"Oh, the boys'll look after theirselves, I 'spect," Mary laughed. She picked up her daughter from her crib and walked behind them to the door. "I hope you girls have a wonderful first day," she called to Alice and Ida May as they set out. Then she added, "An' don't you worry none 'bout your Edgar Lincoln, Minerva. I'll keep a good eye on 'em both. You take as long as you need at school, an' arrangin' downtown for your likenesses to get taken."

"Bless you," Nerva called back, joining the farewell waves from her daughters. After enrolling the girls, the plan she had discussed with Mary was to schedule a sitting with L.A. Kingsbury, the photographer down on Main Street. She wanted to send their likenesses to Brainard as soon as possible, for it had meant so much to them to receive his likeness the few weeks before. She had always felt insecure and apologetic about her writing skills, but likenesses – their likenesses – how that would thrill Brainard and cheer his day! She smiled to herself at that thought as they walked to school.

***

"You must be the Griffins, I believe. Heard you'd moved up here, and was hoping you'd start with us right away." The genial balding man who welcomed them was the schoolmaster, Mr. W. L. Kellogg.

Hum, mused Nerva. *Kellogg – that's a family name on Brainard's side. Wonder if we're kin? Wouldn't that be special!* "Yes, sir, I'm Minerva Griffin, an' these here are my daughters, Alice Jane and Ida May." She stepped behind them so he could see them better. "Moved up here from Alba to share housing with my sister, Mary Durand, whilst both our husbands are off to war."

"We're very glad to have you. Alice and Ida May did you say?" Both girls nodded. "My name's Mr. Kellogg. I'll be your schoolmaster." He turned to Nerva. "Have they had schooling before?"

"Alice has done two years back at Alba, an' Ida May's just set to start. But Alice has been a'helpin' her along at home all that time, so she might be just a bit ahead."

Reaching out to shake Nerva's hand, Mr. Kellogg replied, "We can take care of the particulars later, but I'll go ahead and write them in for now." He was obviously referring to the monthly cost of school. Turning to the girls, he added, "We're about ready to start, so why don't we go in and I'll introduce you around?" And with that warm welcome the Griffin girls began their new school adventures.

Nerva bit her lower lip as the girls made their good-byes and Mr. Kellogg led them inside, leaving her alone on the school's front porch. She hurried away from those gathering emotions by heading downtown on her other errand.

She found Mr. Kingsbury's shop at the corner of Broad and Main, and entered to meet the tall, angular photographer, who had been highly recommended by George Wilder, the local grocer. Fashionably dressed, with curls that cascaded to his shoulders, his warm smile accompanied a multiringed hand that was instantly out to welcome her into his studio.

She was impressed. And it took little time for her questions to be explained and for an appointment to be made for the following Saturday.

As she started for home, Nerva decided to make one more stop. This was at the post office, housed – like back in Alba – in Mr. Wilder's store. "Good Morning, Mr. Smith," Nerva greeted the postmaster. "I was wonderin' if'n you've got any mail for me or Mary today?"

"Matter of fact, I do," he replied as he turned to the nest of boxes that filled the corner wall space of the store. "One for you. Here 'tis. From your man. Posted up from Alba. From Bowling Green, Kentucky, looks like," and he handed her the letter. "Nothin' for Mary from Emory. Nope, not today."

She paused to glance over the letter, planning to read it aloud as always when the girls got home. The line from him that really jumped off the page for its accuracy stated:

"I hope that you will have a good time with Mary. It seems as though you would be as thick as three in a bed, so you will have to be much the more pleasant."

She laughed to herself as she thought, *If he could only see how cozy we all are. But we can make it pleasant enough for all. Oh, what a special day this has turned out to be. My girls both at school. Time to get our likenesses taken. An' to top it off, a letter from you, Brainard. You're not here, o'course, but your words'll connect us again just the same!* Her step home was much lighter than her step had been when the day began.

***

"Alice, have you ever had your likeness taken?" Ida May asked the following Saturday morning as they dressed for breakfast. Their appointment at the photographer's shop was for 10 a.m., and she wanted to know what to expect.

"No, silly. 'Course not. Same as you. Why?" Alice put her hairbrush down and tied pink ribbons to secure her pigtails.

"What's he gonna do? What do we gotta do?" The apprehension in her words expressed the nervousness she was feeling about the unknown procedure as she ran her fingers through the short curls at the back of her head.

"All I know is, he'll have his camera, an' we sit in front of it, an' . . . an' we can't move a bit while he does it, or it'll ruin the picture." She patted her sister's arm reassuringly.

"But how does it work?"

"I have no idea. Maybe he'll show us."

"Do you s'pose Ma could go first? So's we could watch an' see?"

Alice stood up. "I reckon so. If you're ready, let's go ask her."

Their mother was already out in Mary's parlor, holding Edgar Lincoln on her lap to keep him clean, waiting to go. Like her daughters, she was dressed in her "Sunday Best" black dress that was topped at the neck with a lace collar, while her son was wearing the customary light-green boy's gown, patterned with small white flowers. His still-blond hair was combed into ridges of curls atop and along both sides of his head.

Nerva readily agreed to their request that she go first, understanding at once their uncertainty in this new experience. She hadn't had her likeness taken either, but was more aware of what to expect. She also knew that if Brainard could do it, so could she.

Mary joined them, holding Louis Lincoln back, as he was raring for his cousin to get down and begin their daily fun. "Not now," she explained. "Edgar Lincoln's goin' away with his ma an' sisters for a bit. But he'll be back soon. Then you can play."

The Griffins walked quickly through the cold but dry air of that November morning. It was only a few blocks to the Artistic Photographer Studio, and Mr. Kingsbury had all his equipment prepared for them when they arrived.

"Edgar Lincoln an' I'll go first," Nerva volunteered, so he led them to the low-backed chair he had set up in front of a plain canvas backdrop lit by the morning sun streaming through his studio's front window. His imposing black-hooded camera sat atop a wooden tripod, ready to work its magic.

She sat down, with Edgar Lincoln drawn in close on her lap. The young boy watched Mr. Kingbury intently as he adjusted the camera's lens from beneath the hood, then slid the chemical covered wet-plate into the slot at the camera's back, and redraped the hood over his head.

"Steady now," he cautioned, "You *must* hold still for the count of three."

Philinda Minerva and Edgar Lincoln Griffin (taken in Spring Valley, MN, November 1862)

Edgar Lincoln peered silently at the camera, but despite his mother's repetition of Mr. Kingsbury's warning, he turned to look up at her when the photographer removed the lens cover and counted, "one, two, three," before replacing the cover.

"Well, that one won't do. Got the back of the little one's head. Won't satisfy his pa at all. Let's try it again, Miz Griffin. And this time, son, just look at the camera's eye, 'cause it's a'lookin' at you!"

Alice Jane and Ida May Griffin, received by their father, December 1862

The second exposure worked much better. But even though Edgar Lincoln kept his eyes focused on the camera's eye, he fidgeted his fingers a bit – not enough, however to require a second retake.

Off to the side, Alice and Ida May had watched it all. Now that it was their turn, the questions – except how it worked – were gone. A second chair was added, and each girl sat down. "I want you to cross your hands in your laps," Mr. Kingsbury instructed, "and look straight into the camera's lens." He repeated the preparatory process as before, keeping up a light chatter of information so they would understand what he was doing. When all was ready, he uncovered the lens, counted to three again, then replaced the lens cover, leaving their solemn young faces clearly recorded on the glass plate for their faraway father.

"I'll have these ready mounted for you by Wednesday, Miz Griffin. Like we agreed, that'll be three fifty for both sittings, if we could settle up now."

Nerva withdrew the bills and coins from her leather pocketbook and handed them to him saying, "I'm much obliged, Mr. Kingsbury, for your help. This'll mean a lot to my man when he gets 'em. Been gone over a year already."

"Glad to help. Glad to help," he repeated. "I expect he'll be ever so glad to see what his family looks like now. A real comfort to him, I'm sure. So you stop by for them Wednesday, and they'll be ready for the mail." Turning to the girls with a slight bow, he added in parting, "Was a pleasure, taking the likenesses of such pretty young misses as you two. Your pa must be mighty proud."

***

After school on the appointed day, Nerva and Ida May walked uptown to the photographic studio, the youngster chattering all the way about how much she loved school as well as repeatedly asking if her mother thought her father would like their pictures. The only assurance Nerva could offer was, "If they look like us, he'll like 'em right enough."

Just as Mr. Kingsbury had promised, the images were ready, carefully mounted in matching closeable wood and brass frames to protect the glass plates from getting scratched or broken. "Here they are. What do you think?" he asked as he handed one to each of them.

"It's just like I look in Aunt Mary's mirror! Pa will see me!" Ida May exclaimed. "Let me see yours."

Exchanging likenesses, Nerva remembered how good she had felt when she first saw the likeness Brainard had sent from Nashville a month before. *Wonder what he'll feel like . . . .what he'll say . . . when he opens these here treasures from his family?*

"Mr. Kingsbury, these're everythin' I'd hoped for. My Brainard'll be touched, you can be sure, when he gets 'em."

"Well, I'm glad to have been a help to you, Miz Griffin. You come in anytime I can help you again."

Out the door, Nerva allowed Ida May's request to carry both likenesses home. "You be careful, though, 'cause they're glass an'll break if you drop 'em."

As they turned the final corner of their five-minute walk, Nerva was surprised to see Alice sitting on Mary's front porch rocker with Edgar Lincoln on her lap, the boy wailing uncontrollably as he held his bare feet that stuck out before him.

"Alice, what's happened? What's wrong?" she called out as she and Ida May hurried up to the house.

Edgar Lincoln reached out for his approaching mother, seeking her comfort, and was gathered up by her, only to burst forth with an even louder agonized cry. "There, there," Nerva said, patting his back. "Ma's got you now, love." Turning to Alice, she repeated, "What's happened?"

Alice explained that the boys had been playing outside, close to the house, as Aunt Mary had instructed. "But, best as I can figure, they got to chasing each other and Edgar Lincoln took off through the woodlot and into the brambles on the far edge. Before he could get out, he had a mess of thorns in both feet. So he just plopped down there and started crying."

"I heard the poor tyke," Mary continued, having stepped out onto the porch with her two children. "The pain must'a been somethin' awful, thorns pokin' out everywhere. I carried him back and pulled 'em out, him a'cryin' for you the whole time. I soaked his little feet in a bucket o' cold water, but you can see that didn't help much, not 'thout you here to hold him."

Nerva continued to press her son to her bosom as the story unfolded, even gently stroking each foot a bit as she looked at the mass of angry welts on his soles, repeating softly, "There, there . . . it's over now." Slowly his sobs subsided, moving to irregular sniffs as he wiped his eyes. "Edgar Lincoln, guess what? Ida May's got somethin' to show you. Somethin' special. Shall we go inside an' see what it is?" With his nod, she carried her wounded son in, followed by the rest, and all gathered in the parlor.

"What do you think of these?" Ida May asked as she laid the two glass portraits on the tea table. "Won't Pa be ever so happy to see 'em?"

Alice quietly beamed. She was anxious to see how they turned out, though she already knew what they would look like, having been there for the taking. Mary, however, clasped her hands and gave an enthusiastic "Yes!" while Louis Lincoln pointed and said, "That's Edgar Lincoln in his Ma's lap!"

Hearing his name, Edgar looked down from his mother's embrace and questioned, "Me? For Pa?"

"Yes, my love, for your Pa," Nerva answered, and looking up at Mary, asked, "Aren't they grand?"

"Grand indeed," Mary replied. "Oh, your Brainard'll be so proud to get these. Bet he shows 'em all around. When you gonna send 'em?"

"I think I'll write a note tonight, then we can wrap 'em up and send 'em off tomorrow."

Thus, accompanied by a brief update of the family news and questions about his health and activities, plus a brief telling of the "poor little wounded feet," the carefully padded and wrapped images were addressed to Corporal Griffin down in Tennessee, ready for mailing in the morning.

Chapter Thirty-One

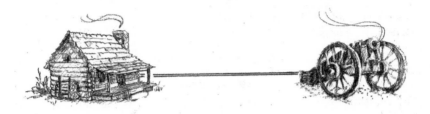

Holidays – Again Without Pa

The combined families knew of Governor Ramsey's proclamation, printed in their newspaper, *The Chatfield Democrat,* that declared November 27 "a day of Thanksgiving and Praise." This was in line with President Lincoln's call for a first-ever national Thanksgiving Day observance for that date. So it wasn't news to them when Brainard noted that fact in his next letter, as well as lamented: *"Oh, how I wish I could spend that day with you. Would it not be a day of Thanksgiving with us if it could be so? Little did I think, one year ago now, that another year would find us still in the South, and apparently no nearer the time to go home than we were then."*

Initially, their plans were to travel in two buggies down to their parents' farm, since Mary's husband, Emery, was still too involved chasing Sioux renegades to come home anyway. But a sudden turn in the weather changed those plans.

"Law me," Nerva said two days before their expected departure, "I don't remember it ever a'snowin' an' a'blowin' like this so early of a season. We can't possibly ride out in this."

"I agree," Mary responded, putting down her morning cup of tea. "We'd best stay put, safe an' warm."

"But I want to see Grampa, and Granma, and . . ."

"I'm sure you do, Ida May, but it'll have to be later." Nerva turned her daughter away from the breakfast table to face the window. "Have a look see outside. There's just no way we could get that far in this."

"But we'll miss Thanksgiving!"

"Not at all," inserted Mary. "We'll have it right here, the seven of us, thankful to be together, and thankful for Louis Lincoln's an' little Hattie's pa, and thankful for yours an' Alice's an' Edgar Lincoln's pa too!"

"An' there'll be aplenty to eat, so don't you worry none 'bout that. With all that food we brung up from the farm, plus one more big fat hen here who won't be alayin' all winter – might's well roast her an' be thankful," Nerva consoled.

She was right. There was aplenty. When mothers and children finally sat down at the table for Thursday's festive meal, the plump roasted chicken was surrounded by numerous bowls of stewed fruits and steaming vegetables. Mary's homemade rolls and butter accompanied the dinner, and Nerva's apple pie was set to finish it.

"I see there's two extra places," noted Aunt Mary to Alice, who had been responsible for setting out the plates, napkins, and eating utensils.

"Yes, ma'am," she explained, "one place each for Pa and Uncle Emory. Just like they are here, too."

"Don't that beat all," Nerva responded with pleasure. "Well, everythin's ready, so let's all hold hands – a family circle – whilst I say the grace." The lively chatter about all the food ceased as hands and hearts were joined in Thanksgiving. "Father in heaven, look down upon us two families, whose husbands an' fathers are gone from us in this terrible war. Take care o' them wher'er they are this day, an' by thy will bring 'em home to us, safe an' whole. And hear our prayer of thanks and praise – for all this food, for precious family, an' for this home to share. Amen."

Her "amen" was echoed around the table, and the feast began.

***

Both girls settled quickly into their new school routine. While the number of students was somewhat larger than at Alba, it was still contained in a single room. A major difference for Alice was that the children were separated into three distinct groups, divided by age and progression. Each group had its own corner of the room, and Mr. Kellogg rotated between them for his instruction time. Alice was placed in the middle group of a dozen, while Ida May joined the eight younger children in the beginners' group.

"Pretty much the same," Alice answered her mother's question one evening about how the Spring Valley school day compared to that back at Alba. "We start each day with recitations. Then we practice reading, or writing, or 'rithmatic in our groups, an' Mr. Kellogg helps us."

"Don't forget playtime," Ida May added, as that was her favorite time because of the new friends she was making.

"Isn't there another part of school you like?" asked Mary.

"Yes, ma'am," she giggled, "lunch."

"I mean something that Mr. Kellogg teaches you," her aunt laughed back.

"Guess I like writing time. And I'm the best in my group, 'cause Alice already taught me how. Didn't you, Alice? And I'm almost good enough to write some to Pa!"

"What a splendid idea, Ida May," her mother responded. "Why don't all three of us, well, an' Mary too, write some to your pa tonight? I been meanin' to answer his last letter, but just haven't gotten to it till now."

And so a fat envelope, containing four sets of questions, news, and expressions of love, was sent on its way the following day to the postmaster of the Second Minnesota Volunteers down in Tennessee.

***

Two weeks into December there was an unusual break in Minnesota's winter weather. After several mild days – so mild that the snow that lay everywhere began to melt – Nerva announced to Alice as they washed the breakfast dishes: "I been talkin' to your Aunt Mary about this. I think we should go down to Alba for a few days whilst it's this nice. We can visit family an' friends, an' see how the home place is a'doin' 'thout us."

"But what about school? We'll miss school if we go," asked Alice.

"Don't you worry your head none about that," answered her aunt. "I'll stop by and tell 'em where you've gone. Besides, you're way ahead, so you won't miss much."

The children already knew they wouldn't be going down there for Christmas, for normally people didn't travel that far for a visit during that time of year. In addition, their Uncle Emory had written that he would be released for a week or maybe more to come home for the holidays, and Mary wanted them all to be together.

"So we'll get to see Granma and Grampa early for Christmas after all!" concluded Alice. She grabbed her mother's wet hands as the excitement of that new anticipation filled her. "Can I go tell Ida May?"

"Yes, go ahead, 'cause you'll need to get your things together right away. It will be early, o'course – not Christmas – an' they're not expectin' us, but I reckon they'll be as glad to see us as we'll be to see them."

"It'll almost be like having *two* Christmases," Alice said over her shoulder as she hurried out to find her sister.

A flurry of activity followed. While Nerva hitched up Ol' Jim to their buggy, then dressed Edgar Lincoln for the half-day trip, the girls gathered what the four of them would need for a few days away. Mary, meanwhile, packed a picnic lunch for them, then sat down to write a brief holiday greeting to her parents and brothers. With all hands thus helping, the Griffins were on their way in less than an hour.

The pleasant weather held, and though the roadway south was muddy from the snowmelt, it was passable all the way. With a stretch stop for lunch, they made the ten-mile trip with ease, the only incident being an axel-high crossing of the Root River during which Ol' Jim had briefly lost his footing.

"I see Grampa's house," a delighted Ida May pointed across the snow-covered fields. "We're almost there!"

"Hud-up," Nerva encouraged Ol' Jim, with less than a quarter mile to go. And, perhaps finally recognizing the route, he responded with renewed vigor to her shake of the reins.

The family soon pulled up in front of their destination and both girls jumped down. Before climbing down herself, Nerva handed the newly awakened Edgar Lincoln down to Alice, and the three children ran to the door of their grandparents' house. It opened wide before they could knock, and there stood their grandfather.

"Polly, come an' see who's come to visit," he called back into the house, then picked up Edgar Lincoln for a welcoming hug. The girls raced past him and into the arms of their approaching grandmother.

"Lord a'mercy! I can't believe my eyes," Polly Griffin said as she gathered them to her bosom like a hen with her chicks. "An' my Minerva too," for her daughter had finally stepped into view on the porch. "I think I'm a'gonna cry."

Ida May backed up in dismay. "Oh, Granma, don't be sad we've come."

"These here are tears of joy, dearie, not tears of sadness. Tears of joy," and she drew Ida May back in once more before she headed to the door to greet Nerva. That allowed the girls to run up the stairs to surprise their cousins.

"Oh, Minerva, dear, it does my heart good to get to see you after all. Was it the change in the weather? How long can you stay? How are Mary an' her babies? And . . ."

Nerva stopped the flood of questions from her mother with a gentle "We'll get to all that soon's we settle in, Ma. Are Allen an' Henry about?"

"Both to town," her father answered. "Needed more salt for the last of the butcherin' soon's it turns cold again. So, how long can you stay?"

"Just a day or two, as we'd best get back a'fore winter sets in again. I'd like to check out our shanty whilst we're here. See if'n everythin's all right. But this'll make do for not comin' down for Christmas."

And so it went, through supper and late into the evening, Uncles Allen and Henry, and Cousins Hellen and Eliza adding to the merriment of the extended family reunited for a day or two.

The next morning, leaving Edgar Lincoln behind, Nerva and her daughters drove their buggy the two miles to Mr. Peters' store. Hiram Winslow – one of the folks they hoped to see – just happened to be there getting supplies, so that eliminated a stop. Both men were delighted to see them and peppered them with questions about how they were getting along up in Spring Valley.

When Nerva inquired about any letters from Brainard, Mr. Peters replied, "There is one, yes. Just came in yesterday. Didn't get it forwarded to you yet, but now I won't have to. Here 'tis, an' any more come here, count on me sendin' them on to you."

Depositing the letter in her apron pocket, she asked, "Could I just get a small bag o' penny candies, a treat for the girls?" Mr. Peters handed her the requested sack of assorted sweets, and she and the girls set off for the nearby settlement of Alba.

They made a brief stop at the school so that Alice could say hello to Miss Cray and her friends. That created quite a stir as everybody wanted to know what her new school was like. But soon they were on their way again, their last stop being the shanty.

Nerva drew out the letter and handed it to Alice. "Would you read your pa's news to us, love, whilst we ride along? We can pretend he's here in the buggy with us, a'tellin' us his story."

Smiling broadly at that thought, Alice unsealed the envelope and unfolded two full double-sided pages from her father. She then smoothed them out in her lap and began to read:

"Camp at the Big Island Ford, Cumberland River, Tennessee. November 27th 1862. My Dear Wife and Children, as it has been some time since I have written to you, or received a letter from you, I will write to you today and let you know how I am and what we have been about…"

As she read his news of marching and foraging and fighting with guerrillas, her mother and sister often broke in to comment on, or ask questions about, what he had written. But it was his story about being shot at by some Rebels that raised the most interest.

Alice's eyes grew big as she read: *"Now, do not be scared for I am not hurt any yet, but the Rebels have got to shoot at me a second time before they hit me, for they shot at me for the first time yesterday, but they shot about a foot to the side of my legs…"*

His story laid out the details of a man trying to convince him to cross over the river in a canoe. When Brainard began to be suspicious and said he wouldn't do it, the man had signaled some others, hidden in the tall grass, to shoot him. Luckily, he was able to jump behind the protection of a tree when *"crack went a rifle, and whiz went a little bullet, about halfway up to my knee, and about a foot from my leg."*

Nerva simply had to stop their buggy when Alice read that line – just to catch her breath and take in what she had heard. "Read that part again," she asked Alice, who complied. Then her mother breathed, "Oh, Lord, he's still safe," and snapped the reins for Ol' Jim to start again.

No one spoke the rest of the way to the farm.

There were no tracks tracing the lane up to the old cabin as apparently no one had come by since the last snow. But Ol' Jim knew well the pathway home, and delivered them safely at the front porch.

"Hope all's well inside," Nerva said again, breaking the heavy silence. She unlatched the door, and right away all three could tell it was not.

"What's that awful smell?" whined Ida May, her hands covering her nose as she gagged.

"Mice," Nerva pronounced firmly as she pushed the door fully open.

"There they are!" shouted Alice, pointing in all directions inside at the scampering rodents. "They're everywhere!"

Sad but true, mouse droppings and chewed fabric lay strewn across the room. There were even several gathered piles, like bird nests, in which tiny pink babies squirmed. With no one occupying the house, dozens of them had moved in to make the shanty their own winter home. The Griffins only entered a few steps into the room, looking around in dismay.

"Must'a come in from the barn an' fields soon's we left," moaned Nerva. "And what a mess they've made."

There was nothing they could do about it, since they weren't planning on staying. So they merely backed out, closed and relatched the door, and after a quick check of the outbuildings, returned to the buggy. As they started back to her parents' farm, Nerva said, "Don't want to take a chance on the weather, so we'd best leave in the morning as soon as we've ate." With both girls nodding in agreement, she added, "Alice, why don't you go ahead and finish the letter?"

She retrieved the half-read letter and continued her father's tale of military actions, his speculations about how long the war would continue (*"Until the whole South is entirely ruined and laid desolate by the sword and bayonet."*), and several questions about their settling in at Spring Valley.

"Pa makes it sound like he won't be back for a long, long time," Ida May observed. "I like it at Aunt Mary's, but . . . when will we get to come back to our own home?"

"We'll just have to wait an' see, dear one. I 'spect your pa's sufferin' a lot more'n we are, remember that," her mother cautioned as she turned the buggy into her parents' lane.

"Grampa, Grampa, Pa's been shot at!" Ida May's mood had quickly changed at the chance to bring this news, and she was shouting and waving excitedly as they approached the house where Almon Griffin stood.

"Shot at? What do you mean?" he answered.

As soon as the buggy came to a stop, both girls jumped down and ran to him with the story. His open outstretched hands flinched with each detail as his granddaughters alternated, in rapid fire, telling the story Brainard had written to them.

"He was just going down to the river to get some water," began Ida May.

"A man on the other side of the river asked him to come over and get him," Alice continued.

"There was a . . . what was it called, Alice?"

"A canoe."

"Yeah, a canoe, but Pa, he doesn't know how to make it go."

"Pa started to get suspicious, thought maybe the man was a Rebel," explained Alice.

"So he said no, and then they shot at him!"

"Good Lord," their grandfather interrupted their story. "Is he hurt bad?"

"No, Grampa, it missed him," answered Alice.

"But he heard it whiz right by his leg," added Ida May.

"And he said they're gonna have to learn to shoot better' an that if they want to hit him," concluded Alice.

The whole story had to be retold, first to their grandmother when they got inside, then to their cousins in their shared bedroom, and then once more when their uncles returned at the end of the day with a haunch of venison from a successful deer hunt.

It was an exciting ending to a wonderful visit.

***

Christmas finally came. Not in the way that any of the Griffins desired, for the husband and father of the family was still away at war. But at least Mary's family knew its full joy, because Emery had

273

arrived three days earlier, given an entire week to celebrate with his wife and children.

He had brought home a number of small pieces of beautiful Sioux feather and beadwork to serve as Christmas presents for each one in his home. Purchased at the Lower Sioux Agency outside Fort Ridgely, where he was stationed, he hoped his family could see that the Sioux were capable of making more than just trouble.

Before he arrived, Ida May and Alice, using a new skill Nerva had taught them, had secretly completed a pair of colorful cross-stitched alphabets, their names and the date embroidered at the bottoms. These were for their mother and aunt. They had also saved up their pennies so they could buy from Mr. Wilder small bags of hard candies for the "two Lincolns," Edgar and Louis.

Nerva had decided, for once, to be extravagant with the fifty dollars Brainard had recently sent. For Ida May, she had purchased her own copy of the beginner's edition of *McGuffey's Reader.* Then, working from a store-bought pattern and its necessary fabrics, she and Mary had stitched and stuffed for Alice a doll dressed in the latest New York fashion, as pictured in the last *Leslie's Magazine* their father had forwarded to his daughters.

It snowed heavily all day the 25th of December, so both families were well content to stay together at home. The gifts were given and received with delight; a hearty stew, along with freshly baked bread and two kinds of pie, satisfied everyone; and an afternoon filled with more of Emery's stories of his adventures pacifying the Sioux held their rapt attention. Then, to bring the day's festivities to a close, Nerva produced two letters from Brainard she had kept back, unreported and unread, so that he could also be a special part of their day.

Besides his typical reporting of military activities, two personal notes stood out for appreciation in the initial letter. The first was to Alice:

"I suppose that the children are in school, as they have a good school. Who is their teacher, and what books do they study? Tell Alice

that she must write a few words to me once in a while so I can see how fast she learns to write." And the second was to both Nerva and then Mary: *"I know that you will not forget me if we are separated from each other for a few more days or months. You seem nearer to me now than before I went away. Kiss the babies for me, and tell Mary to kiss hers for me too. I would like to see her little girl as well as herself, and all the rest of you too, you better believe it."*

But it was two pieces of news in the second letter that brought the greatest satisfaction to their hearts. He was finally able to report:

"When the mail came in last night it brought along your pictures, and I took a good long look at them, I tell you. It did me good to see that familiar look of yours. I could almost imagine that you was agoing to speak to me, 'through a glass.' Alice and Ida look so natural. Everyone that looks at them thinks they are pretty girls. They all remark something about Ida's 'black eyes.' If they will always be as good as they look, I shall be content. But there is one little fat chubby boy sitting in his mother's lap that 'takes my eye.' He looks up as if there was something agoing on that he did not see exactly. He looks well and as pert as a mouse. I hope that I shall be permitted to see all of you as you are before many months."

As if all of that weren't enough to laugh and cheer about, his next item iced the cake:

"I have not yet told you the news. We had an order read to us on the tenth, notifying us of the promotions in Company F. David Brainard Griffin is appointed Corporal. So you may tell Emery that he is not much ahead of me yet as far as office is concerned. I did not know anything about it until the order was read."

Ida May expressed the feelings of all there that evening: "His letters . . . it's almost as if Pa was here!"

Chapter Thirty-Two

Letters to Pa

Spring Valley, Minn   *Christmas Day, 1862*

My Dear Brainard,

Its evening here and the children are all abed so I can finally write a few lines to you, dear husband. I wish you coulda shared this day of joy and hope with us. Im glad to say were all well here, content with the little things we have, but its what we dont have – you! – that leaves such an empty hole. Marys Em is here for a whole month, and the girls ask me why you caint be here to.

I did save back your last two letters to read this morning as a sprise for the girls and to make it seem a bit like you were really here atalkin to us. I would liked to have seen your face when you opened the packet of the likenesses we sent. It sounds like you grinned big. Im glad youre proud enough of your three children to pass em around for the boys to see. I reckon youd be even prouder if you was here to see em yourself.

The girls love your story about bein shot at by the rebels at the river. They tell it and act it out again and again takin turns bein you. Everybody, even Em, cheered and clapped when I read the part about you being raised up to Corpral. Em said hes sure you deserve it.

You asked about their school. It is first rate, even better than Alba, and Alice and Ida May are both very happy there. The schoolmasters name is W. L. Kellogg, and I was wonderin if you two might be kin. You also asked about Marys babe. She named her Henrietta, but we all call her Hattie. Shes as cute as a lil ol bug, tiny yet, but seems alert. Alice and Ida May are so good with her, and thats a big help to Mary. And you should see the two boys play together. More like brothers than cousins. And it warms my heart that he now has a boy for reglar company.

When we left the farm to move up here for the winter Hill still had bout 10 acres to plow for next year. Turns out he was afixin to marry up with the widow Bender. Hadnt told me, so he did that stead of finishin our work. Hes gone to work her place now, so I reckon we wont be able to add the barley field Allen had planned for next spring. I hope theyll be happy together.

The light from the lantern isnt strong, and my eyes are very sore from crochetin most all day, so Id best stop here and get some rest.

We all send you our love and prayers for your safe return.

Minerva, Alice Jane, Ida May and Edgar Lincoln Griffin

Spring Vly, Minn.   *Jan. 28, 1863*

My Dear Husband, Away to War,

It has been a month since I wrote you last. Im so sorry cause I know how much a letter means to you, but all the children have been sick, even Mary, so theres been nary a free moment for me to write. Seems like the whole town is fevered. Schools been closed for now. So far Ive been spared, and Ive been atendin to all in both families. Em left for his fort afore the fever broke out, so I reckon it didnt spread to him.

We have got 5 letters since I wrote. You wont believe it, but one of em you sent back in August when you were down in Pelham, and it just came last week. Musta been laid up somewhere or got lost for a while. Even if its such old news from you, were ever so glad to know where you are and what you are adoin.

Youll be glad to know there was enough of the money you sent to pay the years interest on the farm mortgage. And like you suggested, this month I found a buyer for your reaper machine, and that paid off the note with a little extra to save.

Yes, its true bout the Indians that rose up against us settlers. The ones arrested were tried guilty and 38 of them were hung bout 3 weeks ago. Folks are still feared for their lives up closer there, but I don't think this will ever happen again.

What you report about the fightin at Murfreesboro is terrible for so many families. I must say Im glad you werent in it but could only hear it from the miles away where you were camped.

When I read to the family the part of your letter that said this war should end soon and we should expect you home in a few months, the girls shouted and danced around the room. I didnt want to spoil their excitement, so I didnt remind em how many times afore youve said that.

Youve always said you were signed up for 3 years. Thats half gone already. But if this war should last longer than that, do you think the gov't could keep you longer than those 3 years?

Your boy Edgar Lincoln is agettin about on his own so well now that I thought twas time to get him a real pair of shoes. I tried every store in town and not one had any childrens shoes to sell. Everyone said so much leather was abein used for soldier things there wasnt much left for children things. Ill try later in Chatfield, and even Preston if I have to, and maybe some cobbler will have enough scrap for the little tykes feet.

Im to the end of the page so I need to stop. Im enclosin a letter from brother Samuel back in Vermont. Guess he didnt have your military address. Alice also has a note for you. We missed you on your birthday again, and everybody wishes you to be home for your next one.

Love and greetings from us all,

Minerva, Alice Jane, Ida May and Edgar Lincoln Griffin – to their husband and father.

Mary and hers say hello too.

Dear Pa,

First off I want to tell you happy birthday. We did remember you special that day, but all of us was sick so I didn't write then. We didn't have your favorite dinner that night either, but we talked about last year. It seems so long ago now you've been gone.

Me and Ida May have a good school and we walk there ourselves. We know some good friends already and Mr. Kellogg is a very smart teacher. I like his history lessons the best. Sometimes we even learn about your war.

Aunt Mary had a new baby just before we came. We all call her Hattie. Me and Ida May help care for her, but she is still too small to play with.

Ida May says please I should write you hello from her, but Edgar Lincoln is too busy with Louis Lincoln to answer. I think it is funny they are both named Lincoln, same as the president.

Do you know when you are coming home yet? Uncle Em was here for most about a month. Can you do that?

I will say good-bye for this time, and will write again when Ma writes.

Your daughter Alice

Spring Valley, Minn.   *Feb. 20, 1863*

My Dear Brainard,

Three of your letters came today all in a bundle and I opened em right away. I was beginnin to worry bout you bein hurt or somethin cause youre always so reglar to write. But you said in one of em that the mail wasnt agoin through with the rail line cut by the rebs. So I guess thats why.

Were finally past the sickness here, never got to me, now things are most about normal again. Mary was specially worried for little Hattie, but she came through alright to.

When the girls come home after school today Ill read em your stories. Theyll be laughin as hard as I was bout you turnin a somerset "end over appetite" when your horse tripped. Are you gonna be a horse soldier now? Your story bout it rainin so hard one night the water was arunnin through your tent right under you makes me worry some for your health. You stay warm and dry if at all you can. And Im ever so glad youve become a baker for the boys, so then you can do that for us when you get yourself home.

You wrote some of your thinkin on the presidents freeing of the slaves this year. Does that mean your opinions on slavery are achangin because of what youve been seein? What will happen if they all walk away from their masters? Will it make a diffrence for the war you think? The girls have been askin me bout these things, and I dont know what to say.

Guess I never told you, but neighbor Gates has rented the barn and pastures for the winter. Ill use that to pay a bit extra on the mortgage. We still have plenty of stored wheat, more than well need for us and planting, so I can sell some if somethin happens. Youve been so good sendin money to us, and weve been right careful of all we spend, so you dont need to worry none bout that.

Ill close with love from us all, turn out the lamp, and sleep to dream of your safe return, sames you say you dream of us.

Minerva and your little children

Spring Vally, Minn   Feb. 25, 1863
To our Husband and Father in Tennessee,

As the girls are both busy awritin notes to you for the letter we got from you today, Ill also take a bit of time to put down a few lines as well.

I had wrote in my last letter not to worry bout us agettin along on the money you been sendin us. Now I see you aint been paid for 4 months and dont know when again. The only bill we have due right now is with Mr. Partch, an hes not pressin, so thats good, an well be extra careful to what we spend until you get your pay again.

You say you think we ought to stay up here in Sp. Vly. with Mary, an let my father oversee our farm. But me an the girls are high intent on goin back this Spring an doin our best like before to work the claim for you, ready for you to come home. But Ill speak to Mary again.

Sounds like – with cookin an drill an all – your day is full from sun-up to sun-down. But I see you do get some little time to read an talk with your friends bout the peace that is surely to come. You know it's hard to have you gone, but were proud of you helpin save our Union an the Constitution.

Edgar Lincoln says he wants "to ite Pa" so I'll let him have his say here...

The girls letters are done an Im foldin em inside mine. So here are missives from all your family.

PS. Id like you to start acallin me Minerva now, ifn you dont mind.

Dear Pa,

I miss you. Your letters to us help, specially when they have good stories like your last letter – the one about Company H and the Rebel attack. My friends at school ask about you in the war, so Mr. Kellogg let me read the exciting story to the whole school. A few were afraid when the Rebels rode up and started shooting, but everybody cheered when the battle was over and you told about their empty saddles. Mr. Kellogg smiled, and Ida May was proud too. I am glad your Company didn't have to fight in this battle.

I hope you are still well, and get enough to eat. Please finish this war soon and come back home to us.

Your daughter in Spring Valley Minnesota,

Alice Jane Griffin to David Brainard Griffin in Tennessee

I love you Pa. I miss you Pa. I like school. I learn stuff at school. Please come home. Hattie is Aunt Marys baby. She is very good. I love you Pa.

Ida May Griffin

Alice helped me with the spelling.

Chapter Thirty-Three

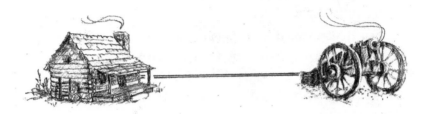

Old Friends, New Dresses

The girls were off at school, the boys playing in the woods close by the house, and Mary napping with Hattie, who hadn't slept well the night before, when Minerva heard a rapping at the front door. She put down the lace collar she was crocheting by the parlor window and looked to see who was there.

On the front porch stood Mr. and Mrs. Wheeler, good friends from the community of Etna, about halfway between the farm and Spring Valley. Behind them were two ladies Minerva didn't recognize.

"Why, hello," she said with glad surprise in her voice, nodding a greeting to each of the four. "What e'er brings you folks up here?"

"Hello yourself, Minerva." Mrs. Wheeler's high-pitched response was followed by a friendly embrace. "You're lookin' well. Oh, this here's Hilda Gillmore. She lives next to your friends, the Bonesteels. And that's Amanda Bassett, who neighbors your hay makers, the LeFevres. Don't 'spect you've met either of 'em yet."

Minerva and the two exchanged polite nods again before Mr. Wheeler broke in. "We got to talkin' 'bout the war an' all last week. Over tea it was, at our place. We thought it was a shame, all the noise them Southern Sympathizers been a'makin' here in Fillmore County. We were all a'wonderin' how our soljers were a'gettin' along. An' your Brainard's name came up."

Amanda stepped forward and continued, "What we were really wondrin' was if there was somethin' we could do for 'em? To support 'em, you understand."

Then Hilda chimed in to finish their explanation for the visit: "We thought maybe there'd be things we could be a'sendin' 'em. Things they ain't able to get, bein' so far from home. An' you could help us know what to send."

"Why don't you all come in an' set a spell? I'll make us some tea an' we can talk about it," Minerva offered. She stepped back to open the door wide and indicated the parlor as she ushered them in. "I'll be just a minute . . . put the kettle on for us. You just make yourselves comf'table there."

"I'll help you, Minerva," Mrs. Wheeler volunteered. "We can start to catch up till the water boils."

"All right. I baked some nut bread yesterday. You slice that up for us whilst I fix the rest, an' we can chat the while." The few minutes of preparation only allowed for the briefest exchange of basic family details before the refreshments were ready to bring in to the others.

"I'm so glad—touched—that you folks are int'rested in our soldiers," Minerva reopened the conversation as they all began to sip and nibble. "But what to suggest?" She paused to reflect. "Reckon I'd best write Brainard 'bout that. He'd know better'an me. Hasn't said much at all 'bout what the boys might need. Reckon he doesn't want to worry the girls an' me."

Hilda set down her cup and earnestly addressed her new friend: "If you'll do that for us, Miz Griffin, we'll start a'talkin' it up 'mongst our neighbors an' friends."

"I'd say we could count on quite a number a'willin' to pitch in," added Mr. Wheeler. "No sense askin' any of them Copperheads, though."

"I just don't understand how folks can be so dead set against a'keepin' our Union together," agreed his wife. Turning, she asked, "How does all their ruckus make you feel, Minerva dear?"

"It hurts, o'course. What with my husband gone a year an' a half now, offerin' his life, if need be, to keep us whole. Hurts 'at others just want to give in. 'Peace at any price' they say, 'stead of 'Union at any price' like Brainard. Course it hurts him even worse. When he reads stories in the papers – 'specially *The Chatfield Democrat* – 'bout the complainers here, he gets all livid. Calls 'em traitors to our nation. He wrote that again just last week."

"Well, we feel diff'rently. We're *for* our boys down there, a'doin' all they can for President Lincoln. An' that's why we want to help." Amanda got up and walked across the room to stand in front of Minerva. "You'll write soon, won't you, an' ask him what we could best do?"

"Been meanin' to write 'im anyways, just to keep up on things." Minerva then orally rehearsed the list she'd already gathered in her mind: "Our late snow, and Mr. DeGrooat's help shovelin' us out again; he'll wanna know 'bout the noise them Southern sympathizers been amakin' here; oh, an' the gospel meetin's we got to last week – guess I could send 'im that printed sermon; an' I weighed in Edgar Lincoln on the grocer's scales yesterday . . . Well, you can see I've got lots to write about."

As the others stood to leave, Minerva said she'd write that very night and let them know as soon as she could what he said. She thanked them again for coming and for being concerned. Satisfied, and committed to help, her four visitors made their good-byes and returned to the Wheeler's carriage, tied up at the hitching post. In an hour or so they would all be back in their homes, to await Brainard's answer. *My, my, how just plain good people are, deep down. Warms my heart,* Minerva pondered as she closed the door behind them.

***

The visitors' conversation had awakened Mary and she emerged from her bedroom to inquire as to who had come calling.

"Old friends an' new friends from close to home," Minerva responded. She explained the purpose of their call, and reviewed the discussion and her promise to write.

"Awful nice o' them, isn't it? But Mary, I'd like to run an errand. I've been a'waitin' for you to finish up your rest. Would you mind attendin' to my boy for a while?" Seeing Mary's nod of agreement, she continued, "Alice Jane's been complainin' a bit 'bout always havin' to dress the same as Ida May. I promised her I'd look into it, so I'm meanin' to go down to the mercantile to see what they've got for dress material. Thought we might get a start on it tonight. What do you think?"

"I think that's a grand idea," Mary said. "She's a'growin' up fast, an' it's only right she should have her own look by now. You go, see what you can get, an' I'll watch the boys."

With that affirmation, Minerva put on her coat and bonnet and walked around the house to call in Edgar Lincoln. Both boys came running, and she told them where she was off to, and that Mary would be in charge until she returned. Kissing them both on their foreheads before they headed back into the woods to continue their play, she started for town.

Some parts of town life were better than farm life. The mercantile was one of those, for it had a much broader selection of dry goods on hand than Minerva had encountered anywhere since she and Brainard had left Vermont almost ten years before. Sewing supplies were among its special features, so she was delighted to have many pieces to choose from. Two cotton fabrics in particular caught her eye: a blue and pink floral print, and a green and white gingham check. The bolts of cloth were passed down to her from the high shelf by an obliging clerk. As she hesitated, fingering both of them and imagining which one would do best for Alice, she came to a different decision. *Why take only one? I'll take 'em both, an' make up somethin' new for Ida May whilst I settle Alice with hers.* So the requested yardage was cut off the two bolts for her, along with matching thread and ribbons for each. After they were wrapped and tied into a carrying package and paid for, she thanked the clerk for his help and walked back out to the street.

She had checked the store's wall clock and, before starting for home, realized *Goodness. I'm purty close to the school, an' it's near about time for 'em to be let out. Guess I could s'prise 'em an' walk 'em home!*

So when the children came rushing out of the schoolhouse at the end of their day, Alice and Ida May were thrilled to see their mother waving to them. Joining her, they took turns reviewing their school day for her as they walked. Then Ida May pointed to her package. "What's that, Ma?"

"This is our evenin' project. Prob'ly take us the rest o' the week. A new dress for both of you," she pronounced with pleasure.

Alice immediately looked down, to hide her disappointment at what she guessed would be another set of identical dresses.

"I see that pout, Alice Jane Griffin. But put it away," her mother scolded with a light laugh, "as these dresses won't be the same. Hold on till we get home an' you'll see."

"Yes, Ma," she responded, though still not sure what to hope for.

When they arrived, the three went round to the back of Mary's house to call in the boys. But they were nowhere to be seen, and there was no response to their repeated calls.

Actually, the pair of mischievous tykes were hiding behind the stack of firewood, trying not to giggle. After tiring of playing hide-and-seek with each other, Louis Lincoln had suggested, "Wanna hide from our mas when they call us?" And Edgar Lincoln, still more the follower than the leader, had agreed. Hunkered down, they grinned at each other and waited to be discovered.

With a growing sense of unease, Minerva left her daughters behind to continue calling and hurried into the house. "Mary, do you know where them boys are?"

"Just checked on 'em a few minutes ago, Minerva. They're not out back?"

"Me an' the girls been a'callin' to 'em since we returned. No sign of 'em anywhere."

"Well, I'll get Hattie. We'd best head out to the woods where they love to play. Reckon they're just havin' themselves too good a time to answer you. But I told 'em to stay close by."

"Oh, Lord," Minerva sighed. "What if somethin's happened to 'em? An' both our men folk's gone. Oh, Lord . . ."

But before they reached the back door, in traipsed the young culprits, heads lowered and bodies herded by Alice and Ida May. "Found 'em," Alice announced, "hidin' from us behind the wood pile. Thought they'd have some fun with us."

A mixture of fear and anger, then relief, stopped Minerva's reaction for a moment, but finally she swept her son into her arms, for her mother's heart proved stronger than the need to punish or scold. Then she held her boy at arms' length and calmly said, "I know it was just a game for you. But I worried so when you didn't come. It wasn't fun for us 'cause we didn't know it was a game. You must *always* answer when I call, Edgar Lincoln Griffin!"

That settled, the two families divided three ways: the mothers to prepare supper, the girls to tend to little Hattie, and the boys to continue their play, just a bit subdued from their normal exuberance. When supper was ready, they all gathered for grace and sat down to eat. "We're gonna sew our own dresses tonight," Ida May announced.

"Are you now?" responded Aunt Mary, as if she didn't know. "And pray tell, what colors will they be?"

"Don't know yet," answered Alice. "Ma's still keepin' it a surprise. But she did say we wouldn't be dressed like twins this time. Right, Ma?"

"That's so, my dear. Somethin' special for each of you. An' you can see soon's we're done with supper."

Aunt Mary then added, "Tell you what. I'll take care of the cleanup and the little ones tonight so you can start right away."

It wasn't long before Minerva opened the two packages for her daughters and laid the two lengths of fabric out on the cleared parlor floor. Both girls gave little cries of delight as their eyes took in what their mother had chosen. The blue floral print had tiny pink rosebuds in twisting designs. Its blue would highlight the gray-blue of Alice's eyes. And the green of the gingham check was very close to Ida May's favorite color. Such lovely new dresses for spring were beyond anything they could wish for – except for their father's return, of course.

On top of the fabric, the girls each spread out her favorite dress, as their mother had instructed. Then, using her thin slice of soft marking stone, Minerva chalked outlines around each of the pieces that would make up the finished dresses. "This'll show you where to make the cuts," she explained. "An' I want you, Alice, to do that cuttin'. I'll watch over you, but this'll be good practice for you."

"But I wanna make my own dress, Ma," wailed Ida May.

"Not this time, love. Watch 'n learn. You'll have a'plenty to do with just the sewin' to make it your very own."

Somewhat mollified, Ida May watched intently as her sister – first tentatively, but eventually with more confidence – cut her own fabric into two sleeves, three bodice pieces, and the long rectangle which would be gathered into pleats along one edge to make the skirt. The younger girl edged in even closer when Alice then began repeating the process with the gingham check. All the while, Minerva murmured her approval at the careful way Alice was handling the scissors, encouraging her daughter's growing confidence.

By the time all the cutting was completed, and the pieces neatly folded and stacked for each dress, there was only time enough left that evening for each girl to stitch the seam of her first sleeve. "It'll be like a tube," their mother had explained, bringing the long edges together, "only turned inside out so's the stitchin's all done on the inside not to show."

Ida May's fingers had not been steady enough to thread her needle, but with her mother's help she was soon copying Alice's stitching of the arm-length seam. "Looks like I can leave you two whilst I make sure your brother's tucked into bed," Minerva said, patting each girl lightly on the shoulder. "I'll be back soon's he's asleep."

"We'll be fine, Ma – won't we, Ida May?"

That was the process over the next several evenings, each sister working on the same piece of her own dress, with their mother hovering over them offering instructions and encouragement. Only twice did Minerva require Ida May to rip out a length of her stitching because her work wasn't careful enough.

Finally they were done. The three pieces had been sewn together after being turned right-side-out and pressed, button holes and buttons added, a bit of lace attached at the neck lines for a collar, and a band of matching colored ribbon sewn to the waist as an accent.

Smoothing out the finished garments, Minerva instructed, "Now the two of you go put these on. I'll gather everybody here in the parlor an' you come in to show off your handiwork." To herself she added, *I'd best write Brainard tonight to tell him what our growin' up girls have done for themselves. An' won't he be tickled to learn Edgar Lincoln topped in at the grocer's yesterday at twenty-six pounds? But for my heart I'll ask 'im 'bout them Union forces the paper says were captured at Franklin, just to make sure it wasn't him. Oh, Lordy, if it was..."*

Alice and Ida May nodded excitedly to each other, picked up their new dresses and hurried away to their family's bedroom to change. "If only Pa was here to see us," whispered Ida May as Alice buttoned up the back of her dress.

"I know ... But let's hope he gets to see us in 'em real soon," her sister replied.

Chapter Thirty-four

April Letters from Pa

Triune Tenn April 2nd 1863

I am as well today as usual, and I hope that I shall remain so during my term of enlistment or during the war, which I hope will be ended before another Winter. We are anxious to end this contest and return to our families and friends, but we do not wish to go home before we can do so honorably, and have our country at peace . . .

I received a letter from you last night, dated March 23d. I am glad that you all keep well, for I should not like to hear that any of you were sick, and I not able to get home. I am glad that your neighbors see a little to your welfare, if nothing more than to shovel the snow off from your wood pile. I wish that you would give Mr. DeGrooat my best wishes. I hope that all in Spring Valley will try to encourage those who have enlisted in the cause of their country, by urging them on and by kind words and kind acts to their families and friends in their absence.

We are expecting four months pay this week or next, and then I will send you forty or fifty dollars. You had better keep the most of it for your own use, for it may be a long time before we are payed off again.

I think that you have made the girls some very nice dresses, even if they were dear. If you lived in the South you could not get them anything, at any price. I do not see how they are agoing to live another year. Wherever we go they do not raise anything. So unless they give up soon, they will be almost in a starving condition by another winter.

As it is getting late and this sheet is nearly full, I shall have to close. I should like to talk to you all night if I could, but I must stop and bid you good bye with a kiss.

In Camp near Triune April 11, 1863

I once more have got down upon my knapsack, with my pen in hand, to write a few lines to you. It has been a number of days since I last wrote, and I have been aputting it off, in hopes that I should get a letter from you, but I will not wait any longer.

I was asking Capt. Barnes if he knew Mr. Gaskill in Spring Valley, and he said that he did, and that Sargeant Gaskill of Co. B was a son of his. So I went to Sgt. Gaskill and told him about you had wrote about his brother being sick. He had not heard of it, and is now anxious to hear from his folks. We are all anxious to hear of our friends, no matter what the source, so when you write you must write about all the friends of the 2nd.

I sent three papers to Alice the other day, so she must excuse me from writing this time. We have not got paid yet, but expect to in a few days.

Write as often as you can and oblige your husband and friend, so good bye.

Camp Steadman, Triune Tenn April 16, 1863

I will write a few lines to you this afternoon, in order that you may know how I am.

I received a letter from you two days ago, which was dated the 4th in which you sent my brother Samuel's likeness and his letter. I was glad to learn that you were all well and that you had received the $20 I sent. I received a letter today from Mary's Emory. He was well, and expected his unit to move in a short time, to where he did not know. I hope we both will be permitted to join our little family circles before another fall. Do not blame yourself for getting whatever you and the children need, for I think you sacrificed enough comfort when you let me go into the army. I hope that we both shall live long enough to be amply rewarded for all our trials, and that we shall again see our country at peace . . .

I see that you are having an early spring. I hope that you can raise enough on your place to eat and some to spare. If you have any way of paying off our little debts, do it in any way your are a mind to, but I want that you should keep enough money by for your own use.

I do not think of any more to write this time . . .

Friday morning April 17th 1863

Good morning "Nerva." It is a pleasant morning here, how is it there? I will send you five dollars in this letter and will try to send you some in my next. We are to be payed in a day or two, for four months. When I am payed I am agoing to send Harpers Weekly to Alice and Ida. I had thought some of getting a furlough this spring if I could, but I have given up the idea, for it would be only a few days that I could be with you, and when I had to come back you would feel worse than you would not to see me at all. I should like to see you all well enough, but it will hardly pay.

You have never told me how much your taxes were last winter. I wish that you would. How much is a good cow worth up there? Or a two year old steer? What is wheat worth?

I will close this letter again, and bid you all good bye, again.

Camp Steadman, Triune April 27th, 1863

I will write a few lines to you this morning. I am well, as usual, and hope that you are all as well.

I received a short letter from Samuel, which I will send to you. I will send you ten dollars in this letter. I am looking for a letter from you, which will tell me all about the folks upon the Prairie, as I suppose that you are there now. I should like to be there with you, but there is no use of wishing ...

I must stop for the want of something to say, so good bye one and all, this from your beloved husband.

Chapter Thirty-Five

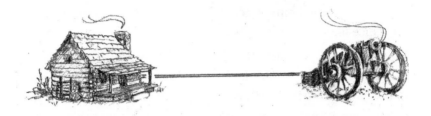

Trouble, Travel, Sickness at Home

"Ma! Ma! Did you hear the news?" Alice's voice was high and wild, arriving well before she burst through the door after school. Her younger sister was several steps behind her, and both girls were breathless from running.

Minerva laid aside the soldier's socks she was knitting and stood to greet her daughters. "News?" she asked. "Good or bad?"

"It's Mr. Douglass. He brought Pa's letter, remember?"

"Yes, Alice, I know Tom Douglass. What about him?"

"He got in a fight by our school. Knocked a man clear to the ground. And a bunch of people gathered around and everybody was shouting and angry."

"We saw it all," inserted Ida May. "Was lunch time, and we were all outside."

"Why would Tom Douglass do a thing like that, I wonder?" Minerva murmured, troubled that the war-injured volunteer would get so upset as to hit another man.

Alice's answer made the reason plain: "Mr. Kellogg called us all back inside. He said the other man was one of those Copperheads for the South, and that's what sparked the fight."

Ida May clung to her mother's waist and began to cry. "We watched out the window. The sheriff came . . . arrested Mr. Douglass . . . hauled him off to jail. What'll happen to him, Ma? He's such a nice man."

"I don't know, love. But I'd best write your pa 'bout all this, 'cause they're good friends an' all. Reckon I'll head downtown first, though, to see if I can learn any more. Will you girls see to your brother for a bit whilst I'm gone? Then I'll write him tonight. Need to let him know his money's come through safe besides."

She spoke briefly to her sister, alerting her to the news and explaining her errand. Mary assured her all would be fine while she was gone, and that she'd start supper for the two families.

It seemed all the town was buzzing about the day's event. There had been heated arguments, to be sure, over the issue of the war, but it had never come to blows before. Minerva learned that the Southern sympathizer had subsequently been arrested as well, so both sides took some satisfaction. However, no one she spoke to hoped such a thing would ever happen in Spring Valley again. She returned home, prepared to write the distressing news to her husband.

***

The first week of May was the last week of the school term. Both girls had done very well, with Alice's marks the top of her age group. Now it was time for Minnesota's growing season, and across the state even the children's hands were needed to help ensure the production of enough food to see their families through the coming winter.

So Minerva announced one morning that it was time to head down to their farm to check on the planting of their field crops. Her father had leased the land from her, and had used the fenced area and barn for his cattle over the winter, and by now was looking to the spring planting of oats, wheat, and sorghum.

"What about our shanty, Ma? Remember all the mice?" Alice's question drew Ida May close enough to hear the answer.

I 'spect we won't be a'livin' in it anymore. By now it'll be plum ruint. I'd planned for us to stay with your granma an' grampa instead. That way we don't have to worry none 'bout food or bedding and such like. How's that sound?"

"But our garden . . . We won't have our garden then," objected Ida May.

"We'll just stay at Grampa's place," her mother countered. "We can still have our own kitchen garden like always, an' grow plenty enough to eat an' store. You just wait an' see. An' the barn's fine. It's only our ol' shanty we won't be usin', least not till your pa gets back."

The girls reassured, Minerva posted a note to her parents, explaining her plans, and got started on preparations for the visit. While she made sure the buggy was prepared for the trip, the girls sorted out the spring clothing the family would need. And Mary, though welcoming the use of her spare room again for a while, spoke of how much she would miss all of them. "We won't be astayin' all summer," Minerva assured her. "Just a couple of weeks to get our garden in an' see some friends there. We'll be back a'fore you know it!" she laughed.

Before the week was out, on the kind of May day that only occurs where there's a real transition from winter to spring, the Griffin family was packed and loaded, had made their good-byes, and was on their way home. With Ol' Jim's steady pace, the twelve-mile trip – including a couple of stretch breaks to snack from the basket Mary had prepared – was traveled by early afternoon. All along the way, the children played a game of looking for things they had seen on earlier trips and noticing new things no one remembered. And Minerva quietly mulled the lists of what she wanted to do and whom she wanted to see.

"There's the turn to Grampa's house," Ida May was eventually able to announce, meaning they were less than a mile from their destination.

Almon and Allen were outside the barn tinkering with the hitch to the harrow when Ol' Jim turned up their lane. Looking up, they realized at once who had arrived. "Hurry in an' tell your ma Minerva an' the children are here," Almon told his son. So she, too, was out to welcome them when the buggy came to a stop and the girls jumped down with Edgar Lincoln.

"Bless my soul, if'n you young'uns ain't agrowin' like weeds. Just look at you," their grandmother welcomed them, drawing all three in with her open arms. But her hug was only momentary for the three then raced across the farmyard to where their mud-spattered grandfather and uncle waited.

"Grampa! Uncle Allen! We're here!" Ida May whooped as she ran to them. Right behind her, Alice and Edgar Lincoln added their cheers to her greeting.

Both men held up their dirty hands in caution as the youngsters arrived. "So, you're back?" Allen laughed. "Wonderful! But we're a mite muddy here, so you'd better wait till we get cleaned up for us to show you how glad we are to see you." But Edgar Lincoln couldn't hold back his love for his menfolk. He ran right into their arms anyway, without the slightest care for getting dirty.

By that time Minerva had climbed down to greet her mother, so the children raced back. "It does my old heart good to see you, Minerva dear. An' the young'uns there, so spry an' happy. Oh, let me hug you again," Polly exclaimed as the three returned to her side.

Smiling up at her grandmother, Alice inquired, "Where's Hellen and Eliza?"

"They took some eggs to Mr. Peters to trade for some Sody Salluratus an' spices for pies. Should be back soon. They haven't talked 'bout nothin' else 'cept seein' you two ever since we got your ma's note."

"We'd like to rest a while, Ma. But then we ought to ride over to our place just to see what we need for puttin' in our kitchen garden." At that, her mother smiled, then looked away – as if she knew something she should not reveal. "Is that all right?" Minerva continued. "We'll be back in time for supper, of course."

"That's just fine. I'll have our evenin' meal ready 'bout six. That should give you a good couple hours at least. Your room's made up for you an' Edgar Lincoln. Girls'll be tuckin' in with Hellen and Eliza."

"Thanks so much, Ma . . . I'll go say hello to Pa an' Allen. Let the children run 'round a little. Then we'll be off."

She wandered over to where the men folk stood, and the men – still muddy – called out to her the same caution they had given the children. Their obvious pleasure at her return was evident in their warm grins. The only thing that seemed strange to her was she thought she saw the two men winking at each other . . .

It wasn't too long before the family was on its way again, this time just the short distance to their own place. The chattered speculation as Ol' Jim pulled them home was all about what they expected to find. But none guessed the surprise that awaited them.

The apple trees beside their lane up to the shanty were in full bloom, of course, and most of the spring planting and sowing already completed, with only the small corn acreage yet waiting for the air and soil to warm up enough for the seed not to rot. But as she came to the top of the lane, with the shanty and barn in plain view, Minerva suddenly understood the turn-away smile and winks she had earlier observed.

"Well, I'll be," she murmured.

"What?" asked Ida May beside her.

"Look'ee there. Pa an' Allen have done readied the garden space for us."

Sure enough, the kitchen garden plot had been plowed and harrowed for them, breaking up the winter clods and creating clean rows ready for sowing. Knowing why they were coming, her father and brother had done the hardest part Minerva was expecting to do.

"Looks like all we need are the seeds an' the sets for the potatoes and onions, an' we can start planting tomorrow," Alice observed.

"You're right. But I'd like to check the shanty first. If we don't dawdle, we could make it to Mr. Peters' for seeds an' such, an' still get back in time for Ma's supper."

As the family walked around the outside of the shanty, it distressed Minerva to see the weakened areas between the logs, caused as much by being unheated through the past harsh winter as by the numerous gnawing mice that replaced them as residents. "Oh my, what'll your pa think of this? When he gets back I reckon we'll have to start all over again for a house to live in."

The girls heard the despair in her voice, so were silent as they walked, merely pointing at damage and glancing at each other for mutual support. Their silence allowed Minerva to sadly embrace her own feelings of loss and pain. For Edgar Lincoln, however – too young to make connections between what he saw and what it would mean – it all seemed like just another game of exploration.

Alice arrived back at the front porch first and unlatched the tightly shut door. She thought she was prepared, but when she pushed it open, the sight of the scurrying rodents, and the nauseating odor they had created, overwhelmed her so much that she couldn't even stay to shut the door.

***

Leaving Edgar Lincoln with his grandmother, and joined by Hellen and Eliza, Minerva was able to oversee the planting of the entire kitchen garden the following day. Rows of beans, beets, carrots, turnips, onions, and parsnips were sown and marked. Hills of pumpkins and squash were raised and planted around the edges. And the cut pieces of potato she had prepared the night before were carefully set out with the "eyes" up for faster sprouting.

Minerva and her daughters spent a second morning planting foot-tall white willow sprigs along the north side of the tiny creek that ran for half the year below the shanty. She and Brainard had recently discussed this addition in their exchange of letters, so she was glad to get fifty of these quick-growing starts from Mr. Peters.

"We'll go up to the woodlot an' work our way down," she said as they arrived. "We'll be a team. Alice, find yourself a stout poking stick to make the holes. I'll follow with this bundle and drop a willow start into each hole. And Ida May, you come behind and circle around to stomp the dirt in tight on all sides. Shouldn't take us too long, then I'll drop you off, as we agreed, at the schoolhouse to see your friends whilst I make a few quick stops to say hello to the folks 'round Alba. That sound good?"

Alice, excited about seeing her school friends again, was happy to complete the morning's tasks. Only Ida May pouted a bit, still tired from the previous day's work, but agreed reluctantly as she wanted to visit Alice's old school too.

When the tree planting was completed, the three washed up at the well, ready for their afternoon visits. "I'll be back for you in 'bout an hour or so," Nerva informed the girls as she dropped them off at the Alba schoolhouse. "Have a good time with your friends. An' please give my regards to Miss Cray."

The girls nodded and raced up the steps and inside as their mother headed off, patting her apron pocket to check that the letter she had brought was still there, then settled back for the short journey up to the Wheelers' farm.

With a light heart at all they had accomplished – despite the condition of the shanty – she soon arrived at her destination. Mrs. Wheeler had just finished taking down her dried morning wash as Minerva pulled Ol' Jim to a halt in front of their house. Her friend waved Minerva to come into the house as she called up to her husband, "Guess who's come to see us? It's Minerva Griffin, that's who." So both of them came out onto the porch to welcome her and usher her inside.

"H'ain't got much time to visit," Minerva began. "Left the girls at school an' need to get back for 'em. Been here a couple o' days puttin' in our garden and such like. But I wanted you to know I heard back from Brainard 'bout your question o' what to do for the boys in the war."

"That's so good you've come, Minerva, 'cause we're ready to start anything that'll help," Mrs. Wheeler said, turning to her husband for confirmation: "Ain't we, dear?"

"Well, I've got his letter here, an' I want to read you what he says. Just his opinion, mind you, but he's the one we asked. Might be a diff'rent answer 'an you were athinkin' I 'spect, but he says it'll help just the same. Here 'tis."

The Wheelers listened intently as she read:

"*You wanted to know what I thought about the people sending clothing to the soldiers. If anyone thinks they ought to do anything for the soldiers, let them help the families of those that are in the army, for I think that they need it if anyone, for they have sacrificed everything as it were in giving up the presence, and comforts of a son, husband, and father, perhaps to shed his blood on some distant battlefield, or to wear his life away in the tedious marches and cold nights. How many a family has already lost all that is near and dear to them in this wicked rebellion, and how many more will be sacrificed before it ends? We are here atrying to do our duty to our country, and if there is anyone who wants to aid in any way, I think that they could not do it in any better way than to help the widows and orphans, and those that are deprived of the enjoyment of being in the presence of a husband and father. You may think that I say this for self interest, but it is not so, for the government furnishes all the clothing to the soldiers that they can wear or carry with them. If they should send any to them, ten chances to one they would not get them, or would not be permitted to wear them . . .*"

As Minerva lowered the letter, having read as far as she intended, Mr. Wheeler spoke up: "I understand what he's sayin' there. Guess it'd be more of a comfort to the boys to know we was helpin' out their families whilst they're gone."

"Yep, we can easy do things like he suggests. If'n that's what the boys need, then that's what they'll get from us. I'll talk to the others soon's I can, an' we'll see what we can do."

Minerva was relieved when she left the Wheelers, the girls quite pleased with their school visit when their mother picked them up, and Edgar Lincoln delighted at their return to the farm, though he had had a wonderful time playing with his cousins and grandparents. In all, it was a very successful day.

By the end of the week, with the farm tasks and visiting completed, it was time to return to Spring Valley so Alice and Ida May wouldn't miss any more school. Polly was in tears when it was time to say good-bye to her daughter and grandchildren. Almon, more stoic, simply said again how good it had been for them to come, and assured Minerva that he would take good care of their farmland and garden.

With the usual "Hud-up," Ol' Jim made the wide circle in the farmyard, thus heading the Griffin family back down the lane to the road that lead north to the place that now seemed more likely to be "home" until Brainard's return: Spring Valley.

It was not a warm welcome that they met upon their arrival, however, for they found a large part of the town in the grip of a very debilitating sickness known as "The Ague." Mary and Louis Lincoln already displayed the classic symptoms of alternating sweating fevers and shivering fits, along with painfully aching joints. At least for the moment, baby Hattie was spared, but Minerva knew immediately what she and her three were up against.

"I'll nurse Mary and Louis Lincoln," she announced to her daughters. "An' it'll help me heaps if'n you two can see to little Hattie and keep Edgar Lincoln away the while."

"You mean for us to skip school?" Alice asked.

"No, I want you to go, an' I'll manage whilst you're there. But when you get home, I'll surely need your help."

That plan lasted but a single day, however, for with only five still-healthy children attending, Mr. Kellogg closed the school. Not only that, but the ague had gotten to Edgar Lincoln his first day home, and he was already very sick when the girls came home.

"I've everybody to bed all right, but I'd like to check on the neighbors if I could. Mary told me she thinks they're all down too. An' I need to write your pa 'bout all this, though I know he'll only worry himself sick for us."

"I'll play with Hattie, Ma," offered Ida May.

"And I'll start us a soup for supper," chimed in her big sister. "Maybe they can keep at least some warm broth down."

"You're such good girls. Makes me proud to be your ma." She gave them each a grateful hug before she continued, "I don't 'spect to be too long," and Minerva was out the door.

That became their routine for the next several weeks, Minerva and the girls caring for the others, until the sickness had finally run its course. It had hit Edgar Lincoln particularly hard, and he was the last one of the household to recover.

Chapter Thirty-Six

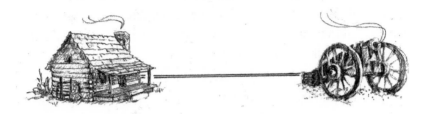

Strange Dreams, Unknown Packages, New Clothes

"I don't understand why Pa burns our letters." Ida May was reacting to what her father had written, as the two sisters, just returned from school, sat together on their bed discussing the letters the family had received that week.

"He doesn't have any place to save 'em, silly. Remember," Alice answered, "he sleeps in a tent and has to carry everything he owns – even the tent – when he's on the march."

"Still, it doesn't seem right to me, but I guess that's true. But won't he be proud to see the way Ma's been savin' all of his for when he gets back?"

"He surely will," agreed Alice. "Quite a stack already. Most about eighty, I think. Did you see Ma had to get a longer ribbon to tie 'em up this time? We can't even read all of 'em at one time like we used to when he was first gone."

"The part I liked in the last one was about them men dressed up as ladies an' puttin' on a dance for the others. What a show that musta been! I wonder where they got the dresses."

Alice mused for a moment on that question, but decided she couldn't even speculate. She changed the subject instead. "Lookin' through all those pictorials he keeps sending us, one thing I wonder 'bout is if he sees as many Negroes as they always picture, an' if they're really as bad off as they seem?"

Ida May, in turn, had no answer. So they sat with their silent thoughts a bit longer, each reflecting particularly on their father's comment that he was worried about Edgar Lincoln's health, and that he wanted his family to be, as he wrote, "unbroken at the end of the war."

It was Ida May who broke the silence. She felt compelled to share something that had been troubling her all day. "Had a strange dream last night..."

"Oh? What was it about?"

"Well, in my dream it was the day Pa left us. We all waved good-bye, then I ran up the hill to see him one more time, remember? Only he never came down the road . . . I didn't get to see him again after all."

"That is strange. But dreams are funny, Ida May. Can't tell what they mean or if they mean anything at all. So don't worry none about it," Alice responded, patting Ida May's crossed hands in a reassuring way. Eventually she suggested, "Let's go play with the little ones. That'll help Ma an' Aunt Mary to fix supper."

***

The end of May a string-tied packet was waiting for them when the girls stopped at the post office after school. Fingering the brown paper wrapping as they walked home, neither girl could guess for sure what it was, though they agreed it might be another likeness of their pa.

"Ma, you try to guess what it is before you open it," teased Ida May when they arrived home and she handed the packet to Minerva.

"Sakes alive, child, how'm I s'posed to know?" she said, fingering the packet just like they had.

"Guess," insisted Alice.

"Well, from the feel of it, it might be a book or somethin' like that. Let's just open it an' find out." And with that, she untied the string and tore open the paper, revealing its contents, indeed, to be a thin book. She read its grand title to the girls: *A Record of the Members and Actions of Company F of the Second Minnesota Regiment of Volunteers.*

"That's Pa's Company!" Alice declared with amazement and pride.

"Is Pa in it?" asked Ida May as she watched her mother thumb through the pages.

Minerva sat down, the girls joining her, one on each side, close enough to see for themselves. "Here at the beginnin's a list o' all the men, an' yesiree, there's your pa's name, right there, pointing as she read, "Corporal David Brainard Griffin, Fillmore County."

"What else does it say?" Ida May asked as she squeezed in closer.

"Well, looks like the rest of it's a history, a history of all they've been through. Do you want to hear it?"

During the reading that followed, all three repeatedly interjected thoughts like: "I remember way back when Pa wrote about that," "Didn't your pa write us once 'bout how that happened to him?" or "I don't think Pa ever told us about that at all."

When she finished the company's story, Minerva turned the small book over and back several times, appreciating this new contribution it made to the family's understanding of and connection to all that Brainard had been through during the twenty months he had been gone. "This here's purty special," she finally said. "Lets us know a whole lot more 'bout what your pa's been up to. Makes me almost cry that he sent it to us."

Alice excused herself to prepare her things for the brief summer school session set to begin as a result of the three-week closure for the ague. That gave Ida May, who was already prepared, a chance to confide to her mother the previous night's reoccurrence of the disturbing dream she had earlier described only to her sister. The details of the dream were the same. The unease it aroused in her was the same. And her mother's assurances echoed those Alice had given. "Ida May, love, just leave it be. It's only a dream, nothin' more. Don't fret yourself over it. You'll see your pa again . . . when he comes amarchin' home."

Her mother's words and comforting embrace were just what the young girl needed.

***

After nearly a month of wasting away, fighting off the lingering ague, Edgar Lincoln finally began to beat it and reemerged relatively unscathed because of the loving care lavished upon him by his family. The friends and neighbors that Minerva had been ministering to had, one by one, also finally recovered. *Praise be, Brainard doesn't have to hear he's lost his only son after all,* Minerva thought as she watched him begin to run and laugh again with his cousin. She had written her husband twice about how sick their boy was, but now, bit by bit, each day as his appetite and energy returned, he was almost back to his old rambunctious self. *What a joy to my heart he is, an' to his pa too.*

I know what'll make him feel even better, she realized about a week after his recovery was evident. *That boy's ready for pants 'n' boots. Yep, needs pants 'n' boots. An' wouldn't Brainard be right proud to see him so? Be a perfect use of them 'leven dollars he sent us last week!*

The switch for young boys from the girlish gowns of infancy to shirt and pants was usually around the age of two. Edgar Lincoln, however, had been somewhat delayed in learning to use the outhouse for his "nature calls." They all had encouraged him, and perhaps the example of his slightly older cousin had done the trick, as he had recently gained that awareness and control, and it was now time to acknowledge his achievement.

"Edgar Lincoln, got a surprise worked up for you," Minerva said after lunch that day. "I want you to go to town with me, an' then we'll meet up with your sisters as soon's their school lets out. Whatcha say?"

"Louis Lincoln go?" the boy asked.

"No, my dear. This surprise is just 'tween you an' me."

"What is it?" he inquired.

"That's the surprise, love. You won't know till we get there."

"Me like it?" he continued his probe.

"I'm sure you will. Yes indeed. But let's go find out," his mother teased him. Hand in hand, they walked down to the Main Street block of shops and into the dry goods store. Minerva led her son up to the counter, where she was greeted by the proprietor, Thomas Watson.

"Howdy, Miz Griffin. How can I help you today?"

Pushing Edgar Lincoln forward, she said, "He needs his first pairs o' pants an' boots."

"Growed up enough, has he? Well, let's just see what I've got for him." He walked to the far end of the counter and lifted down several stock boxes from the back shelf. Returning with the stack, he opened them out on the countertop for Minerva to look at.

The different sized pants were made from either the newly produced cotton denim or the more traditional woven wool. Both kinds were dyed blue, and came either belted or bibbed. *Hum, he needs sturdy fir sure, so that's prob'bly the denims, an' the bibs'll give him a mite more protection when he's a'tumblin' around* . . . "We'll take a pair like this," Minerva finally decided, laying her choice aside. "Will it fit the young'un?"

"You hold 'em up to him, but I'm sure they'll do fine. Looks like you might have to tuck the legs up a bit at the bottom. That'll even give him some room to grow," replied the proprietor. "Now the two of you set yourselves down over there, an' I'll see about fixin' him up with a nice pair o' boots as well."

He soon returned with three sizes of black brogans, the common form of work boots of the day. The smallest of them fit Edgar Lincoln just fine when Minerva added the extra pair of woolen socks she had thought to bring.

She also drew out of her handbag the plain bleached cotton shirt she had stitched for him while he was recovering. It was just a shortened copy of the nightshirt he wore to bed. Changing from the gown he wore to the store to his new shirt, pants, and boots, the boy was instantly transformed into the image of a small young man. He left her side and began proudly marching up and down the short aisles of the store.

"Oh, if only your pa could see you right now. I'd best write him tonight and tell him all about how growed up you are, an' how fine you look in them new clothes."

"Tell Pa? Pants an' boots like him. Me a big boy now!" he proclaimed to the smiling adults.

"Why, he still needs a hat to top off that outfit," said Mr. Watson. "I'll throw it in for free, 'cause of his pa."

After thanking him for his help, and paying for the items Edgar Lincoln now wore, they left the mercantile store, and the boy pranced all the way to his sisters' school. When they were let out, he reveled in the adulation he received from them as the family walked the rest of the way home together.

"Why, look at you. Don't you look grand!" his Aunt Mary greeted him as he entered the house. "Louis Lincoln, come look at your cousin," she called to her son. A bit older, Louis had transitioned to pants several months earlier, and proudly proclaimed Edgar to be "now like me!" With that, the two took off upon their normal game of chase around the house.

Minerva could hardly get him to take his new clothes off when it was time for bed later that evening. "We'll lay 'em right here beside you while you sleep. An' they're yours to put on first thing in the morning," she promised him.

As soon as he was down, she began her letter to Brainard, relieved to finally be able to describe the end of their little one's terrible illness, and pleased to inform him of his son's new shirt, pants, and boots.

***

The next letter writing project was in response to three letters they had received in quick succession from Brainard. Minerva invited the girls to join her in the parlor after supper to help write back, while Aunt Mary settled the three little ones into their beds. "Let's do it together," she had said, "so's it comes from all of us, 'stead of just me this time. Your pa'll really like that."

They sat around the small table at the window, making use of June's lengthening daylight for the writing process, and each one suggested a few news items of the family as well as things to respond to from his letters. Minerva ran her hand lightly over the blank paper, then dipped her pen in the inkwell and, after dating the page, began: *"Our Dear Husband and Father . . ."* She decided to start by writing about the gospel meetings they had recently attended in Spring Valley with Mary, which were led by their long-time friend Reverend Westfall. After reading back her description of the three evenings to the girls, Ida May spoke up to remind her, "You didn't say anything 'bout those special prayers for Pa an' the others that everybody made."

"Bless you, child, you're right. I'll add that so he knows. 'Twill be a comfort to him for sure. Then what next?"

"How 'bout finding that nice close-by pasture to rent for our Grisey that'll make milkin' her so much easier than last year?" suggested Alice. "Or how good we're doin' at school?"

When she had finished writing bits about both of those, Minerva added the farm news that her brother, Allen, was opening for cultivation a few more acres of their prairie grassland with the oxen team of Duke and Dime, which her father had purchased from them after Brainard's enlistment. "Guess I'd also better let him know how tired my eyes get at night doin' fine needlework for you young'uns, though I don't want him to worry none 'bout me—just to know."

"Wouldn't he get a chuckle out of seein' Mr. Nichols a'teachin' all the schoolboys how to march around like soldiers? He sure makes it look like fun instead of like war."

Ida May's suggestion filled the page to the bottom, and as she turned the paper over to the other side, Minerva said, "We'd best write somethin' 'bout his letters, too. Alice, I've got 'em here. Why don't you be a good girl an' read 'em to us again? Remind us what he says, then we can answer back."

The others listened intently as Alice read her father's last three letters. Brainard described with great enthusiasm a "Grand Review" at their camp in Triune, Tennessee, of twenty-three regiments totaling fifteen thousand men before General Granger. He also recounted his own regiment's recent fifteen-mile night march in the rain to the embattled town of Franklin, only to discover that the attacking Rebel cavalry had already departed before they could arrive to help. Both those were to be mentioned when Minerva continued her writing, but the piece that elicited the most comment was his calculation that only thirteen months of his three-year enlistment remained – if the war lasted that long – and thus he would soon be mustered out.

"Then Pa's comin' home, right?" insisted Ida May. "They can't make him stay any longer'an that, right?" She stared at her mother, waiting for an answer.

Minerva looked away from her daughter into an uncertain future, finally responding, "I'll ask him 'bout that, to let us know what to count on, but . . ." She shrugged her shoulders and let out a long-held breath, wishing she could give those promises to her children. "He'll be home, soon's he can . . ."

By the time she had finished writing all their responses, only enough room for their farewells and signed names remained on the back side of the sheet. The letter was long, newsy, and complete, ready to be folded and the envelope addressed, then sent on its way bearing their love for the soldier so deeply missed.

Chapter Thirty-Seven

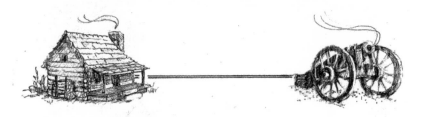

Looking to the Past and to the Future

When June's summer school session came to an end, the Griffin family planned a return to their farm – again staying with Minerva's parents – to check on and help with all that needed doing there. Their kitchen garden was to be their primary focus. "All them rows of veg'tables will need lots o' weedin' an' tendin' to by now," Minerva warned the girls. "So you can't just play with Hellen an' Eliza, though I 'spect they'll be plenty o' time for that too."

As for the field crops, she mostly wanted to be able to report to Brainard that the growing season was coming along nicely under the supervision of her father and brother. They had already managed to get the first cutting of hay cured and into the barn, but she hoped to describe the progress of their oats, wheat, sorghum, and corn.

"We'll prob'bly stay through July," she had informed her mother by letter. And while Minerva and Mary waited out on the porch for the girls to bring out their tote bags filled with clothes they had packed for the stay, she said, "Why don't you think about comin' down for a few days, Mary, 'stead o' bein' up here alone?" Before Mary could answer, the two boys who shared the president's name came chasing around the house one last time. Each mother laughed as she caught up her own son, both finding it impossible to corral the wriggling creatures as off they raced again.

"They do enjoy each other so. Partin' now'll prob'ly be hard on 'em," Mary observed. "So I reckon we'll just have to come down for a spell while you're there. I'll write Ma before we're ready to set off."

Alice and Ida May appeared with their bundles, and as Minerva walked with them to the waiting buggy she turned to Alice with a request. "Would you go catch your brother? Him an' Louis Lincoln are out back. Tell 'im we're right ready to set off."

"Yes, Ma," she replied, and left to fetch him while her mother and sister climbed aboard. She soon returned, raised Edgar Lincoln into her mother's arms, and settled in herself. With many affectionate "Farewells," they were off.

Nothing slowed their journey south, but still they were all both tired and glad to arrive at the grandparents' farm. Polly had a room prepared for their stay, and Allen's offer – "Help you any way you need" – reassured Minerva it wouldn't be just up to her and the girls at their own farm. Leaving the children behind, there was still enough daylight that long summer's evening for her to make a quick survey of the fields with her brother, and also to make plans for addressing the needs of the kitchen garden.

"Crops're lookin' right smart, Pa," she reported to Almon as the family sat down to supper upon their return. While they ate, she outlined for her daughters her plan for the following day. "We'll divy up the garden an' each take a piece. You two'll be doin' row weedin' whilst I tend to the squashes an' beans. Couple o' days should do it. Oh, an' Ma, I think there's beans to bring back if'n you want 'em."

"Can always use more, Minerva. Plenty o' mouths to feed," Polly chuckled as she surveyed the five grandchildren at her table. "But why not take Hellen an' Eliza? They have nothin' to do here. Bet you could get that garden done in one day if you did. An' I'll keep little Edgar busy here so's you don't have to mind him."

Minerva looked at the two girls, both of whom were nodding enthusiastically. "All right," she said. "That's just what we'll do then."

Her own daughters beamed, not only at the thought of two additional hands for the work, but also at the prospect of spending the whole day with their cousins.

***

"It *will* be as exciting as last year, won't it, Ma?" asked Ida May.

"We'll just have to wait an' see when we get there, love," Minerva answered.

"But will there be sky rockets again, like Grampa shot off? They were *so* beautiful."

A laughed, "Won't know till we get there," was the only answer she received.

The exchange was in response to the fact that a couple of days before, the Griffins had learned that several of the Beaver Township families were planning on traveling up to Chatfield for a big Fourth of July celebration to be held there. Many had already made arrangements with family or church friends for places to stay, so Minerva immediately wrote a note to Reverend Westfall to see if he could arrange accommodations for her family as well. With all the crops in and flourishing, and the first of two cuttings of hay already completed, little would need tending to while the farm families were away for the festivities. Minerva's mind was set at ease when she heard back from Reverend Westfall that, indeed, he could do so.

Three of the area families who had men serving in the Second Minnesota Regiment – the Griffins, the Baldwins, and the Nichols – decided to travel the twenty-six miles together to support each other. The wagon road lay north to Spring Valley, then northeast through the villages of Fillmore and Jordan, and on to Chatfield, the largest city in Fillmore County. The three families agreed to start out from the tiny hamlet of Etna, some five miles away for the

Griffins, but less than half of that for the others. That meant Minerva would have to get the children started early.

It was mainly a matter of getting her family dressed and fed, as their small pasteboard traveling cases were already packed. "Hurry up now, young'uns," she kept saying, though the sun was barely up. Her three children reacted with displeasure at the earlier than normal beginning of their day, but at least the girls understood the need to set off on their trip as soon as possible.

The buggy was heavily loaded with all four passengers and their three-days baggage aboard, but Ol' Jim was up to it and started trotting smartly down the lane at Minerva's "Hud up, Jim!"

The Fourth of July, 1863, began clear and warm, a hint of the heat to follow as the day progressed. But it was still quite pleasant and the first miles passed swiftly for the young family. While their mother tended to the horse and buggy, the children spent most of the time playing their favorite "I Spy with my Little Eye" guessing game as they traveled, using items along the way or out on the horizon for their choice of things to be guessed. Edgar Lincoln particularly delighted in the animals, furred and feathered, that their passing buggy spooked out of the brush that lined the lane.

The buggies of the Baldwins and Nichols sat beside the road at the approach to Etna, both families standing in light conversation while their horses chomped the ubiquitous prairie grass that gave nourishment to so many animals, large and small. "Here they come!" shouted Horace Nichols, the first to see the dust of the approaching Griffins.

"Right on time, too, I'll say," added Martha Baldwin, checking the small watch she had pinned to her blouse. "Let's give 'em a chance to stretch a bit an' then be off."

As Ol' Jim slowed to a walk, Minerva was able to wave broadly to the others. Alice and Ida May joined in, but since neither family had any children it was without much enthusiasm. Edgar Lincoln had long before fallen asleep in Alice's lap. Minerva guided Ol' Jim up beside the other horses and pulled him to a stop. As soon as she loosened the reins, his head dropped to the ground to begin feeding like the others.

"Why don't you step down an' stretch your legs a bit?" Mrs. Baldwin offered. "Then we'll head on up to Spring Valley. Should be there by lunchtime, an' we can pic-i-nic somewhere along Valley Creek."

Mr. Nichols chimed in: "It'll still be a long stretch up to Chatfield, but we should make it all right afore anything starts."

"Sounds just fine," Minerva replied and gave her daughters permission to alight from the buggy. "I'll climb down soon's I lay little Edgar out."

A few minutes later, all ready to continue, the three families set out in what became an alphabetical parade: Baldwins, Griffins, and Nichols. The day warmed into the low nineties, yet, traveling along in a constant breeze, the heat wasn't tiresome. The two hours it took them to reach the creek below Spring Valley, however, had everyone ready for a good break and a meal. Minerva's children especially relished the time to run and play along the banks of the creek, while the women huddled in gossipy conversation and the men tended to the horses.

Starting again an hour later, quite refreshed, they entered Spring Valley, pausing for a brief exchange at Mary Durand's house, then down its Broad Street of shops and offices to where the lane turned northeast toward the villages of Fillmore and Jordan. On they traveled through the long afternoon until at last they came to Chatfield and the three families parted for their separate accommodations. It had taken all day, and who could tell whether the humans were any less tired than the horses?

Alice and Ida May had only been to Chatfield twice with their mother, and Edgar Lincoln not at all, so their eyes were wide and pointing fingers were active as Minerva headed Ol' Jim along the streets lined with houses and shops, right to the main square. Around the central park sat the Root River Bank, the Case & Sawyer Real Estate firm, the publishing office for *The Chatfield Democrat,* several law offices, the large L. Bemis & Son Mercantile, an official post office, and the newly built Methodist church. It was at the latter they were to meet their hosts for their stay, the Reverend and Mrs. Tainter, friends of the itinerant Reverend Westfall.

"Hello, you must be the Griffins," said a tall, black-suited man of moderate age who stepped out from a small group of people chatting by the church steps. His gracious smile was clearly evident, even through his generous beard, and as he tipped his hat he extended a hand to Minerva, announcing, "Welcome, I'm Nahum Tainter, pastor of the Methodist flock here, and my wife and I are very glad to share our humble home with you and your children for this celebration." From behind, he pulled forward a short, red-cheeked, plumpish woman, saying "And this is my wife, Lucinda Tainter." Her plain dress and hat were black satin, and the black ribbon rosette pinned to the arm of her dress was a clear indication she was still in mourning for someone close.

Nerva wondered, *Was it her child? That would give answer to the spare room we're to stay in. P'raps she'll want to talk a bit whilst we're here – mother to mother.* She stepped down from the buggy, and with a wave of her arm introduced Alice, Ida May, and Edgar Lincoln as they descended to the street.

"What fine-looking children you have there, Missus Griffin – I'm sure the pride of both you and their father," Reverend Tainter remarked. After pausing a moment to gaze at his wife, he said, "I understand from Reverend Westfall he's away down in Tennessee in this dreadful war forced upon us by the traitorous Southerners."

"Yes, sir. He's actually down in Mississippi now. He's been gone two years this September, an' we sure do miss him."

"I well imagine you do. It must be right hard to manage your farm alone, with your children still so young."

"I do have my father and brother close by," Minerva explained. "We even live with them, as our shanty has fallen to ruin. They're a great help. But so are my girls," she added, wrapping her arms around their shoulders. "I'm blessed to have 'em."

"I'm sure you are, Missus Griffin. Well, let's get your things inside. It's almost time for the parade to begin."

Nahum Tainter led the horse and buggy around to their stable behind the parsonage next to the church, while Lucinda Tainter, without a word, escorted the Griffins with their meager belongings inside to the room that would be theirs for the night. Minerva paused at the door and shut her eyes a moment, causing Ida May to run into Alice. She was remembering her own loss of a child ten years earlier. *I hope we get to talk. Looks like she needs it.*

In the small room the guests found a quilt-covered bed that took up more than half the room. It was to be shared by Minerva and her daughters. Lucinda then slowly pulled a small trundle bed out from underneath. This was where Edgar Lincoln was to sleep. The room was tight, but tidy, and would do nicely, they assured her, so they set down their traveling things and returned to the front porch.

"Ah, here you are. And just in time," said Reverend Tainter. "The parade's started. Can you hear?"

From the other side of the park, which was filled with hundreds of spectators, came the sounds of a military air being played by nearly a dozen local musicians: horns, fifes, and drums. Around the square they marched, followed by various dignitaries as well as a number of uniformed soldiers either too old or too wounded to be presently serving. Twice around they went to the cheers of the flag-waving crowd. Then they came to a halt right in front of the church steps, from where the speeches were to be given.

As was happening that day in cities and towns all across the North, tribute was again being paid to the soldiers of the American Revolution who enabled the Union, as well as those then fighting to maintain that Union. Dozens of area men whose families were in attendance were recognized by name for their service, and a strong sense of pride swelled up within Minerva when Brainard's name was read. "That's your pa they're atalkin' about," she whispered to the children during the applause that followed each name, to make sure they caught the significance of the moment.

Mr. Jason Easton, president of the Root River Bank, then stood up and, with his hands raised, asked for their attention. When the crowd had sufficiently quieted, he began his oration: "I have it under good authority that this day, this remarkable Fourth of July, has witnessed two, count them, two events that may well lead to the conclusion of the terrible war of rebellion in which we are engaged."

Folks immediately began murmuring, as everyone began to wonder with their neighbor about this unexpected news. Once again, he raised his hands for quiet, and when he had it, continued: "Over in Pennsylvania, at a place called Gettysburg, our Union Army, led by General Meade, has won a glorious victory over the Confederate forces of their General, Robert Lee. They were vanquished from the field!"

A cheer rose up from the crowd, and the excited buzz continued for several minutes until all turned back to Mr. Easton, who was shouting he had more news to tell. "That's not all," he claimed, "for on this very day as well, our General Ulysses Grant has accomplished the fall of that infamous citadel on the Mississippi, Vicksburg. The city and its army have surrendered!"

The whooping roar from most of the crowd expressed the great pleasure of all but the few attending "Copperheads," those Northern sympathizers of the Southern cause. Minerva knelt down before her children to make sure they understood the significance of that wonderful news, for it might mean the soon return of their father.

The festivities were brought to a close with the firing of six sky rockets, which burst one after the other into red and blue stars that filled the sky above the crowd. Their light revealed the joy and wonder in the children's faces at such a marvelous spectacle. "This is even better 'an last year!" Ida May proclaimed to the little brother who was holding her hand.

When the last sparkles had fled from the sky, Lucinda Tainter invited the Griffins in for a bite of sweets to conclude the celebration.

The children especially, but Minerva as well, were all tuckered out from the day's long journey and the excitement of the commemorative festivities. So Lucinda was not surprised when Minerva said at the table, "I'll help you tidy up here, Lucinda, but looks like I need to get my young'uns off to bed purty soon. 'Sides, the Baldwins and Nichols want to head out as early as possible tomorrow, so ..."

Mrs. Tainter broke in, "You just tuck your lovely children in, Minerva, yourself as well. Nahum'll help me with the cleanup, won't you, dear?"

"Of course, of course. You get yourselves a good night's rest so tomorrow can go easy," replied Rev. Tainter.

"You're very kind, the both of you," Minerva said as she lifted her nearly asleep son and indicated to her daughters it was time to go upstairs. She had them stop at the doorway so all but the littlest could thank their generous hosts, then ushered the girls toward their bedroom.

The children were quickly asleep, but before she herself drifted off she thought to herself, *Looks like I won't have a chance after all to offer Lucinda a chance to talk. I'm sure she's lost a child ...*

***

A cool front of midsummer rains swept across the prairie soon after they arrived back at her parents' farm, delaying for several days their return to Spring Valley. "This'll be so good for finishin' the crops," Almon had commented. "Things're gettin' a bit dry, but this'll all soak in for 'em."

Returning from a final visit to her farm, Minerva was able to confirm her father's observation. Though hard on the leaking shanty – "It looks like it's about to fall in on itself" – the acres under cultivation and the kitchen garden seemed to be in prime condition – "'Specially our potatoes. There'll be plenty for Brainard to enjoy when he comes home."

With the rains finally passing on to the east, Minerva went into Alba for some supplies her mother needed. Mr. Peters' greeting was reserved when she entered his store. "Is anything atroublin' you?" she asked, as this was not his usual demeanor.

"P'raps you don't know, Minerva . . . An' I'm not sure I'm the one to say, but . . ." He paused a moment, looking at the floor and rubbing his hands together in an uncomfortable manner, then hesitantly spoke. "Mrs. Boynton was in here 'bout an hour ago . . . Said she'd heard some bad news . . . Bad news 'bout the Second Minnesota . . ."

Minerva froze, body and soul. *That Sophrena Boynton again! But what if it's true this time?* Managing a deep breath, she encouraged him to "Go on . . ."

"Heard they was all cut to pieces . . . Cut up as they moved on the Rebels at a place called Tullahoma . . . No particulars 'bout your Brainard, just that it was his Second, an' they was all done in . . . After a moment's silence, he concluded, "Hope he's all right, Minerva . . . With all my heart."

"We've been away from home these three weeks, Mr. Peters. So I ain't heard a thing from him or about him. Till now, that is." A low whistling sigh escaped her lips before she continued, "Headin' back to Spring Valley tomorrow. Guess we'll learn somethin' then. But thankee for your concern. Hard news to hear. Pray it's not true."

"I'll do that . . . I surely will," he promised. "Now, what is it you'll be aneedin'?"

As she drove the buggy home with her mother's requested supplies beside her, Minerva resolved: *I'll not tell the children. Nor Ma an' Pa neither. Not till I know somethin' for sure.*

***

The following day, after dropping off the children and their traveling cases, Minerva told Mary she wanted to make a quick stop downtown to see if there was any news from her husband. "That's fine. The cousins are so glad to see each other again, they won't be a bother at all," Mary assured her.

A bit reluctant, Minerva entered Wilder's Mercantile a few minutes later and walked up to the post office counter. After an exchange of greetings, she asked the inevitable, "Got any letters for me?"

Mr. Smith's "Indeed I do" didn't quiet her anxiety, but when he added, "Your man must be quite a writer. I believe there's three more awaitin' for you," her heart began to sing *He's alive! If he's awritin', he's alive!*

After thanking him for those precious communications, she sat in the buggy parked out front to preview their contents. Finding no mention of any difficulty at Tullahoma or beyond, she knew that once more Sophrena Boynton was wrong. It was with renewed confidence that she returned to her children, ready to share with them the continuing story of their father's service to his country. One highlight for her in that reading, she knew, would be his confirming news about Gettysburg and Vicksburg; another, his descriptions of safely marching into and beyond Tullahoma, which reassured her Sophrena's "news" was again mistaken.

After the letters were read and discussed, and the children were all tucked into bed, Minerva at last had the opportunity to pen the following:

"Brainard, dear Husband,

We are all well, and hope you are the same. There were three letters from you awaitin for us when we returned from Ma an Pas after the big July 4 celebration up in Chatfield. Twas a parade, speeches, an sky rockets that thrilled the children so. We all wished you coulda been there. Heard about Gettysburg an Vicksburg there, but ever so glad you could tell us its all true. That scoundrel Gen. Bragg – will you ever catch up to him? Your thought that the end of the war was in sight, an might allow you to be home afore winter, made the girls dance around the table, I tell you. We specially loved your story bout crossin the Elk Riv. with a rope ana thousand men takin a swim together. Whata sight that musta been.

Gettin those letters was just what I was aneedin, for my heart had been sorely tried. It was told to me that your 2nd was all cut up at Tullahoma. But from all you write, I see it just wasnt true. Brainard, I want you to know how proud we are of you an what your adoin for our Country. More here had ought to be there with you, stead of makin a noise against the war, terrible as it is. Course we wish you was here with us, but we know your service is needed for our peace an freedom. So you be faithful in all you do, an well keep aprayin for your safe return. Surely now its but a short time til this will all be over, making our prospects for the future look good.

I am sendin you the never ending love an prayers of your family, one an all . . .

Minerva Griffin

***

"Will you be goin' down to Pa's? Wheat an' oats must about be ready for harvest," Mary asked her sister as July turned to August.

"No, don't think so. Wasn't plannin' to anyways. Pa said he could manage 'thout us when we was there last," Minerva replied.

"Would you be of a mind to helpin' me put away for winter some o' the fruit that's hangin' ripe? Maybe some preserves an' dried apples, an' such like?"

"O'course, Mary. The girls'n I'd be glad to do that with you. Alice was just askin' a day or so ago if'n we was gonna do that out at the shanty. When'ja have in mind?"

"I'll have to get my jars ready. S'pect I still have plenty o' dryin' string. But we'll need a pile o' sugar, an' toppin' wax too. But it looks like there's plenty o' ripe fruit around already."

"Let me call my girls in, an' we can start out gatherin' apples from folks. Get the sugar an' wax whilst we're out as well. That is, if'n you don't mind atendin' to Edgar Lincoln the while. You get your jars and kettle ready, an' we'll take care o' the rest."

"That should work out just right, Minerva. It'll be fun. I've got plenty o' baskets for you to gather in. I'll get 'em as you call your girls."

It wasn't long before the three set out, and only a couple of hours for them to bring back two half bushels of neighbor's apples for drying, and nearly a half bushel of plums for preserves. The girls had also spied an unpicked blackberry patch, and offered to go out again while Minerva washed the fruit. In no time they returned with two full pails for more preserves.

The peeling, slicing, stringing, pitting, and slow cooking would wait for a morning start, but Mary, Minerva, Alice, and Ida May had everything ready for a long day of starting to prepare for winter.

***

Weekly letters from Brainard arrived through August, and each described the Union Army's gradual movement south, across the steep Cumberland Mountains, and down to the Tennessee River, inexorably toward Chattanooga, where Gen. Braxton Bragg had ensconced with his Confederate Army. Several letters contained money for the support of his family and to help pay down the debt on their land. In one he addressed the untrue story Minerva had heard about his regiment being badly mauled:

"I was sorry to hear that someone had reported that the 2nd Minn. was all cut to pieces in their advance on Tullahoma. But it is not so, for we did not lose a man, as you have learned In my letters. But it must have been hard for you to hear such reports, and then not to receive any letters from me for so long a time..."

"I just couldn't bear to tell you," she explained to her daughters. "Not until I knew for sure either way. But you can see it's all turned out for the good."

Two other times he commented on her descriptions of the deplorable condition of their shanty:

"Let the old shanty rot down, or anything else, until I return, and then we will fix up something to live in, in some shape or other..." and *"I was glad to hear that you had all been up to your father's once more, and that you found everything in good shape on the farm except the old shanty. It seems that it is getting rather lame, and about to fall. It has stood us pretty well, I think, but I hate to see it fall, for we have passed many a happy day under its roof. But if I live to get home, I think that we can soon rig up something for a shelter, and that does not worry me at all..."*

After Minerva read one particular section, Alice asked, "Please, Ma, read that part once more. I want to see the picture in my mind as clearly as he wrote it." So she read again:

"I wish that you could see me sometime when I receive a letter from you. I hasten to my tent and open the seal that was closed with your hands, and draw forth the little missives of love from you and the children. God bless you all, you would think that I was foolish I expect, for I cannot always keep back the silent tear that steals down my cheek. But they are tears of love and joy to hear from the loved ones at home, if only a few words. And if any one gives me more joy than another, it is the ones with a little missive in them from Alice. I want to see you all very much, but I shall have to wait a few more months . . ."

In response to that moving passage, Alice asserted, "Ma, you should write Pa tonight. I can write a note too, and I'll help Ida May add something, 'cause that means so much to Pa, like he says."

"Well, I been meanin' to pass on the news of George Spaulding gettin' hisself married, an' how Jerry's wife had another baby girl last week. Those'll tickle him for sure. He'll also be glad to hear his money's comin' through to us all right, an' that I've nearly paid off the farm. Course, he'll want to know how your grampa's doin' with the harvest. An' maybe he ain't heard yet 'bout Chief Little Crow bein' killed up north, which'll surely end the uprising. So's I've got plenty to write about. Let's do it!"

That double letter was traded the following day for another long letter from him, written on the south bank of the Tennessee River, for the Union Army was crossing over on a fifty-foot raft that his own Company F had built. And though he had described the process in great detail, Ida May had a hard time picturing her own father actually constructing a raft big enough and sturdy enough to transport thousands of soldiers across such a big river. "That'll be the *first* story I ask him to tell me when he gets home," she declared, causing her mother and sister to begin speculating what they would ask him to tell first.

Chapter Thirty-Eight

Letters from Georgia

Since the opening of the new school term in September, Nerva had allowed the girls to stop by the post office on their walk home to check for mail. Alice and Ida May took daily turns asking Mr. Smith if there was anything for them or for their Aunt Mary, and if there was, she got to carry it home.

Toward the end of the month, on a day when it was Ida May's turn to inquire, Mr. Smith said, "Yes, indeedy. Came in today." As he turned to fetch it from their box he continued, "Let's see . . . Postmarked down in Georgia. From your pa all right. That's new for him, Georgia, ain't it?"

"Georgia?" Alice questioned, stepping forward to see what he had handed Ida May. "Well, Pa did say in his last letter he expected to be in Georgia when next he wrote. Chasin' the Rebs wherever they go, you know. Remember that, Ida May?"

Stuffing the treasured letter into her pinafore pocket, Ida May nodded, but turned, without even a thank you to Mr. Smith, to hurry home. She was too excited about the news she carried from her father to stay and chat. That left Alice to politely thank the postmaster before she chased her sister out the door and up the street.

"Ma, another letter from Pa," the young girl called ahead when she spied her mother sitting on the front porch waiting for them. Waving it over her head, she raced up the steps and plopped the envelope triumphantly into Minerva's lap. Alice arrived just a few steps behind, panting from the effort of running all that way with her heavy book bag.

"Land sakes alive . . . Thank you, love, for bringin' me such welcome news! Alice, dear, since Ida May got to carry it home, why don't you be the one to read it?" which was *just* what Alice had hoped her mother would say.

Nestled between her mother and sister, Alice handed the letter back to Ida May and generously offered, "Why don't you open it, an' then I'll read it?"

Ida May's small fingers shook with excitement as she carefully tore open the back of the envelope and pulled out two folded half-sheets of paper. She opened them up and noticed, "One's from Pa, an' the other's from . . . Aunt Mariah," as she passed them to Alice, but held onto her father's envelope. She then closed her eyes so she could concentrate on her father's words.

Alice read his typical introduction:

"In Camp at the foot of Coon Mountain, Georgia Sept 7th 1863. My Dear Wife, I will write a few lines to you this evening in order to let you know where we are and how we get along. I am well as usual, and stand the march first rate."

After some details of that march into hot and dusty Georgia, he wrote he had received a letter from his sister, which he was enclosing. "That must be this one," Alice surmised as she passed the other sheet to her mother. She continued reading his description of where they were, then stopped to take a deep breath when she came to his words:

"We have got orders to have three days' rations in our haversacks, and forty rounds of cartridges in our cartridge boxes, so you see we

may get into a skirmish before long. There has been some cannonading this evening in the direction of Chattanooga..."

"Lord a'mercy, he's into it again," Minerva whispered, as Ida May moved to the other side to cling to her mother.

Alice took another deep breath, but her voice still choked a bit as she read the closing lines: *"I will write as often as I can until the campaign is over. May God bless and protect us all, is the wish of your husband and father. D. B. Griffin."*

The three of them simply stared into empty space, each contemplating in her own way the news and the farewell he had written.

"Well," Minerva finally broke the silence, "Sounds like he's still all right. But he musta faced this other fight since he wrote that. We'll have to wait a bit, I 'spect, for him to write us how that all turned out. Pray God his news'll be as good as always before..."

After her daughters went inside, Minerva wondered if she needed to protect her daughters. *P'raps his news won't be so good next time. P'raps... Should I get the mail 'stead o' them, just in case? Or would they then start to worry, athinkin' I'm aworryin' 'bout their pa? Guess I'd best let 'em go ahead for the mail, an' trust it'll all come out right...*

***

Their wait was a week. Checking each day, the girls got the same answer from Mr. Smith, "Nope, nary a thing for you today." Their disappointment was mirrored by that of their mother, who often was waiting on the porch as before.

But finally Brainard's next letter arrived, indicating he was still alive and well. Alice got to carry it home, and like Ida May the week before, she was waving it for her mother to see as they ran up the street. Minerva stood and called to her, "News from your pa?"

"Yes, Ma. Another letter from Georgia," she replied as she handed the missive to her mother.

Minerva caught her breath, pressing the letter to her bosom as her mind rejoiced: *He's safe. Still Safe. Thank God he's safe!*

"Can we read it now?" asked Ida May, the longing in her voice more powerful than the mere words. She tugged on the crook of her mother's arm, as if to demand an affirmative response.

"Of course, love. Let's sit an' I'll read it." And so she began . . .

In Camp at the foot of Lookout Mountain, Georgia September 11th, 1863 My Dear Wife and Children, As I have a few moments to spare this afternoon, I will improve them by writing a few lines to you. We are upon the march again after Bragg, as that celebrated individual has skedaddled once more. He has left Chattanooga without a fight, and gone south to find another ditch. Our army went into the place on the ninth without meeting any resistance. We lay in the last camp, ready to march at a moment's notice, until yesterday morning when we were awakened at three o'clock and started at daybreak . . ."

As Minerva continued to read, Brainard's words fascinated his daughters with their vivid descriptions of the people, the villages, and the mountains his regiment had to march past, through, and over. "Pa's such a good writer," Alice interjected. "I wanna be as good as him someday."

"You will, my dear. I'm sure o' that. Just work hard at school. Make us both proud. And you, too, Ida May," Minerva said, turning to her other daughter.

Then the tone of his writing became more serious as he explained what was happening. They had received news of a Rebel attack on their leading division across Lookout Mountain, and so were ordered to cross that high ridge as quickly as possible to aid in their comrades' defense. The girls both gasped in horror when their mother read his account of discovering that at least 150 Union soldiers had already been killed or wounded, and another sixty or so captured before they could arrive. He immediately offered his family some comfort, however, by writing: *"We all stand the march first rate, and are willing to march a good while longer if it will end the war."*

Minerva read on about them having to forage for food because they were issued only half-rations. Then he had written a series of comments upon the latest letters he had received from them, as well as his formal farewell.

"Ma, read that last part again, please. The part about us," asked Alice. She *did* want to hear all of it, of course, though secretly what she longed to hear again were his words of praise for her.

So Minerva read again:

"I received your letter of the 1st on the 9th and was glad to hear that you were all well, and that you were enjoying yourselves in drying fruit and making preserves. I hope that you will have the pleasure of my company when you eat some of them. It seems that you have had a frost rather early for Minnesota even. I hope that it did not spoil all of the corn for you, nor your sorghum either, for I may want some of it, if I live to get home, and I hope I shall. How much do you have to pay for wood, do you have any trouble in getting it, and in getting it cut up into stove wood? I hope that Emory will be at home so that he will get you fixed up for winter, a little. I should like to be there at the same time, but I do not see any way for me just now, and I guess that I shall stick to it nine months more. I think that Alice does very well in writing to me. I think that she does very well if she gets fifteen verses to recite at sabbath school. I hope that they will all be good children, and learn well. I suppose that they all grow fast, so that I should hardly know them. We have received orders to have three days rations in our haversacks, and be ready to march at a moment's notice, so I cannot tell where I shall be the next time I write to you. I will try and keep you posted while we are on the march. I will bid you all a good bye. D. B. Griffin

"I think we should set aside special some of what we made, to make sure Pa gets some." Ida May looked up to her mother as she spoke, an earnest pleading in her voice. "Otherwise, we might eat it all up before he returns."

"That's a right nice idea, Ida May. Maybe a small box marked 'Brainard' so's we don't touch it. An' a whole jug of our molasses when it's made. You know how he loves to spread it on his mornin' cakes. An' won't he be pleased to know when I write him that both our sorghum an' corn on the farm were far 'nough along not to be hurt by the frost?"

Minerva's inner thoughts were already elsewhere, though, for she was again troubled by the fighting he faced. As her daughters chattered about what he had written concerning Alice, her mind tumbled: *You talk so brave, my love. I know you're sure everythin's workin' out for good. Oh, if only you were done an' home . . . But what if . . . it's now your time? What if . . . maybe just a wound, not too bad? Wouldn't want the girls to read that kinda news all unprepared like. Guess I'd better catch the mail from you till you're through this an' write us again. Please, please take care o' yourself, an' let us know you've come through all right . . .*

***

"Sorry, Miz Griffin, no letter for you today." Mr. Smith's response to Minerva's inquiry had been the same every day for two weeks, and she had to press down a growing fear over Brainard's silence. *It's been this long before. Prob'ly no chance to write, a'chasin' the Rebs again. But . . . .maybe he can't . . .* Her thoughts confirmed her decision to tell the girls she'd be checking for letters instead of them, though she hadn't explained her reason.

Finally, her heart leaped when Mr. Smith pulled a letter from her box one morning as she walked up to the post office window. He extended it to her hesitantly, "This here's from Georgia all right, but not from your man." He paused, then added, "Hope it's not bad news . . ."

Minerva took the letter without looking at it. Wishing to be alone when she did, she mumbled a thank you and left the store. She crossed the street into the small city park and sat down on the corner park bench. First she read just her own name. It was written in an unknown hand, so she looked at the sender's name: "Captain D. B. Loomis, Co. F, 2nd Minnesota Volunteers." As her mind raced through the myriad possibilities of the letter's message, most of them bad, her chest began to tighten from the pounding of her heart and sudden intakes of gasped-for breath.

As she cradled the letter in her hands, she realized there were some heavy bulges within, perhaps coins or medals. Her curiosity overcoming her fear, she turned the envelope over and began, with trembling fingers, to unseal it. But she stopped, realizing she needed to be away from public eyes – at home – when she read its contents. Though traveling that distance in her stressed condition seemed more than she could manage, Minerva forced herself to her feet and walked home, the still unopened letter held close.

She felt she needed to know what she faced before she shared whatever news there was with Mary, so she sat outside on the porch and for a few moments simply stared at the dreaded envelope. Eventually she opened it. And it carried her worst fear . . .

Chattanooga, Tenn September 30th 1863

Mrs. David B. Griffin

Madam:

It becomes my painful duty to inform you that your husband, formerly a member of my company, was killed in the desperate battle which took place near here on the 19th & 20th of this month. But he fell as becomes a soldier while in the discharge of his duty.

The final statements of his accounts with the Government have been sent as required to the Adjutant General in Washington.

His clothing was all lost upon the battlefield, but I enclose you 10.55 the amount of money found among his possessions.

Respectfully

Your Obedient Servant

D. B. Loomis, Captain

Co F 2nd Minnesota Volunteers

Minerva bolted to her feet, gasping for breath as she tossed the letter aside. "Oh . . . no . . . no . . . Not my Brainard!" Heavy sobs escaped her lips, and swaying and slowly turning, a sinking feeling washed over her. Her moans were loud enough for Mary to hear inside, and she rushed to the porch to see what had happened to her sister.

"It's my Brainard . . . killed in battle . . . so far from home. This awful war has taken my husband!"

"Oh, no! Nerva, I'm *so* sorry . . . Was that in a letter today?"

"There 'tis," she said, pointing to the captain's letter at her feet even as she turned away not to look at it. "Go ahead an' read it. Does he say how it happened? Or what happened to his body?"

Mary picked it up, and quickly scanned the text, gasping as her sister had done when she read the mortal news. "No, none o' that, just that 'twas a desperate battle . . . and that he died like a good soldier . . . Come, let's go inside," she said, tenderly tugging on Minerva's hands, "inside where you won't have to see anyone."

Dully obedient, Minerva let herself be led inside to their parlor. The two sisters sat together, holding onto each other for support – Minerva afraid for her now-fatherless children, and Mary newly afraid for her still-fighting husband.

Minerva had much to process as the harsh reality began to come into focus, and she expressed her concerns: "How will I tell the children? How will we survive 'thout him? Why . . . why did this happen to such a good man? An' how, how did it happen? Where is he now? I wanna *know!*"

Fortunately the young boys weren't interrupted in their backyard play, and baby Hattie continued to nap her way through the entire incident. So the two mothers had time, not only for this radical news to settle in, but to begin to envision its effect on the Griffin family's future.

The farm was still there for them, just not the shanty. Minerva's parents and brothers would surely be sufficient support if she decided to return to the prairie, though Mary assured her there was no need for her and the children to go. Mary also suggested she write to a couple of the friends Brainard had been serving with, in the hope of learning some of the details of his death and burial.

In the end, there was another flood of tears, yet this one brought a mix of both grief and release, and slowly an exhausted quiet returned. Minerva then picked up the letter and read it a second time. "It's fine for 'a soldier in the discharge of his duty,' fine for 'The Cause,' but what about *his family*? What about *our* hopes and dreams?" An emerging bitterness and resentment now battled with her beginning efforts to resign herself to the reality of this awful and final news. "Oh, *how* will I tell my children . . . how will I *tell* my children?"

***

When the school day came to an end, Mr. Kellogg bade farewell to his students, and the noisy bunch hurried out of the schoolhouse by twos and threes, off in the differing directions that lead them home. Alice and Ida May were the last to leave, as Alice needed to check with Mr. Kellogg regarding a writing practice assignment she still had to complete. But when those instructions were clear, they, too, headed for home.

"Wonder what's for supper," Ida May mused as they turned the last corner and Aunt Mary's house came into view.

"Wanna race to find out?" Alice challenged. Aware that her younger sister wasn't nearly fast enough for a race between equals, she added, "How about I'll even give you a three-count head start. What do you say?"

Ida May didn't say anything. She just laughed as she burst ahead as fast as her shorter legs could go. Alice quickly counted to three, then took off after her, her book bag bouncing off her back with each stride. She had nearly caught up to her sister by the time they reached the house, but Ida May leaped up on the porch first, and turned to laugh again and pronounced, "Beat you!" when Alice arrived.

Alice joined in the laughter, asking, "When did you get so fast? No count of three for you next time!"

They entered the house and headed for the parlor, still giggling together. Ida May shouted, "Ma, we're home!" But both girls stopped at the doorway when they saw their mother, sitting stiffly, a letter held upright in her lap, and their Aunt Mary standing behind her, a hand resting gently on one shoulder. The taut faces and reddened eyes alerted the girls that something was wrong.

"What is it, Ma? What's happened?" asked Ida May as she rushed toward her mother.

Not moving from the doorway, as if she wanted to protect herself from what she now feared, Alice asserted: "It's Pa, isn't it? Something's happened to Pa!" She still held her ground as Ida May, halfway across the room, whipped around to face her, then turned back to face her mother.

"Yes, my loves, it's your Pa. He . . . he won't be comin' home . . ." When she finished this simple statement, she laid the letter down, lowered her head almost to her lap, and began to cry again. But not wanting to further distress her daughters, she swallowed hard, and with a mother's strength of spirit, raised her head and reached out her arms to invite them to come to her.

Eyes and ears intent on all of her mother's responses, Alice raised her right palm, fingers slightly spread, and deliberately asked, "What do you mean? He's been hurt bad?"

"No, Alice . . . this here letter from his captain tells us . . . two weeks ago . . . he was killed in their battle."

Ida May screamed, "No! That can't be! Not my Pa . . . not dead . . . not Pa!" And she turned and ran from the parlor to their family bedroom and threw herself, sobbing, on the bed she shared with her sister.

Alice stood in the doorway for a moment, stunned by the awful news, but finally crossed the parlor and crumpled down beside her mother, seeking the comfort and security that now only one parent could provide. Minerva gathered her in her arms and began to stroke her hair.

***

Supper that evening was a very quiet affair for everyone but the three youngest children. While young Edgar Lincoln, Louis Lincoln, and Hattie remained for the moment blissfully ignorant of the day's tragic news, the others listlessly stared at their plates. All hunger for food was gone, replaced by a different hunger: the emptiness and numbness that descends with such a terrible loss.

The real depth of the disquietude didn't reveal itself, however, until the girls knelt together for their normal bedtime prayers. Ida May stood back up and turned to her mother. "I ain't gotta thing I want to say to God. He let my pa get killed." It was a defiant statement from her seven-year-old lips, and Minerva was shocked.

"Oh, love, you can't say that. I know inside your heart's as broke as mine . . ." With one hand on Ida May's head and the other on her back, she drew her daughter in and cooed, "God loves us. He does. He loves your pa, too, sure enough. An' he'll take good care o' him till we're all back together again in heaven. If'n you can't talk to God tonight, I'm sure he'll understand and wait for you to be ready once more . . . Now you two just lay yourselves down, and we'll talk it all through in the mornin'. We'll be all right. An' Pa's safe with God now. Think on that, 'stead of him agettin' kilt."

Alice rose from the bedside where she had still been kneeling to take Ida May's hand and drew her into bed beside her. In each other's arms they managed to lay aside for the moment their anguished present and unknown future, to sleep the child's blessed sleep, unburdened and restorative. Perhaps too exhausted by the emotions of the evening's news, Ida May's strange dream of trying to wave good-bye to her father didn't come to her that night.

Sometime later, Minerva opened the door a crack to check on her three children. Observing their innocent sleep, she wished her night could be the same, though she knew from her aching heart that wouldn't be possible. There was just too much to think about . . . and to remember.

She had left Mary in the parlor, for she was writing the dreadful news to Emery, and most likely needed the freedom to include her anguished pleas for him to make sure he was safe. "I do need to do this, Minerva. But soon's I'm done, we can talk more about the future," she had assured her heartbroken sister.

It was well past midnight before their conversation finally dwindled, neither one able to see further into the future than the following day. The emotional content was still too fresh, and the pile of unknowns too deep for them to yet wade through. And so, drained as never before in their lives, the two parted to their own bedrooms of little ones, to toss in fitful slumber until the new day dawned.

"My darlings," Minerva whispered to her daughters when the sun was fully up. "Come, let's leave the little tyke to sleep a bit more. Quiet now . . . You dress, an' I'll set us out a bite o' somethin' to eat."

The girls got up and dressed silently. Neither one was able to talk about what had happened or what lay ahead for their little family. They were relieved when their mother announced as they entered the warm kitchen a few minutes later, "I want you to stay home from school. There's so much we've gotta talk about an' work through if'n we can. All right?"

Her daughters nodded in agreement, and accepted the tea and toast their mother had prepared to help them start their day. "Who's gonna tell Edgar Lincoln?" Ida May asked, tearing off a length of buttered toast and looking at it blankly.

"I will, Ida May. That's my job. I'll think o' some way to do it proper. But I want us all to be together when I do."

"What'll you say, Ma? Think he'll understand? Why, he doesn't even remember Pa, just what we've told him." Alice's comments went right to the core of one of the issues that had troubled her mother's attempt to sleep.

"Best I can figure, for him, for you girls, and for me, too, is the plain truth: your pa went off to war, an' sometimes a pa just . . . doesn't come back. It'll always be up to us . . . the three of us . . . to tell him what his pa was like when he's old enough to understand." Her voice broke on those words . . .

***

339

That day and the weeks that followed seemed to drag more slowly than Mary's mantle clock regularly announced. Minerva made the customary wide black crepe ribbon bow to hang on the front door. Neighbors who saw it, or who had heard the news downtown, stopped to pay their respects and offer whatever assistance the family needed. Minerva often let them read the captain's letter for themselves. Almon, Polly, and Allen drove their buggy up for a day that was spent in tearful remembrance and support. Without room for them to stay in Mary's already crowded house, they had to return home that evening, but promised to come again. There was to be no funeral for Brainard because there was no body, but special mention was made and prayers offered that Sunday at the community church.

The single highlight of the week occurred when Mr. Gaskill came to call. Minerva expressed her consternation at the lack of details she had been given in the captain's letter, and Mr. Gaskill immediately offered: "I'll write my son, Minerva. As sergeant, he'll surely know what happened. I know he'd be right glad an' proud to get an answer to any question you've got."

Quickly writing a pleading note of inquiry, Minerva handed it to Mr. Gaskill to include in his letter to his son. "I'm ever so grateful for this, Mr. Gaskill. Anything he can tell us'll help me an' the children understand what happened. An' that'll ease up the healin' as well."

By the end of the week the Griffins were able to begin making some plans for their future. Their intention was to go back to the prairie homestead they all – especially Brainard – had dearly loved, and with the offered help of Minerva's family, somehow make it work. For their real intention was never to forget the husband and father who had been so central to the life of their family.

"I'll bundle up all his letters an' keep 'em safe. But for family times, whenever you want, we'll get 'em out an' I'll read 'em all to you, again an' again. Even these last three letters from Georgia. It'll be almost like he's still awritin' to us," Minerva told her daughters. "Ain't you glad we saved all of 'em for that? An' I'll tell you 'bout your pa's and my mem'ries growin' up in Vermont, an' comin' to

Illinois where you was born, Alice Jane, in that ol' rickety covered wagon, an' then amovin' on to Ioway, where Ida May got herself added to our family, then o'course our move up here to Minnesota Territory. An' one day, when Edgar Lincoln grows up a bit more, we'll read 'em all to him, too – an' that way he'll get to know his pa, his pa who went to war . . ."

EPILOGUE

The story of Corporal David Brainard Griffin's death is known from the official record and from at least three letters that Minerva received from his companions. He was killed by a shot through his forehead in the opening minutes of the Battle of Chickamauga at the age of thirty-three, two years after his enlistment in the Union Army. Because his brigade was forced to withdraw by overwhelming forces, Brainard's body and effects were abandoned, to be buried that night by a detail of Confederate soldiers. His body was subsequently removed to a mass grave of unknowns at Chattanooga National Cemetery.

Minerva continued to work their farm for several years with the help of her family. It took her three months to prove her formal marital status and the parentage of their children in order to receive a military widow's and orphans' pension totaling eight dollars a month. Despite that – or perhaps because of that – she became quite active in the Women's Relief Corps, dedicated to rendering assistance to the widows and orphans left by the Civil War. In 1868, five years after Brainard's death, Reverend J.M. Westfall officiated at her new marriage to Warren D. Andrews, who had served in Company A of the 2nd Minnesota and was undoubtedly known to Brainard Griffin in Company F. Sometime in 1875, the family relocated in Spring Valley, which is where she died twenty years later, and where she now lies buried between the two stones that memorialize her Civil War husbands.

Alice Jane married Manuel Beardsley Hutcheson, a maternal cousin of Laura Ingalls Wilder, in 1873. Minerva sold the farm to them in 1881, and it was sold by them in 1886, prior to their move to Whittier, California. There Alice remained childless, died a widow in 1928, and is buried next to her husband.

Ida May married Jacob LeFevre, her childhood neighbor (see Chapter Twenty), at her mother's home in 1880. The couple started farming and began their family in Nebraska, but eventually migrated further west to Granger, Washington, to raise their brood of five sons and a daughter. One of those sons became my maternal grandfather, as well as my mentor-image of an educator. Ida May lived until 1943, a year after I was born, and is my connection to the American Civil War.

Edgar Lincoln, last in this branch of the family bearing the Griffin name, tragically died after ingesting poison hemlock in 1870 at the tender age of nine. He is buried between his mother and his father's military memorial marker.

Review Requested:
If you loved this book, would you please provide a review at Amazon.com?
Thank You

ᵀA information can be obtained
w.ICGtesting.com
ᶦn the USA
ᵑ0644200818